Contemporary Debates
on Civil Liberties

Contemporary Debates on Civil Liberties

Enduring Constitutional Questions

Edited by

Glenn A. Phelps
Northern Arizona University

Robert A. Poirier
Northern Arizona University

Lexington Books
D.C. Heath and Company/Lexington, Massachusetts/Toronto

Library of Congress Cataloging-in-Publication Data
Main entry under title:
Contemporary debates on civil liberties.

Bibliography: p.
Includes index.
1. Civil rights—United States—Addresses, essays,
lectures. I. Phelps, Glenn A., 1948–   . II. Poirier,
Robert A., 1941–   .
KF4749.A2E53 C64 1985   323.4'0973   84–40816
ISBN 0–669–10224–5 (pbk. : alk. paper)

Published simultaneously in Canada
Printed in the United States of America
International Standard Book Number: 0–669–10224–5
Library of Congress Catalog Card Number: 84–40816

The paper used in this publication meets the minimum requirements of
American National Standard for Information Sciences—Permanence of
Paper for Printed Library Materials, ANSI Z39.48–1984.

To Cathy and Michael

Contents

Preface and Acknowledgments

THE information revolution threatens to inundate even the most attentive reader with a tidal wave of new material. In this light any author is confronted with the question, Why this book? The question is fair. Our response is one we believe will be understood by anyone who has taught an undergraduate course in civil liberties. Having taught such courses ourselves, we have never failed to be impressed with the genuine student enthusiasm for class discussions of civil liberties questions. The enthusiasm exhibited in those discussions, unfortunately, is often characterized by more heat than light. Many of these discussions end in frustration for all concerned because students usually lack sufficient ammunition in their intellectual arsenals to go beyond general assumptions. Too often, partisans in the debate are left with the woefully inadequate, "Well, that's just the way I feel."

Contemporary Debates on Civil Liberties is our attempt to address that problem by arming readers with the kinds of evidence and reasoning helpful to a resolution of some of these lively issues. We have chosen to focus on thirteen famous Supreme Court cases and the enduring questions of civil liberties that they raise. These cases were selected not merely for their notoriety but also because the constitutional, moral, and philosophical issues that they address continue to challenge and perplex U.S. society.

The many excellent texts and casebooks in the field are often unable to treat these individual cases with anything more than a cursory reading. Each chapter of *Contemporary Debates on Civil Liberties,* though, begins with an introduction that invites the reader to take a more comprehensive look at the featured case and its significance. These introductions highlight the relevant facts, analyze the reasons undergirding the Supreme Court's opinion, and assess the significance of the case for the ongoing civil liberties controversy at issue.

Each introduction is followed by an essay supporting and an essay opposing the central proposition posed by the case. Contributors include notable authors from such diverse fields as jurisprudence, journalism, and social science, as well as legal philosophy.

Drawing on our concerns as teachers, we have selected these essays for their style as well as their substance. We believe that the cogency, clarity, and avoidance of cumbersome legalese represented by these essays will stimulate rather than inhibit clear thinking. If *Contemporary Debates on Civil Liberties* encourages readers to think about the hard questions regarding the role of rights and liberties in a democratic society, then we will have succeeded in our task.

Acknowledgments

A number of individuals have shared, at various times and in various ways, in the development of this enterprise. Our political science colleagues at Northern Arizona University continually offered encouragement and thoughtful suggestions. Their generous good humor created a working environment that should serve as the definition of collegiality. John Ostheimer, Chairman of the Political Science Department; Henry Hooper, Associate Vice President for Academic Affairs—Research and Graduate Studies; and Richard Foust, Director of the Bilby Research Center, provided essential financial and administrative support. Linda Tudan, our graduate assistant, proved to be indispensable to the project. Her boundless enthusiasm cannot be seen in these pages, but her research skills, as represented by her coauthorship of chapter 13, can be. Christine Poirier was able to revive her talents as a former English major to set us both straight on some gross abuses of the language that, fortunately, will not now be permanently ensconced in print. Perhaps most important, we wish to extend our sincerest thanks to Evelyn Wong, Kimberly Poole, Sharon Ritt, Teresa Redmon, and the NBI word processor for assistance above and beyond the call of duty. Finally, we thank Margaret Zusky and Martha Cleary, our editors at Lexington Books. Their enthusiasm for the project nearly exceeded our own.

1
Engel v. Vitale: Is Jefferson's "Wall of Separation" Breached by Prayer in Public Schools?

Robert A. Poirier

THE First Amendment states that "Congress shall make no law respecting an establishment of religion." This phrase, known as the Establishment Clause, reflects the concern for religious liberty among the founders of the United States. At a minimum the phrase means that there cannot be an official state religion or preferential treatment given to one religion over another. Thus the Establishment Clause provides the constitutional basis for the singularly American notion of separation of church and state.

Seemingly clear in its intent, the Establishment Clause has not been so easily interpreted. In a nation that prides itself on having been founded on Christian values and in which most of its citizens profess belief in a major Christian sect, how can the government maintain a religious neutrality as suggested, some say demanded, by the Establishment Clause? If the state acknowledges the spiritual needs of the citizenry, would it not be obligated at least to provide the climate in which religion can thrive? In facilitating the environment for religious activities, how can the state avoid giving one sect preferential treatment over another? Finally, by not providing a favorable environment toward religion, is the state being hostile to religion?

Engel v. Vitale (370 U.S. 471, 1962) is a case that still generates controversy more than two decades since the decision. The case raises the question of the constitutional propriety of prayer in a public school setting. *Engel* created such a storm that its most vocal critics have organized a fight in Congress to amend the Constitution to allow for prayer (or a moment of silence in some versions of the legislation) in the nation's public schools. Also being considered is a statutory provision to remove public school matters from the jurisdiction of federal courts. Thus far the statutory and amendment remedies to the *Engel* decision have failed in the Congress, but activity in this matter is likely to continue at least through the 1980s.

By allowing prayer in a public school, is the state merely allowing a climate for citizens to meet their spiritual needs, or is it infringing on the Establishment Clause? In *Engel* the Court was specifically asked to determine the constitutionality of the daily recitation of the Regents' Prayer in New York State. Composed by officials of the New York State Board of Regents, the prayer went as follows: "Almighty God, we acknowledge our dependence upon Thee, and we beg Thy blessings upon us, our parents, our teachers and our country." Innocuous and nondenominational on its face, this prayer was to be recited in public schools at the beginning of the school day following the pledge of allegiance to the flag. Although recitation was voluntary for the children, local school boards were required to use *this* prayer if the decision were made to include a daily prayer.

In a momentous 6-1 decision, the Court struck down the Regents' Prayer as an unconstitutional infringement of the Establishment Clause. The Court's opinion pointed out specifically that it was not the business of government officials to compose prayers or prescribe them for anyone. One year later two companion cases from Pennsylvania and Maryland school districts, *School District of Abington Township v. Schempp* and *Murray v. Curlett* (374 U.S. 203 1963), dealt with recitation of the Lord's Prayer and Bible chapters in morning exercises. Once again the Court ruled against these religious practices in public schools.

It was in *Abington* that the Supreme Court articulated two of the three criteria used to determine whether the Establishment Clause has been violated. Justice Tom Clark wrote for the majority:

> The test may be stated as follows: what are the purpose and the primary effect of the enactment? If either is the advancement or inhibition of religion then the enactment exceeds the scope of legislative power as circumscribed by the Constitution. That is to say that to withstand the strictures of the Establishment Clause there must be a secular legislative purpose and a primary effect that neither advances nor inhibits religion.

The third criterion for the Establishment Clause is the test for "excessive entanglement" between government and religion developed in *Walz v. Tax Commission* (397 U.S. 664, 1970). In *Walz* the Court reasoned that tax exemptions for churches did not violate the Establishment Clause because the tax benefit was not sectarian and was given to a wide variety of nonprofit institutions, including churches. These institutions were providing essential public services; the tax exemptions were offered as a reward and were not intended to promote the interests of any one institution to the detriment of others.

The "excessive entanglement" criterion, however, was at the heart of *Walz*. Chief Justice Warren Burger reasoned that without tax exemptions for churches, the government would be required to interfere more directly in church financial affairs in order to assess effectively the level of taxes due the state. The objective of separation of church and state, the Court argued, was better served by a system of tax exemption, especially one that treated all nonprofit institutions equally.

The Court's decision in *Walz* recognized the necessity of a church-state relationship of "benevolent neutrality." This view holds that absolute separation is unworkable and that in fact some state involvement might be necessary to preserve the spirit of the Establishment Clause. At what point does that involvement become an unconstitutional "entanglement"? As always, the Supreme Court finds itself in the role of balancing competing claims based on different interpretations of the Constitution.

Proponents of school prayer advocate not only the propriety but the need for state involvement to preserve certain fundamental values putatively universal in U.S. society. They see no conflict between school prayer and the Establishment Clause because, they stress, the accent is on "voluntary" participation. In fact, many proponents cast the issue in Free Exercise terms by arguing that the religious liberty to pray, as well as the free speech right, has been abrogated by the school prayer decisions. This constitutes state hostility to religion and not the "benevolent neutrality" that is minimally required.

Opponents of school prayer are concerned that the line will be crossed if school prayer is given constitutional blessing. They argue that it is not possible to skate on the thin ice of "benevolent neutrality" in this matter because the state will inevitably become entangled in the ensuing sectarian squabbles over the type of prayer to be used. Citing the views of the leadership of most mainstream U.S. churches and the *Engel* Court's concern over government-composed prayers, opponents see school prayer ultimately as a threat to religious liberty because it transfers spiritual authority from the churches into the hands of temporal institutions. Furthermore, opponents insist that the "voluntary" aspect of school prayer is an inappropriate standard because school children are an impressionable and captive audience. Children are not likely to have the courage to remove themselves from their peers in order to avoid prayer recitation. To do so stamps any child as different and out of step with majoritarian values. Hence, school prayer, according to opponents, displays the opposite side of the free speech coin: the issues of compulsory affirmation of belief and the right not to speak.

Resolving these conflicts is not easy because, like the abortion issue, prayer evokes strong emotional responses and is intertwined with moral considerations beyond the realm of legality or constitutionality. The controversy will undoubtedly increase in intensity as proponents and opponents raise the ante by emphasizing the interaction among the Free Exercise, Establishment, and Free Speech clauses. For example, in *Widmar v. Vincent* (454 U.S. 263, 1981) a campus Christian group stood before the Court on free speech grounds to win the right to use state-owned facilities in the same manner as any other recognized campus organization. In *Stone v. Graham* (449 U.S. 39, 1980) the Court struck down a Kentucky law that required posting the Ten Commandments in every public schoolroom. Using the "secular legislative purpose" test, the Court said that the "pre-eminent purpose for posting the Ten Commandments . . . is plainly religious in nature" and served "no secular legislative purpose, and is therefore unconstitutional."

Aid to parochial schools further illustrates the government's dilemma. How can the state adhere to the "benevolent neutrality" principle without becoming hostile to religion or infringing on the Free Exercise Clause? Beginning with the well-established case of *Everson v. Board of Education* (330 U.S. 1, 1947), which made the Establishment Clause applicable to the states and advanced the "child benefit" theory, the Court has wrestled with many such school aid cases.

Parochial schools are operated primarily by the Roman Catholic church and, more recently, by numerous fundamentalist Protestant sects. They are funded through private donations from parishioners, tuitions, and church subsidies. Proponents of state aid to these schools have consistently argued that such aid benefits the child without materially advancing the church as an institution, a principle endorsed by the Court in *Everson*. They also stand on the Free Exercise Clause by positing the plausible argument that aid helps the church continue the religious education of its members and thus promotes continued freedom of religious expression. Economic arguments are also raised. Church leaders insist that closing parochial schools would put more strain on already overburdened public school budgets. Opponents argue on Establishment Clause grounds that state aid to parochial education amounts to preferential treatment of particular religious institutions and activities.

Court decisions have examined parochial aid by utilizing both the "child benefit" and "valid secular purpose" theories. Hence, *Board of Education v. Allen* (392 U.S. 236, 1968) upheld free textbooks for parochial students, a decision reaffirmed in the instances of similar state aid plans in *Meek v. Pittenger* (421 U.S. 349, 1975) and *Wolman v. Walter* (433 U.S. 229, 1977). *Everson* involved transportation, whereas *Allen, Meek,* and *Wolman* involved textbooks, but all four cases were held together by the common thread that the Court was unwilling to reject aid that benefited parochial students directly.

Indirect aid, however, such as teacher salaries, tuition grants, and physical plant expenditures, has been rejected as an infringement of the Establishment Clause. In *Lemon v. Kurtzman* and *Robinson v. Dicenso* (403 U.S. 602, 1971) the Court firmly rejected such state programs because they involved "excessive entanglement" between secular and religious institutions to the detriment of the separation principle. But the Court's willingness to endorse federal aid to *higher* education institutions even for the improvement of physical facilities is an indication of how the Court has unevenly applied the three-criteria test for the Establishment Clause. Institutions of higher education, the Court reasoned, were not fraught with the danger of "excessive entanglement" because the students were beyond the age of religious indoctrination, the facilities funded were "religiously neutral" (classrooms, labs, and so on), and the one-time nature of the grants did not necessitate any continuous government surveillance of a college's administration.

The future of aid programs or of school prayer is uncertain. It seems likely, however, that the three-pronged test of "purpose and primary effect," "advancement or inhibition of religion", and "excessive entanglement" will remain on the constitutional landscape.

The articles in this chapter continue this debate. Erwin Griswold, one-time solicitor general of the United States and dean of the Harvard Law School, insists that an absolute "wall of separation" is neither required by the First Amendment nor a fair reflection of U.S. traditions. Geoffrey Stone counters that the school prayer and Bible-reading decisions were reasonable and judicious and that efforts to pass a school prayer amendment are ill advised.

[Is Jefferson's "Wall of Separation" Breached by Prayer
in Public Schools?]

Yes: The School Prayer Decisions Are Reasonable

Geoffrey R. Stone

E NGEL and *Schempp* are founded upon a perfectly sensible understanding of the establishment clause. They are in accord with the
Court's precedents and are consistent with the language, purposes,
and history of the first amendment.

The practice of government sponsored prayer in the public schools impli-
cates the most fundamental values underlying the first amendment. Unlike
other establishment clause questions, the school prayer issue does not involve
the mere *neutral* provision of wholly *secular* government services, such as fire
and police protection, to both religious and secular institutions. Nor does it
involve the mere *neutral* and essentially *passive* acquiescence of government
in the conduct of both religious and secular activities on government property, such as the distribution of leaflets on public streets. Rather, government
sponsored prayer in the public schools involves *direct* and *active* government
involvement in the encouragement and structuring of perhaps the most basic
form of religious activity—prayer itself. For government to compose, select,
or promote prayers to be recited by children in a setting dedicated specifically
to the inculcation and "preservation of . . . values" would clearly seem to
undermine the constitutionally compelled separation of church and state.

Three arguments are most commonly offered in opposition to this conclusion. First, it is sometimes said that *Engel* and *Schempp* are predicated
upon a misguided notion of "neutrality." Under this view, the establishment
clause "command[s] impartiality . . . [only] as among the various sects of
theistic religions, that is, religions that profess a belief in God. But as between
theistic religions and those nontheistic creeds that do not acknowledge God,

Geoffrey R. Stone, from "In Opposition to the School Prayer Amendment," 50 *University of
Chicago Law Review* (1983), pp. 827–835.

the precept of neutrality . . . [does] not obtain." Accordingly, so-called "non-denominational" prayers, such as the Regents' prayer invalidated in *Engel,* pose no establishment clause issue.

At the outset, it should be emphasized that the proposed constitutional amendment cannot be defended on this basis, for as its proponents concede, "[t]he proposed amendment . . . does not . . . limit prayer in public schools . . . to 'nondenominational prayer.' " In any event, this understanding of the clause seems inconsistent with the central premise of religious tolera-tion upon which the First Amendment is founded, for under this view the establishment clause would not protect the members of such faiths as "Bud-dhism, Taoism, Ethical Culture, Secular Humanism and others." A more inclusive and more reasonable interpretation, long embraced by the Court, holds not only that the establishment clause forbids "governmental prefer-ence of one religion over another," but also that it takes " 'every form of prop-agation of religion out of the realm of things which could directly or indi-rectly be made public business.' " Under this interpretation, government can-not "constitutionally pass laws or impose requirements which aid all religions as against non-believers, and [it cannot] aid those religions based on a belief in the existence of God as against those religions founded on different beliefs."

Moreover, even if the less inclusive interpretation were supportable, the very concept of a "nondenominational prayer" is self-contradictory. There are well over fifty different theistic sects in the United States, each of which has its own tenets regarding the appropriate nature and manner of prayer. Any effort to compose a truly nondenominational prayer must thus produce, at best, a sterile litany virtually devoid of true religious meaning. Indeed, even the Regents' prayer in *Engel* embodies numerous sectarian presumptions—that it is appropriate to pray orally, in unison with others, and in public; that it is appropriate to invoke divine blessing for one's parents; that the appropri-ate subject of prayer is a unitary, immanent, and metaphysical "God" who is "almighty"; that the appropriate relationship of human beings to "God" is one of supplication and dependence; and that it is appropriate to "beg." Finally, even if one could compose a meaningful nondenominational prayer, there is the very real and widely recognized danger that the "official promo-tion of common-denominator religious practices" could contribute to the development of an "official folk religion" and thus undermine the "vital-ity . . . of the historic faiths." This is, of course, one of the evils that the first amendment was designed to prevent, for as the Court observed in *Engel,* one of the assumptions underlying the establishment clause is "that a union of government and religion tends . . . to degrade religion."

A second objection that is occasionally lodged against *Engel* and *Schempp* turns on the notion that the school prayer issue involves a conflict between the establishment clause and the free exercise clause and that the

Court did not give sufficient weight to the free exercise interests of those students and parents who desire government sponsored prayer in the public schools. This argument was first elaborated by Justice Stewart in his dissenting opinion in *Schempp*. He argued that "a compulsory state educational system so structures a child's life" that "parents who want their children exposed to religious influences" might not be able adequately to "fulfill that wish off school property and outside school time." Although Stewart conceded that such parents would have a right under the free exercise clause to send their children to private or parochial school, he maintained that this consideration was "too facile to be determinative" because, as the Court had recognized in *Murdock v. Pennsylvania*, " '[f]reedom of speech, freedom of the press, [and] freedom of religion are available to all, not merely to those who can pay their own way.' "

This argument proves too much, for it would logically authorize not only school prayer, but "state sponsorship of the full panoply of denominational instruction available in private schools." Why, after all, should the line be drawn at one highly ritualistic prayer? Moreover, Justice Stewart's reliance on *Murdock* is fundamentally misplaced, for there is a critical difference for First Amendment purposes between the proposition, established in *Murdock*, that government may not unreasonably *tax* religious activity, and the proposition, put forth by Justice Stewart, that government may affirmatively *promote* such activity. Finally, it should be emphasized that the school prayer issue does not pose a "true" conflict between the establishment clause and the free exercise clause, for as even Justice Stewart appeared to concede, the refusal of government to sponsor prayer in the public schools would not itself violate the free exercise clause. . . .

The third argument that is occasionally advanced in opposition to *Engel* and *Schempp* is that "the history of the Establishment Clause . . . [does] not support the Supreme Court's conclusion that public prayer in schools is unconstitutional." In his opinion for the Court in *Engel*, Justice Black suggested that the result was virtually dictated by the intent of the Framers. In fact, it seems fair to say that Black's use of history was somewhat "overdrawn," for a careful review of the record indicates more ambiguity than Black acknowledges. This is not to say, however, that the claim that *Engel* and *Schempp* are contrary to the intent of the Framers is any less "overdrawn." As is often the case, the appeal to the intent of the Framers yields mixed and conflicting conclusions. The point, of course, is not that history is no guide. It is, rather, that resort to the intent of the Framers is a slippery business that must be approached with caution.

There are essentially three facets to the historical attack on the Court's decisions. At the most specific level, it is argued that "the Framers of the First Amendment did not intend to forbid public prayer." To support this contention, the critics of *Engel* and *Schempp* point out, for example, that the First

Congress, which drafted the First Amendment, "retained a chaplain to offer public prayers" and, "the day after proposing the First Amendment, called on President Washington to proclaim 'a day of public thanksgiving and prayer.' "

Although the Framers of the First Amendment did not intend to forbid such public prayer, that is not the issue. For as the Court made clear in both *Engel* and *Schempp,* those decisions turned on the very special characteristics of *school prayer.* In *Engel,* for example, Justice Black explained that "nothing in the decision reached here . . . is inconsistent with . . . [the] many manifestations in our public life of belief in God . . . [Most] patriotic or ceremonial occasions bear no true resemblance to the unquestioned *religious exercise* that the State of New York has sponsored in this instance." Similarly, in *Schempp,* Justice Clark expressly distinguished the clearly "religious" exercises that were "prescribed as part of the curricular activities of students who are required by law to attend school" from such matters as the inclusion in oaths of office of the final supplication "[so] help me God" and the traditional commencement of legislative and judicial sessions with an opening prayer.

Thus, that "the Framers did not intend to forbid public prayer" generally tells us very little about their intent with respect to the very special problem of government sponsored prayer in the public schools, where the environment is dedicated to the inculcation of values and "where immature and impressionable children are [especially] susceptible to a pressure to conform and to participate in the expression of religious beliefs." And, of course, the Framers themselves gave no distinct consideration to the particular question of devotional exercises in public schools, for education as the Framers knew it was confined almost exclusively to private schools. Finally, even if the Framers had expressed an intent on this question, it is not at all clear that it is sensible for their intent to control our present understanding of the clause. The religious composition of our society and the general structure of American education have changed fundamentally since the enactment of the first amendment. We may well be truer to the intent of the Framers if we look not to their specific intent based on their immediate circumstances but to whether, in the light of changed circumstances, a challenged practice tends to promote the type of interdependence of religion and state that the first amendment was designed to prevent.

The second facet of the historical attack focuses on the Court's interpretation of the establishment clause at a more general level. In attempting to come to grips with the ambiguities of the clause, the Court often has sought guidance in the writings of Thomas Jefferson and of James Madison, the original author of the First Amendment. Indeed, to "anyone conversant . . . with Madison's Memorial of 1785" and with the Court's reliance on Madison's views, the decision in *Engel* "ought scarcely to have been surprising." Critics of the Court's decision maintain, however, that the Court has paid too much attention to the views of Jefferson and Madison and not enough attention to the views of others who contributed to the framing of the First Amendment. These critics argue that a consideration of the other views would lead to an understanding of the clause considerably narrower than that embraced by the Court. The Reagan Administration argues, for example, that a consideration of these other views would demonstrate that "the concern the Congress wished to address by the amendment was the fear that the federal government might establish a national church, use its influence to prefer certain sects over others, or require or compel persons to worship in a manner contrary to their conscience," and that "in addressing that concern, Congress did not want to act in a manner that would be harmful to religion generally or would defer to the small minority who held no religion." This interpretation is not wholly implausible, but neither is the Court's. To the contrary, on any fair reading of the record there is "sufficient historical evidence to justify" the Court's interpretation. At best, then, the contrary interpretation warrants the traditional Scotch verdict: not proven.

The final facet of the historical attack turns not on the intent of the Framers, but on the observation that "there has been a long tradition of including some form of prayer in the public schools ever since their inception." Although the existence of such a "tradition" may be relevant to constitutional interpretation, it is hardly dispositive. Otherwise, such landmark decisions as *Brown v. Board of Education* and *New York Times Co. v. Sullivan* would not stand. In any event, at the time of the *Engel* and *Schempp* decisions, the "tradition" of school prayer was not nearly as firmly entrenched as the proponents of the proposed amendment would like to believe. By 1962, a number of states had outlawed school prayer entirely, and only twenty-two states had actually sanctioned it by statute or judicial decision. A 1962 survey revealed that less than half the school systems in the United States conducted Bible readings and only about one third of the systems required prayers at the beginning of the school day.

The central holding of both *Engel* and *Schempp* is that government sponsored prayer in the public schools violates the establishment clause because its purpose and primary effect is to aid religion. This conclusion is founded upon a reasonable understanding of the First Amendment. Moreover, these decisions have clearly withstood the test of time. Despite dramatic changes in the makeup of the Court, *Engel* and *Schempp* have never been called into question. To the contrary, they remain important and vital components of the Court's contemporary interpretation of the First Amendment. Thus, those who support the proposed constitutional amendment must forthrightly recognize that they seek to overturn not just two decisions of the Supreme Court, but an established precept of our First Amendment jurisprudence. . . .

Is Jefferson's "Wall of Separation" Breached by Prayer
in Public Schools?

No: Absolute Is in the Dark

Erwin N. Griswold

I VENTURE the thought, quite seriously, that it was unfortunate that the
question involved in the *Engel* case was ever thought of as a matter for
judicial decision, that it was unfortunate that the Court decided the case,
one way or the other, and that this unhappy situation resulted solely from the
absolutist position which the Court has taken and intimated in such matters,
thus inviting such litigation in its extreme form.

What do I mean by this? I have in mind at least two separate lines of
thought. One is the fact that we have a tradition, a spiritual and cultural
tradition, of which we ought not to be deprived by judges carrying into effect
the logical implications of absolutist notions not expressed in the Constitution itself, and surely never contemplated by those who put the Constitutional provisions into effect. The other is that there are some matters which
are essentially local in nature, important matters, but nonetheless matters to
be worked out by the people themselves in their own communities, when no
basic rights of others are impaired. . . .

First, as to the long tradition. Is it not clear as a matter of historical fact
that this was a Christian nation? Of the immigrants who came to previously
British North America by the time of the adoption of the Constitution, virtually all were Christian, in all the degrees and types of persuasion which come
within that term. Are the Mayflower Compact, Ann Hutchison, Cotton
Mather, Jonathan Edwards, and William Penn, and many others, no part of
our history? It is true that we were a rather remarkable Christian nation, having, for various historical and philosophical reasons, developed a tolerance in
matters of religion which was at once virtually unique and a tribute to the
men of the seventeenth and eighteenth centuries who developed the type of
thought which came to prevail here. But this was not a purely humanistic
type of thought. Nor did it deny the importance and significance of religion.

Erwin N. Griswold, from "Absolute Is in the Dark; A Discussion of the Supreme Court on Constitutional Questions," 8 *Utah Law Review* (1963), pp. 173–177.

It is perfectly true, and highly salutary, that the First Amendment forbade Congress to pass any law "respecting an establishment of religion or prohibiting the free exercise thereof." These are great provisions, of great sweep and basic importance. But to say that they require that all trace of religion be kept out of any sort of public activity is sheer invention. Our history is full of these traces: chaplains in Congress and in the armed forces; chapels in prisons; "In God We Trust" on our money; to mention only a few. God is referred to in our national anthem, and in "America," and many others of what may be called our national songs. Must all of these things be rigorously extirpated in order to satisfy a constitutional absolutism? What about Sunday? What about Christmas? Must we deny our whole heritage, our culture, the things of spirit and soul which have sustained us in the past and helped to bind us together in times of good and bad?

Does our deep-seated tolerance of all religions—or, to the same extent, of no religion—require that we give up all religious observance in public activities? Why should it? It certainly never occurred to the Founders that it would. It is hardly likely that it was entirely accidental that these questions did not even come before the Court in the first hundred and fifty years of our constitutional history. I do not believe that the contentions now made would occur to any man who could free himself from an absolute approach to the problem.

Jefferson is often cited as the author of views leading to the absolutist approach. His "wall of separation" is the shibboleth of those who feel that all traces of religion must be barred from any part of public activity. This phrase comes from Jefferson's reply to the Danbury Baptist Association, dated January 1, 1802. It is clear that he wrote it deliberately, and with planned effect, as, before issuing it, he sent it to the Attorney General for comment with a note saying that he thought of answers to such addresses as "the occasion . . . of sowing useful truths and principles among the people which might germinate and become rooted among their political tenets." What Jefferson wrote was a powerful way of summarizing the effect of the First Amendment. But it was clearly neither a complete statement nor a substitute for the words of the Amendment itself. Moreover, the absolute effect which some have sought to give to these words is belied by Jefferson's own subsequent actions and writings.

This matter has been thoroughly investigated by a number of writers. The most recent, and perhaps the most dispassionate of these, is Robert M. Healey, whose book, entitled "Jefferson on Religion in Public Education," was published in 1962. Professor Healey shows that Jefferson denied "that the government was without religion." On the contrary, he contemplated that "those areas of religion on which all sects agreed were certainly to be included within the framework of public education." And he continues, "Jefferson was indeed against government support of any kind for any one or more churches," but "it is not true that he was against support of religion in general or against any form of religion in public education."

The seeking of motives in such cases is dangerous and fraught with difficulties, especially when the motives are likely not to be clearly appreciated by the authors of statements or opinions, or by commentators. On this, Professor Healey may shed some light. He says: "Jefferson's attempts to relate religion to public education reflected his belief that his own religious persuasion was not only right but neutral, and therefore a constitutionally acceptable basis for developing moral adults and fostering religious freedom." And he adds that Jefferson's actions "reveal an unconscious but powerful drive to put his own religious beliefs in a position of unusual strength. . . . That his efforts to foster religious freedom in public education might result in the virtual establishment of his own beliefs . . . undoubtedly never occurred to him in any convincing fashion." Might the same words be applicable to our present advocates of absolutism?

Similarly, though Catholic reaction to the *Engel* decision has been varied, it may be that some of it is motivated by the thought that if public education can be completely secularized (so that, as it has been said, "religion" in such quarters becomes "a dirty word"), then there will be an increased public demand for sectarian education which can combine religion with general education. This could then be an argument in favor of parochial schools, and as the public schools decline, the argument for public support of parochial schools can be advanced in one guise or another. Thus, as so often happens, the absolutist approach may be its own worst enemy, and may result in a situation which will in effect destroy public education, and thus go far to defeat the very results the absolutists want to achieve.

Now let me turn to the other point—that there are some matters which should be settled on the local level, in each community, and should not become great Supreme Court cases. This can be presented on an essentially legal level, in terms of "standing to sue," and this has been thoughtfully developed by my colleague, Professor Sutherland. What I have in mind is not really different, but I would like to consider it in less technical terms.

The prayer involved in the *Engel* case was not compulsory. As the Supreme Court itself recited, no pupil was compelled "to join in the prayer over his or his parents' objection." This, to me, is crucial. If any student was compelled to join against his conviction, this would present a serious and justiciable question, akin to that presented in the flag salute case. The Supreme Court did not give sufficient weight to this fact, in my opinion, and relied heavily on such things as the history of the Book of Common Prayer, which, under various Acts of Parliament, was compulsory on all.

Where there is no compulsion, what happens if these matters are left to the determination of each community? In New York, under the action of the Regents, this determination was made by the elected authorities of the School

District. It was, indeed, a fact that a large number of the School Districts in New York did not adopt the so-called Regents' prayer. This may have been because they could not agree to do so, or because the situation in particular school districts was such that all or a majority did agree that they did not want to have such a prayer or that it was better to proceed without a prayer. Where such a decision was reached, there can surely be no constitutional objection on the ground that it was a decision locally arrived at, or that it amounts to an "establishment" of "no religion." But, suppose that in a particular school district, as in New Hyde Park, it was determined that the prayer should be used as a part of the opening exercises of the school day. Remember that it is not compulsory. No pupil is compelled to participate. Must all refrain because one does not wish to join? This would suggest that no school can have a Pledge of Allegiance to the Flag if any student does not wish to join. I heartily agree with the decision in the *Barnette* case that no student can be compelled to join in a flag salute against his religious scruples. But it is a far cry from that decision to say that no School District can have a flag salute for those who want to participate if there is any student who does not wish to join.

This is a country of religious toleration. That is a great consequence of our history embodied in the First Amendment. But does religious toleration mean religious sterility? I wonder why it should be thought that it does. This, I venture to say again, has been, and is, a Christian country, in origin, history, tradition and culture. It was out of Christian doctrine and ethics, I think it can be said, that it developed its notion of toleration. No one in this country can be required to have any particular form of religious belief; and no one can suffer legal discrimination because he has or does not have any particular religious belief. But does the fact that we have officially adopted toleration as our standard mean that we must give up our history and our tradition? The Moslem who comes here may worship as he pleases, and may hold public office without discrimination. That is as it should be. But why should it follow that he can require others to give up their Christian tradition merely because he is a tolerated and welcomed member of the community? . . .

Let us consider the Jewish child, or the Catholic child, or the nonbeliever, or the Congregationalist, or the Quaker. He, either alone, or with a few or many others of his views, attends a public school, whose School District, by local action, has prescribed the Regents' prayer. When the prayer is recited, if this child or his parents feel that he cannot participate, he may stand or sit, in respectful attention, while the other children take part in the ceremony. Or he may leave the room. It is said that this is bad, because it sets him apart from other children. It is even said that there is an element of compulsion in this— what the Supreme Court has called an "indirect coercive pressure upon religious minorities to conform." But is this the way it should be looked at? The child of a nonconforming or minority group is, to be sure, different in his beliefs. That is what it means to be a member of a minority. Is it not desirable, and educational, for him to learn and observe this, in the atmosphere of the school—not so much that he is different, as that other children are different from him? And is it not desirable that, at the same time, he experiences and learns the fact that his difference is tolerated and accepted? No compulsion is put upon him. He need not participate. But he, too, has the opportunity to be tolerant. He allows the majority of the group to follow their own tradition, perhaps coming to understand and to respect what they feel is significant to them.

Is this not a useful and valuable and educational and, indeed, a spiritual experience for the children of what I have called the majority group? They experience the values of their own culture; but they also see that there are others who do not accept those values, and that they are wholly tolerated in their nonacceptance. Learning tolerance for other persons, no matter how different, and respect for their beliefs, may be an important part of American education, and wholly consistent with the First Amendment. I hazard the thought that no one would think otherwise were it not for parents who take an absolutist approach to the problem, perhaps encouraged by the absolutist expressions of Justices of the Supreme Court, on and off the bench. . . .

2
Wisconsin v. Yoder: Are All Religious Beliefs and Practices Guaranteed by the Free Exercise Clause?

Robert A. Poirier

IN the classic *Democracy in America,* Alexis de Tocqueville remarked that "religion is a distinct sphere" and observed that democracy promoted a "multitude of sects."[1] The distinct sphere of private religious activity protected by the Free Exercise Clause of the First Amendment has enjoyed a long history relatively free from government intrusion and hostility. Even private discrimination and hostility toward the practices of religious minorities, although certainly present, has been quite insignificant in the United States when compared with the experiences of other countries. Under the protection of the First Amendment and the general level of tolerance found in the United States, there has been, particularly in the past two decades, a veritable explosion of religious sects and cults operating on the fringes of the religious scene that would make even Tocqueville less sanguine about religious freedom in a democracy.

Despite the recent cult explosion, most Americans' religious experience remains within the mainstream of Christian denominations, which collectively comprise the large majority of the religiously affiliated public. The beliefs and practices of these denominations would raise few eyebrows or concerns today, although they might have done so in times past. Religious organizations do exist, however, whose beliefs and activities test the limit of permissibility under the Free Exercise Clause because of challenges to established orthodoxies, or more important, because of practices that provide a real or imagined threat to the health, safety, and general welfare of the community. Most recently we have seen in communities or witnessed through the media the following examples of religious activities testing the limit of tolerance in society: Rev. Jim Jones and the Jonestown mass murder-suicide, the practice of snake handling and poison drinking as religious exercise, the Rev. Moon and the Moonies, the Hare Krishna cult, religious cults that advocate free sex, the cultic use of drugs as in the case of the Rastafarians, the itinerant evangelicals who claim to have the power to heal physical ailments.

In these examples we are once again confronting, as in national security and other public order issues, the question of rights as absolutes or as relative to the interests of the larger society. Theoretically the Free Exercise Clause of the First Amendment disengages government from involvement with the "exercise" of religion. Separated by a comma from its sister Establishment Clause, suggesting that the two religion clauses were intended to serve different purposes, the Free Exercise Clause is bound in the spirit of separation of church and state envisioned by the Framers and is inexorably entangled in the contemporary debates on religion and politics. Referring once again to an observation of Tocqueville, sooner or later every issue becomes a judicial matter.

Such has been the case with the Free Exercise Clause. The case of *Wisconsin v. Yoder* (406 U.S. 205, 1972) is one example of many cases before the Supreme Court dealing with the fundamental question, To what extent can one claim exemption to universally applicable laws on the grounds of religious freedom? Questions corollary to this one are whether government can compel behavior that is violative of religious beliefs and whether it can prohibit behavior that is a required religious practice.

In the *Yoder* case the respondents were members of the Old Order Amish religion and the Conservative Amish Mennonite church. Traditionally known for their industriousness and success as farmers, the Amish have always been exemplary law-abiding and peaceful citizens. Despite a life-style considered odd by the standards of the modern world, it would be unfair to categorize the Amish as extremist. Their conflict with the law was relatively uncomplicated. Amish beliefs require members to disassociate themselves from the worldly values of the modern world and live an austere, simple life of physical labor. The Amish agree with the importance of learning reading, writing, and arithmetic, but they believe they have no need for high school education and in fact consider such education a threat to their life-style and, more important, to the tenets of their faith. Thus, the Yoders had run afoul of the compulsory education law in the state of Wisconsin that required school attendance until age sixteen. The state contended that it had an interest of "sufficient magnitude to override the interest claiming protection under the Free Exercise Clause" and prosecuted the Yoders for violating the school attendance statute.

The first task before the Court was to determine whether Amish beliefs were based on deep religious conviction or merely a matter of personal life-style. Agreeing that the Yoders' beliefs were "deeply religious", the Court next had to ask if the reasons for the Wisconsin law were compelling enough to interfere with Amish religious convictions. Conceding the state's right and obligation to require education so as not to foster ignorance, the Court argued that "a state's interest in universal education . . . is not totally free from a balancing process when it impinges on other fundamental rights and interest." Carefully balancing the state's right to educate children to function in society against the Amish community's religious convictions *and* their strong emphasis on vocational agricultural education for *their* society, the Supreme Court ruled in favor of the Yoders's request for variance from the school attendance law.

The *Yoder* case broke some new constitutional ground in the difficult problem of "free exercise" in two significant ways. The first concerns the issue of the belief-action dichotomy established in the first test of "free exercise," *Reynolds v. U.S.* (98 U.S. 145, 1878), decided by the Supreme Court. At issue was the Mormon practice of polygamy for which Reynolds was convicted. Claiming violation of his right under the First Amendment, Reynolds appealed but lost his case before the Supreme Court. Citing popular opinion and some scholarly research, the Court felt confident that polygamy was deleterious to morality and that its prohibition was compelled by the necessity to protect society.

The *Reynolds* decision gave a great deal of freedom to the state to regulate religious behavior. Reinforcing the belief-action test in 1940, *Cantwell v. Connecticut* (310 U.S. 296) leaned in the direction of the "free exercise" claimant but insisted the state had an obligation and right to protect citizens from harm even if the actions were perpetrated in the guise of religion. The Cantwell doctrine, as it came to be known, emphasized the point that "beliefs" are absolute and beyond the regulatory hand of the state, whereas "actions," by necessity, might require some state-imposed limitations. In so ruling, the Court left an opening to those who might argue that religious "action" was not protected by the Free Exercise Clause. Wisconsin argued this position against Yoder, but the Court firmly rejected that notion and held that, without negating a state's compelling interest in some circumstances, "there are areas of conduct protected by the Free Exercise Clause of the First Amendment and thus beyond the power of the State to control."

The second area of groundbreaking in *Yoder* was that the case opened the Pandora's box of how to avoid violating the Establishment Clause while granting privileges under the Free Exercise Clause. *Yoder* represents the first case to grant an exemption from a valid criminal statute to a specific religion. Since there are extensive precedents interpreting the Establishment Clause to mean that there can be no official state religion or preferential treatment to any particular religion, did the Court violate the Establishment Clause in *Yoder*? A cursory review of the flag salute cases is appropriate here.

Like *Cantwell,* the flag salute cases involved Jehovah's Witnesses (who have been before the Supreme Court in religious freedom cases more than any other religious group) who refused to participate in required flag salute exercises in public schools on the grounds that they were a violation of their religious convictions not to worship any "graven images." The first such case, *Minersville School District v. Gobitis* (310 U.S. 586, 1940), went against the Jehovah's Witnesses and led the way to a considerable amount of private discriminatory and hostile action against the sect by a public seeking a scapegoat for the depressing turn of events on the war fronts of Europe. But three years later the Court reversed itself in *West Virginia Board of Education v. Barnette* (319 U.S. 624, 1943), and here is the difference with *Yoder*: the Court did not grant Jehovah's Witnesses a specific exemption from a universal law. Instead it held that *no one* should be required to salute the flag. Although claiming rights under the Free Exercise Clause for themselves, the Jehovah's Witnesses won rights for all citizens and vindicated the view that the state cannot compel a person to express a belief he or she does not hold.

Cases involving draft exemptions for conscientious objectors also have raised concerns over the clash between the Free Exercise and Establishment clauses. Earlier draft exemption rules allowed members of bona fide pacifist religions such as the Quakers and Mennonites to claim conscientious objector status. The matter lay largely unchallenged until the unpopular Vietnam war resulted in a flood of litigation. In *U.S. v. Seeger* (380 U.S. 163, 1965), the Court, hoping to sidestep the Free Exercise–Establishment conundrum, expanded the category of classes that could claim exemption from military service. Previously one had to show "religious training and belief" in a pacifist sect. *Seeger* construed "religious training and belief" to mean "a sincere and meaningful belief which occupies in the life of its possessor a place parallel to that filled by the God of those admittedly qualifying for exemption." Although retaining a "religious motivation" to qualify for draft exemption, *Seeger*'s "parallel place" doctrine eliminated formal religious instruction as a requirement and avoided the charge that granting pacifist sects the privilege of draft exemption discriminated against those religious beliefs that might lead to moral opposition to combat even if not formulated in the crucible of a pacifist religion. Hence, there was no longer preferential treatment for the Quakers and Mennonites. Then, on the premise established in *Torcaso v. Watkins* (367 U.S. 488, 1961) that theistic belief need not be a requirement for religious belief, the Court in *Welsh v. U.S.* (398 U.S. 333, 1970) effectively eliminated any and all theistic bias in the draft law by expanding the qualifications for consciencious objector status to include motivations other than those religiously based. What remained now was the question of whether the Establishment Clause was being violated by granting a Free Exercise Privilege to those who held moral values leading to opposition to all wars, while denying a privilege to holders of those moral values leading to opposition to a *particular* war. In *Gillette v. U.S.* (401 U.S. 437, 1971), the Court firmly closed the door on any concept of "selective conscientious objection."

Another area involving a clash of state police powers with the "free exercise" of religion concerns the rights of Sabbatarians such as Jews and Seventh Day Adventists, which may come in conflict with laws favoring the interests of a majoritarian Sunday-worshiping society. In 1961 the Court decided in *Braunfeld v. Brown* and *Gallagher v. Crown Kosher Super Market* (366 U.S. 617) that the Sunday closing law of Pennsylvania did not infringe on the religious freedom of Jews even though they suffered an economic penalty for closing on Saturday for religious reasons *and* Sunday for statutory reasons. These cases established the view that a valid state purpose to advance a secular goal would be constitutional even if this placed an indirect burden on religion. Unfortunately the Sunday closing cases failed to yield an effective standard for drawing lines. *Sherbert v. Verner* (374 U.S. 398, 1963), decided two years later, provided an opportunity for a more precise standard. The Court ruled in favor of a woman's claim to unemployment compensation after she, a practicing Seventh Day Adventist, lost her job for refusing Saturday work. The *Sherbert* standard, which was also applied in *Yoder,* holds that the state must provide evidence of a "compelling state interest in the regulation of a subject within the state's constitutional power to regulate," and it must demonstrate "that no alternative forms of regulation would combat such abuses without infringing First Amendment rights."

Any "compelling state interest" test to override a religious freedom claim is subject to the same kind of limitations and pitfalls that the critics of "clear and present danger" have pointed out for that constitutional test. Religious freedom is not an absolute. Similarly, absolute separation of church and state is impossible to achieve; hence, how the line ultimately is drawn between religious freedom and other societal rights might well depend on considerations of public tolerance.

This theme is taken up by the two subsequent essays. Martin S. Sheffer argues that the limits on the Free Exercise Clause should be as narrow as possible—that religious practices are specially protected by the First Amendment. Walter Berns warns of the dangers of allowing religions to be above the law.

Yes: The Free Exercise Clause: Are Standards of Adjudication Possible?

Martin S. Sheffer

THE free exercise of religion guarantee speaks of freedom of religious belief and freedom of religious action. As such it is related to the other substantive rights of the First Amendment—namely, speech, press, assembly, and petition. At the same time, the phrase "prohibiting the free exercise thereof" is designed to mean that Congress and, by virtue of the doctrine of incorporation, the states as well may not restrict or prohibit religious belief and exercise. Yet while the first is absolute, the second cannot be. As Justice Owen J. Roberts said: "Conduct remains subject to regulation for the protection of society. The freedom to act must have appropriate definition to preserve the enforcement of that protection. . . . The power to regulate must be so exercised as not, in attaining a permissible end, unduly to infringe the protected freedom." Yet drawing the line here raises as many questions as it seems to answer, and it involves, as well as emphasizes, the interrelationship between free exercise and the guarantees of speech, press, and assembly.

More directly to the point, the free exercise clause, as well as the non-establishment clause, attempts to mollify the uncertain relationship between the realm of God and that of Caesar. The words of the clause leave much unstated and seem to take much for granted. Is the clause primarily an expression of religious commitment, or are the words intended to justify a democratic and secular experiment? The First Amendment does not explain itself. What is at least clear is the fact that the free exercise clause is not an isolated statement. It may be argued that in the absence of a religious clause, the guarantees of speech, press, and assembly provide sufficient protection for religious belief, religious worship, and religious proselytizing. However,

Martin S. Sheffer, from "The U.S. Supreme Court and the Free Exercise Clause: Are Standards of Adjudication Possible?" 23 *Journal of Church and State* (Autumn 1981), pp. 533–549.

because the free exercise clause is not redundant, it must be interpreted as having a more specific scope in protecting something not protected by the other First Amendment clauses.

The problem of defining the phrase "free exercise of religion" is a difficult, if not impossible, task. Nevertheless, at this point some brief attempt does seem appropriate. Each individual is guaranteed the constitutional right to believe, worship, and practice his religion so long as that individual does not illegally interfere with the rights of others. Thus, there are those "who believe in nothing, those who believe but doubt, those who believe without questioning, those who worship the Judeo-Christian God in innumerably different ways, those who adhere to Mohammed's creed, those who worship themselves, those who worship a cow or other animals, those who worship several gods—to mention just a few of the remarkable variety of expressions of belief that obtain." Any legal definition of free exercise, if one is even possible, will come from the Supreme Court. Its acceptance or rejection by a majority of the people will depend ultimately on their willingness to have the Court substitute its current legal values in defining free exercise for their own psychologically oriented spiritual values. They have usually allowed the Court's definitions to stand.

The free exercise of religion clause means more than no governmental infringement of that inner, spiritual belief already beyond governmental reach. Nevertheless, something is protected against governmental intrusion. As a beginning, one must question what free exercise does not mean. Free exercise, for example, does not mean that the individual may resort to any action which he believes is sanctioned by his religion. At the same time, the individual cannot refuse to obey valid criminal law, even if it is contrary to his religion. In essence, there are limits to the freedom guaranteed by the free exercise clause, and the Court's line-drawing can set limits which are minimal as well as maximal.

On the other hand, in terms of what free exercise may mean, one must distinguish among the freedoms of belief, worship, and proselytizing because each represents a different aspect of the free exercise of religion. At minimum, the freedom of religious belief means that the government cannot impose upon the individual an official or acceptable belief, or one which he must say he believes, for freedom of belief means much more than no allowable compulsion. It also means that the individual is guaranteed freedom from any intellectual conformity resulting from the embarrassment of his refusal to be compelled initially. Ultimately, it means, in the words of Joseph Tussman, the right of individuals "to provide or maintain a general environment conducive to the development of desired moral and intellectual attitudes and beliefs." All forms of coercion vis-a-vis religious belief are intolerable and should be constitutionally voided. . . .

In refusing to permit the state to define as harmful (and therefore as actionable behavior) anything it believed undesirable, the Court, in *Wisconsin v. Yoder,* held Old Order Amish parents immune to criminal punishment for violation of a compulsory education law. In reaching that conclusion, Chief Justice Warren E. Burger "tested" religion in terms of its longevity. If one's religion has been long recognized as legitimate, and everyone has perceived those actions to be religious, one must be accorded the protection of the free exercise clause. Even the claim of the state as *parens patriae* could not be sustained (absent the overriding charge of direct criminal conduct) in the face of the minority's judicially protected right to believe and to practice a minority point of view.

The same general result obtained in the California case of *People v. Woody,* where the state supreme court overturned the conviction of American Indians for the religious use of peyote. Finding that the religious use of peyote had a long history among various Indian tribes and that the sacramental use of peyote was the cornerstone of the Navaho religion, Justice Mathew O. Tobriner could find no sufficiently compelling reason for prohibiting a practice so central to the religion: "Peyote . . . is the *sine qua non* of defendants' faith," and the state's regulation of peyote thus tore out "the theological heart of Peyotism."

What was troublesome, of course, was, and still is, the distinct possibility that courts would equate "traditional" and "orthodox" with "religious." It is hoped that courts would not apply one interpretation of the free exercise clause to religious actions the judge found personally acceptable and another (and more restrictive) interpretation to unorthodox religious groups. The creation of "one rule for well established religions and a different rule for religions 'newly discovered'" must never be allowed. Moreover, Lionel H. Frankel suggested that "it is precisely in its dynamic infancy that a new religious doctrine will seem most threatening to the old order. It is at this stage that it is most likely to be met by some form of community resistence. The First Amendment must surely apply to protect new religions as well as old from governmental restraints. . . . "

Assuming that the Supreme Court is not yet ready to accept a comprehensive system of freedom of expression, consider the following test: Any law that compels an individual to perform a duty contrary to his religious belief or the dictates of his conscience must be presumed unconstitutional. The burden of proof (a showing of a compelling and overwhelming state interest) falls exclusively on the state. Any law which, in its application, is demonstrated *prima facie* to be religious in its primary effect must once again be presumed unconstitutional. Once the Court distinguishes between laws that compel and those that command nonperformance of an act, the task is easier. At the same time, no distinction should be made between religion and conscience—even nontheistic conscience.

On the other hand, where criminal conduct of a sufficiently dangerous nature (or a clear and imminent danger) is involved—and this does not mean drug or child labor laws—the law would be presumed constitutional even against a free exercise claim. A specific type of criminal enactment—for example, a command that individuals not handle poisonous snakes during religious rituals—would not involve any presumption of unconstitutionality because of the compelling state interest at stake. Other laws regulating criminal conduct (such as those present in the *Leary* and *Prince* cases) would not stand if such conduct is believed by the individual as an "inexcusable duty" in a bona fide cause and it involves only the individual and other consenting persons. In other words, even here the most important interest protected by the free exercise clause (and the one the state cannot infringe) "is the prevention of the severe psychic turmoil that can be brought about by compelled violation of conscience."

Such a standard can be applied by the Court in the following way. First, the Court must define religious "effect," namely: "State action abridging the individual's freedom to adopt, observe, or propagate his religion (or irreligion) through programs of assistance, or systems of regulations, exercises a religious effect." Second, once such a definition is agreed upon, the Court must decide whether the free exercise clause will allow such effect. To that end it must ask whether the purpose and primary effect of the law is secular and does the state have a compelling interest to decline alternative means involving no secondary religious or conscientious effect? Third, "if the plaintiff tenders *prima facie* proof of a secondary religious effect, the government must rebut the inference of the secondary effect, *or prove that it has considered alternative means free of such effects and that it has over-bearing reasons for not adopting them.*" Fourth, the Court must determine whether the state has even considered alternative means. Fifth, the Court must judge whether the challenged statute has possible alternatives put forth by the state that is attempting to justify the impractibility of alternative means. If the state has not considered less restrictive measures, the Court cannot sustain the claim that none exist. Under these circumstances the law must be judged unconstitutional.

The Court has occasionally taken judicial notice of these standards (at least in part) and applied them to concrete fact situations. Thus, in *Sherbert* the Court said: "An incidental burden on the free exercise of religion may be justified by a compelling interest in the regulation of a subject within the state's constitutional power to regulate [but] it would plainly be incumbent upon [the state] to demonstrate that no alternative forms of regulation would combat such abuses without infringing First Amendment rights." In *McGowan,* Justice Frankfurter's concurrence suggested much the same approach and also implied that the same standards can be used in establishment cases as well: "If a statute furthers both secular and religious ends by means unnecessary to the effectuation of the secular ends alone—where the same ends could equally be attained by means which do not have the consequences for the promotion of religion—that statute cannot stand." Finally, the California Supreme Court held in *Woody* that, notwithstanding the secular purpose and primary effect of a narcotics control law, the statute must fall because the state could not show a compelling interest in enforcing it against the Native Church of America and imposing a secondary burden: "The state's showing of 'compelling interest' cannot lie in untested assertions that recognition of a religious immunity will interfere with the enforcement of the state statute."

This is properly a generous set of standards for free exercise (both religion and conscience) interests. It is recognition that in God's domain, when Caesar is to trespass, Caesar must do so with honesty, consideration, and under extraordinary circumstances: "The presumption is against rather than in favor of the validity of legislation which on its face or in its application restricts the rights of conscience, expression, and assembly, protected by the First Amendment." Such a standard, when properly applied, would have struck down as void on its face, or void in its application, or void in its secondary effect, many of the laws upheld by the Court in the free exercise cases. Ultimately this standard would encircle the free exercise clause with a preferred position as the clause itself encircles belief, worship, and proselytizing with a corresponding preference.

One additional point: It has been suggested that the free exercise clause enjoys a preferred position in the eyes of the Court. More specifically, this means that "when a preferred position is assigned to a constitutional right, two results follow. The presumption of constitutionality will no longer suffice to validate a statute which invades such right [and] moreover, as a second consequence, the preferred position test requires the use of the reasonable alternative, a statute 'narrowly drawn to prevent the supposed evil.'" Hence, there remains the clear and present danger plus imminence test, greater and more searching judicial scrutiny, the alternative means rule, and the reversal of the presumption of constitutionality all attesting to the viability of the concept of preference in free exercise cases. Preference must be accorded to the free exercise guarantee because it has substantive meaning within the context of the First Amendment, it is concerned with the life and soul of the individual in the attainment of capacities, and it is related to the interest of minority groups. A violation of the free exercise clause does much more than erode a basic principle. It is essentially an infringement that is real, never abstract, and it is a wrong with injury—for severe psychic turmoil has been caused by the compelled violation of conscience. Thus, . . . the protection of substantive freedom is basic to the workings of the democratic process.

Religion is human behavior and as such ought to be given by society the freest possible latitude to develop, William James insisted that "a true thought is a thought that is an invaluable instrument of action." So to speak of the free exercise of religion as a negative or passive concept (and to protect it accordingly) is to fail to understand the true, inner meaning of religion or of its ultimate value to a free political society. Failure by the state to allow an excessive toleration and latitude for free religious exercise, and ultimately conscience as well, denies the state its necessary cultural and political progress in order to maintain free institutions.

A man cannot exercise the innermost thoughts of his conscience or practice his unorthodox religious beliefs without disturbing his fellow men. His right to such a free exercise must be guaranteed and protected. For the Supreme Court to reverse its development of the meaning of religious liberty from *Cantwell* to *Welsh* would at once be both unacceptable and disastrous. For the Supreme Court to do less than guarantee and protect the right to believe, worship, and proselytize would make the words of the First Amendment and the historical meaning they convey empty ideals. To do less, moreover, would be to confirm what Albert Camus believed to be "the most incorrigible vice." That is to say, "The evil that is in the world always comes of ignorance, and good intentions may do as much harm as malevolence, if they lack understanding. On the whole, men are more good than bad; that, however, isn't the real point. But they are more or less ignorant, and it is this that we call vice or virtue; the most incorrigible vice being that of an ignorance that fancies it knows everything and therefore claims for itself the right to kill." That ignorance is also the willingness of the state and its political and judicial institutions to turn its back on or balance with other contending but less important interests the unique dimension of free religious exercise. . . . It is, once again, God's domain and Caesar may not trespass upon it.

$$\left[\begin{array}{l} \textit{Are All Religious Beliefs} \\ \textit{and Practices Guaranteed} \\ \textit{by the Free Exercise Clause?} \end{array} \right]$$

No: The Importance of Being Amish

Walter Berns

T HE Amish have won from the Supreme Court of the United States a special exemption allowing them, and so far only them, to ignore an otherwise valid statute. It is not part of my purpose here to speculate about the reasons for their unprecedented success—and it is unprecedented, for, although many groups have tried, none before the Amish has ever succeeded. But if it were my purpose, I would attribute their success to the fact that when it comes to culture there is no group more counter than the Amish, and in this day of bourgeois diffidence, that sort of thing matters.

The facts of the case, *Wisconsin v. Yoder,* decided by the Court on May 15, 1972, are these: Wisconsin's compulsory school attendance law requires parents to cause their children to attend school, either public or private, until they reach the age of sixteen; Yoder, a member of the Old Order Amish religion, refused to permit his daughter, Frieda, fifteen at the time, to attend school beyond the eighth grade, and specifically refused to permit her to attend high school. There was no disagreement (or at the least none that appears on the record) between him and his daughter on this score; both agreed that it would be profoundly contrary to the Amish religion and way of life for her to attend the public high school, and no doubt they are right about that. (Indeed, if I credit half the stories I hear, what goes on in the high schools is profoundly contrary to my way of life too, and mine is a long way from being Amish.) . . .

The court was not unsympathetic to his claim, finding that the compulsory school attendance law did interfere with his freedom to act in accordance with his sincere religious belief, but concluding nevertheless that the requirement of school attendance until age sixteen was a "reasonable and constitutional" exercise of governmental power. The circuit court affirmed, but the Wisconsin Supreme Court reversed, holding that the conviction violated the free exercise clause of the First Amendment. This decision was affirmed by a divided Supreme Court of the United States, the Court's opinion being written by Chief Justice Warren Burger, usually the most sober of men; the lone dissenting vote, paradoxically, was cast by Justice William Douglas, usually the most liberal if not radical of men. So the Amish will be permitted to pursue their traditional, pious, gentle, yet industrious ways; and that is good. But the rule in Yoder's case is not good.

Jews especially will have no difficulty being sympathetic with Yoder's plight. It is similar, for example, to the plight of the Jewish merchant unable to work out an accommodation with the local officials who insist on enforcing Sunday closing laws. And the question Yoder fought through the courts is also similar to the question litigated, not so long ago, by just such a Jewish merchant. A few states make an exception to their Sunday closing laws for persons who, because of religious convictions, observe a day of rest other than Sunday, and the Supreme Court has suggested this may well be "the wise solution to the problem." Pennsylvania, however, where Abraham Braunfeld had his place of business was not one of these states. He was in the habit of closing his retail clothing and home furnishings business "from nightfall each Friday until nightfall each Saturday"—as the former Chief Justice, Earl Warren, put it in his 1961 opinion for the Court in *Braunfeld v. Brown*—and he sought a court order permitting him to remain open on Sunday. Like Yoder, he hoped to be exempted from a law because of its peculiar impact on him. But at this point there appears a difference between the two cases, and, presumably, it was this difference that proved to be material and accounts for the fact that Braunfeld lost his case. "The impact of the compulsory attendance law on respondents' practice of the Amish religion," said Chief Justice Burger "is not only severe, but inescapable, for the Wisconsin law affirmatively compels them, under threat of criminal sanction, to perform acts undeniably at odds with fundamental tenets of their religious beliefs. See *Braunfeld v. Brown. . .*"

Presumably he referred to Braunfeld's case in order to make the point that, whereas Yoder was being affirmatively required to do something that violated his religious belief, Braunfeld was merely being asked to refrain from something. While the law imposed a financial burden on him—or, at a minimum, put him at a competitive disadvantage—it did not require him to act in a manner forbidden by Jewish law. It did not—and this, one assumes, would be the equivalent case—require him to open his shop on the Jewish Sabbath. To sum it up, the state may sometimes make piety expensive, but it may never require impiety.

That sounds reasonable enough, but one is left with the lurking suspicion that the distinction is not all that clear. What of the case of a person firmly persuaded that salvation requires him to go out onto the highways and byways (or at least onto the streets of Brockton, Massachusetts) and preach the gospel by selling or giving away copies of a religious publication—indeed, a person persuaded not only of the necessity to do this but of the consequences of a failure to do it, namely, punishment by "everlasting destruction at Armageddon"? What of such a person being confronted by a child labor law that forbids him to engage in this kind of activity?

The Court had such a case in 1944, and the person involved, a Mrs. Sarah Prince, made it sufficiently clear to the officer who told her to take her nine-year-old niece, Betty Simmons, off the streets that she would not have been satisfied with the distinction drawn in the *Yoder* case. Mrs. Prince told him that neither he nor anyone else could stop her. "This child," she said, "is exercising her God-given right . . . to preach the gospel, and no creature has a right to interfere with God's command."

Here, clearly, is the case where the requirement that one must refrain from an activity (preaching on the streets rather than, as in *Braunfeld,* remaining open on Sunday) has the affirmative effect of requiring one to act in what is understood to be an impious fashion. Not only was Betty Simmons being required to act in an impious fashion, but if she was right about the divine consequence of failing to preach on the streets—Armageddon and all that—she had had it, for the Supreme Court upheld the law.

THE PROBLEM IS THIS: may a person, because of his religious beliefs, be entitled to an exemption from a valid law? Pennsylvania may require merchants to close their shops on Sunday. Are Jews, because they are Jews, entitled to keep their shops open? The Court said no. In effect, it would be a denial of the equal protection of the laws for Pennsylvania to assess a fine against, say, Ryan, a Roman Catholic, and not against Braunfeld, a Jew, for the same act. Massachusetts may forbid children to engage in commercial activity on the streets. Are Jehovah's Witnesses, precisely because they are Jehovah's Witnesses and required to sell copies of *Watchtower* on the streets, exempt from this requirement? The Court said no. The law is a reasonable health measure, and no one can claim an exemption from it. Wisconsin may require parents to send their children to school until the age of sixteen. Are the Amish, because they are Amish who see nothing but iniquity in the high schools of the community around them, exempt from this requirement? For the first time in its history, the Court said yes to this question.

No doubt it is a difficult question, and no doubt the Justices, silently cursing the Wisconsin school officials for their refusal to find some way of accommodating the Amish without resorting to the courts, would have preferred to avoid it. Indeed, one wonders why they did not avoid it; they would have had a precedent for that. Back in 1944, and again in 1946 in the same case, the Court refused to answer what was probably the most radical formulation ever given this question in American law: does the constitutional guarantee of religious freedom afford immunity from criminal prosecution for the fraudulent procurement of money through the United States mails? . . .

It is easy to understand the Court's reluctance to grapple with the issue involved in this one. The defendants were members of the so-called "I Am" movement who claimed to be Saint Germain, Jesus Christ, George Washington, and Godfre Ray King among others, and to possess miraculous powers, including the power to make the sick well and less generously, the well sick. The Ballards (the name under which they had been indicted and tried) has passed a collection plate through the mails, so to speak, and the government, refusing to credit their miracles, indicted them for mail fraud. They could be convicted, however, only by proof that they knowingly made false representations, and it is said to be no business of any public official in the United States to say what is or what is not a false religious representation. "The religious views espoused . . . might seem incredible, if not preposterous, to most people [but] if those doctrines are subject to trial before a jury charged with finding their truth or falsity, then the same can be done with the religious beliefs of any sect."

So said Justice Douglas, although having decided to send the case back for retrial, it was necessary for him to say it. All he accomplished with it was to provoke Harlan Stone, then Chief Justice, to reply that freedom of worship does not include the "freedom to procure money by making knowingly false statements about one's religious experiences." Stone thought the government should be allowed to try to prove the falseness of some of the claims made, at least the claim to have "physically shaken hands with St. Germain in San Francisco on a day named" and to have cured "hundreds of persons" by means of their special "spiritual power."

In any event, the Ballards escaped punishment, and they escaped it not because a special exemption was carved out of an otherwise valid statute but because almost everyone except Stone was anxious to avoid the trial of such questions, and they should not be criticized for that.

Unlike the Ballards, whom the Justices to a man probably regarded as scoundrels of the worse sort, Yoder and his Amish friends escaped punishment precisely because they were held to be decent, "law abiding," "productive," "sincere," and—viewed from a world beset with a sense of guilt for what is understood to be its ecological sins and its psychological madness—living "in harmony with nature and the soil," the closest thing possible to the virtuous "sturdy yeoman" of the Jeffersonian "ideal." Pervading Burger's opinion for the Court is a muted admission that the Amish (and others similarly situated, to use the legal phrase) may well have been right all along. It is no wonder Wisconsin could not prevail against them; neither could the gates of hell.

Of course, the Court would have us believe that there is nothing novel about the decision or the rule on which it rests. As Burger put it in his opinion only state interests "of the highest order . . . can overbalance legitimate claims to the free exercise of religion"; or again, while "religiously grounded conduct must often be subject to the broad police power of the State [this] is not to deny that there are areas of conduct protected by the Free Exercise Clause of the First Amendment and thus beyond the power of the State to control, even under regulations of general applicability." But this is not the rule that had been applied in earlier cases, including the ones Burger cites; and it surely is not the rule of the case most opposite to Yoder's, the second flag-salute case (1943), which he does not even deign to mention.

West Virginia required school children to salute the flag and recite the pledge of allegiance. Children who refused to comply were expelled and treated as delinquents; and their parents were made liable to prosecution and, upon conviction, a fine and jail sentence. Jehovah's Witnesses refused to salute the flag, on the ground that to do so would constitute worship of the graven image, and their parents brought suit to enjoin enforcement of the regulation.

Here, in every material sense, is the compulsory school attandance case: in each case children and their parents are being compelled, by a statute carrying criminal penalties, to perform acts contrary to their religious beliefs. The Court ruled in favor of the Jehovah's Witnesses, but it was very careful to avoid making them the special beneficiaries of its decision. The flag-salute requirement was held to be unconstitutional, a violation not, however, of the free exercise of religion clause of the First Amendment but of the free speech provision. Stated otherwise, the Court held that *no one,* pious sectarian or militant atheist, could be required to salute the flag. In the school attendance case, on the other hand, the Court held that the statute was constitutional, except as applied to Yoder and the other Amish.

The Court has never before held that one's religious convictions entitle him to an exception from the requirements of a valid criminal statute. This is new law, and of a dangerous sort. It is dangerous because if one is entitled to disobey a law that is contrary to his religious beliefs, and entitled as well to define his own religious beliefs, the proliferation of sects and of forms of worship will be wonderful to behold: drug cultists, snake worshippers, income-tax haters—why, in Shelley's words, the sense faints picturing them all. But there will be no stopping this religious revival (or what, for legal purposes, will be labeled a religious revival), short of permitting public officials, and ultimately the judges, to do precisely what the Supreme Court has insisted they may not do, namely, get in the business of distinguishing the honest profession of faith from the dishonest, the genuine from the spurious. The principle was stated best by Justice Robert Jackson in the second flag-salute case: "If there is any fixed star in our constitutional constellation, it is that no official, high or petty, can prescribe what shall be orthodox in . . . religion, or other matters of opinion or force citizens to confess by word or act their faith therein."

But in Yoder's case the Court took the first step in this heretofore prohibited direction by drawing a line between the religious and the secular; it did this by emphasizing that the exception being carved out for this religious group could not be claimed by other kinds of groups, "however virtuous and admirable" may be their "way of life." No assertion of "secular values" will do, Chief Justice Burger insisted in his opinion. Even Thoreau, who, like the Amish, "rejected the social values of his time and isolated himself at Walden Pond," would not have been entitled to the privilege, because, unlike the Amish, his "choice was philosophical and personal rather than religious."

This, inevitably and with very good reason, proved too much for Justice Douglas. He agreed that the Amish could not be compelled to go to high school, but he insisted that the privilege could not be restricted to those whose objection to a law rests on religious beliefs in a formal sense. So what's wrong with Thoreau's philosophical position? he wanted to know. And the "philosophy" of the conscientious objector who figured it out for himself that "human life is valuable in and of itself"? Douglas wants it known that he adheres to "these exalted views of 'religion,' " and we can expect him to send battalions of his favorite cultists—flag burners, not-this-war-I-won'ters, and the like—through the gap that will be inevitably be blown in that line.

Finally, is it not strange to be told now—after eighteen years of the effort to integrate the public schools, when one of the principle political issues appears to be whether there shall be busing to achieve a balance between the races; when the decision that gave rise to all this in 1954 held that "education is perhaps the most important function of state and local governments," that "compulsory school attendance laws . . . demonstrate our recognition of the importance of education of our democratic society," that, indeed, it is "the very foundation of good citizenship," that, in the famous statement that so troubled the logicians, "separate facilities are inherently unequal"—is it not strange to be told now that it is unconstitutional for a state to require children (or, at least, some children) even to go to high school? Is it not strange that they be permitted to segregate themselves from the rest of the American community? That they cannot be forced to attend other schools or, presumably, to accept other children in their schools? Is this not inconsistent with the law of school integration? Or shall we see the day when a suburban school district, asked to show cause why it should not be integrated with an inner-city school district, will reply the following words:

Said counsel for schools suburbanish:
   "Sure, we admit that we're clannish;
But there's no use your fussing for court-ordering busing,
   'Cause there's no one out here but us Amish."

3
Schenck v. United States: Can the Need for National Security Justify Limitations on Free Speech?

Robert A. Poirier

J USTICE William Douglas once remarked that freedom of speech best
serves "its high purpose when it induces a condition of unrest, creates
dissatisfaction with conditions as they are, or even stirs people to anger."
This view of the First Amendment and the issues that revolve around it
demonstrate that the Free Speech Clause may conflict with other rights and
governmental obligations.

Any society that values freedom of speech as an essential condition of
democracy must come to terms with the inevitable conflict between that value
and the imperative of society to protect itself from destruction. During this
century, the Supreme Court has been asked to settle free speech disputes on
constitutional grounds that have raised a number of questions:

Can the First Amendment be used by those who would advocate the
destruction of society and the democratic institutions that sustain it?

At what point does it become permissible to interfere with speech that
might have the consequence of inciting rebellion or revolution?

Is there a distinction between speech and action, and is it possible to
interfere with the latter without abridging the former?

Does Congress have a valid legislative duty in proscribing certain kinds
of speech in the interest of protecting society from its enemies?

The answer to these and related questions demonstrates that the Supreme
Court never intended to endorse an absolutist view of the First Amendment
as suggested by Douglas's famous statement. Rather, the Court has
endeavored to play the role of balancing this right against wider societal interests and has shown that free speech is a relative right depending on circumstances and conditions. *Chaplinsky v. New Hampshire* (315 U.S. 568,
1942), for example, excludes "fighting words" from constitutional protec-

tion. *Roth v. U.S.* (354 U.S. 476, 1957) removes obscenity from the umbrella of the First Amendment, and *N.Y. Times v. Sullivan* (376 U.S. 254, 1964) suggests that libel is protected only under certain conditions.

But what of the standards for drawing these lines between conflicting rights in matters involving national security? Does the restriction depend on the content of the expression, the contextual circumstances, the method of expression, or the identity of the speaker? In *Schenck v. U.S.* (249 U.S. 47, 1919), Justice Oliver Wendell Holmes explained that

> the character of every act depends upon the circumstances in which it is done. . . . The most stringent protection of free speech would not protect a man in falsely shouting fire in a theatre and causing panic. . . . The question in every case is whether the words used are used in such circumstances and are of such a nature as to create a clear and present danger that they will bring about the substantive evil that Congress has a right to prevent.

Thus was born the famous "clear and present danger" formula, which limits speech according to the circumstances.

Charles T. Schenck, general secretary of the Socialist party, was tried and convicted under the Espionage Act of 1917 for sending out leaflets to potential and actual draftees urging draft resistance and opposing the war effort. Although it upheld Schenck's conviction without finding that his activities created a clear and present danger to society, the Court reasoned that when "a nation is at war many things that might be said in time of peace are such a hindrance to its effort that their utterance will not be endured so long as men fight, and that no court could regard them as protected by any constitutional right." This standard effectively gave government the power to act in anticipation of illegal conduct and prohibit speech if the circumstances were such as to create the clear and present danger of unlawful activity.

The doctrine of clear and present danger was seen as a workable solution to the dilemma of individual rights against those of society. But does it give the government too wide a scope in limiting speech? Fearing that possibility, Justices Holmes and Louis Brandeis, champions of the doctrine, found themselves in dissent in *Abrams v. U.S.* (250 U.S. 616, 1919) when the Court upheld the conviction of Abrams, who had engaged in similar activities but was convicted instead under the Sedition Act of 1918. Attempting to clarify the clear and present danger formula, Holmes argued that Congress could not proscribe all efforts to communicate ideas. Clear and present danger, Holmes wrote in dissent, could be a viable standard only if the speech created an immediate evil. Holmes urged "that we should be eternally vigilant against attempts to check the expression of opinions that we loathe and believe to be fraught with death unless they so imminently threaten immediate interference with the lawful and pressing purposes of the law that an immediate check is required to save the country."

"Clear and present danger" as a doctrine of limitation is not without its critics. Alexander Meiklejohn, most prominent among them, opposed the standard because, by curtailing speech at the moment it becomes effective, it would reduce free speech to a harmless academic discourse.[1] Furthermore, the test is criticized for being vague and because it presumes much judicial wisdom in that the court must make factual judgments on the alleged "danger."

Other standards, like the "bad tendency" test established in *Gitlow v. New York* (268 U.S. 652, 1925), which ruled that because a "single revolutionary spark may kindle a fire that . . . may burst into a sweeping and destructive conflagration . . . [the state] . . . may, in the exercise of its judgment, suppress the threatened danger in its incipiency," occasionally have derailed the Court from the "clear and present danger" formula. Although now abandoned except for obscenity cases, the "bad tendency" doctrine gave virtually no protection to freedom of speech and made that constitutional right subject to the whim of legislative bodies empowered to suppress speech in advance.

After *Gitlow* the Court tenuously adhered to the "clear and present danger" formula until the political issues of World War I and the red scare of the 1920s were replaced by the McCarthy era of the 1950s. Attempts to utilize congressional investigative and legislative powers to weed out Communist influence in the United States took the form of activities and legislation that ran afoul of the First Amendment and challenged the Court to a new round of rulings on national security clashes with free speech. A host of statutes such as the Subversive Activities Control Act of 1950, the Communist Control Act of 1954, and state statutes requiring loyalty oaths for public employees emerged during this period. The first anti-Communist statute to be tested was the 1940 Smith Act in the celebrated case of *Dennis v. U.S.* (341 U.S. 494, 1951). This case clouded the meaning of the "clear and present danger" standard as the justices offered four different interpretations of the doctrine. Chief Justice Carl Vinson paid lip-service to the doctrine but in reality substituted Judge Learned Hand's appeals court opinion of "clear and probable danger" for Holmes's "imminence." Since Dennis had not been charged with any overt acts, the dissenters, Justices Hugo Black and William O. Douglas, feared that the Holmes test had all but been destroyed.

Dennis did serve notice that organized conspiracies to overthrow the government, as the communist party was alleged to be, would have difficulty standing on the First Amendment. This interpretation was short-lived; the McCarthy-era Communist subversion statutes later were weakened by the Court because of the vagueness of terms like "subversive organization," "subversive persons," and "sympathetic association with." Finally, in *Yates v. U.S.* (354 U.S. 298, 1957) the Court drew an important legal distinction between "actual advocacy" and "theoretical advocacy" of an illegal act, with the latter having constitutional protection. Under *Yates,* expressing a theoretical or philosophical belief in the "abstract idea" of violent political upheaval was not sufficient grounds to abridge free speech. The burden was on the government to prove a defendant had actually intended, or urged others, to overthrow the government by violent means.

The "clear and present danger" test was suspended in *Dennis,* leaving its status somewhat unclear, although *Brandenburg v. Ohio* (395 U.S. 444, 1969) demonstrates the Court's continued concern with the Holmes-Brandeis formula. Vietnam era street protests and demonstrations once again juxtaposed free speech rights against the claims of national security and public order. Two cases from this period that reached different conclusions raised the new issue of "symbolic speech." In *U.S. v. O'Brien* (391 U.S. 367, 1968), a conviction for burning a draft card as an act of protest was upheld on the grounds that Congress is empowered to raise armies and that the draft registration process is a reasonable administrative method of achieving this valid state objective. In *Tinker v. Des Moines* (393 U.S. 503, 1969), the Court reversed the decision of the lower court to uphold the suspension of school children for wearing a black armband as a gesture of opposition to the Vietnam war. The Court reasoned that such an act was "akin to pure speech" and was constitutionally protected.

Recent cases involving national security concerns continue to raise the question of the limits of permissibility when valid state objectives are at issue. The first of these, *New York Times v. U.S.* (403 U.S. 713, 1971), involved the publication of purloined secret documents, known as the *Pentagon Papers,* which analyzed the circumstances of U.S. involvement in Vietnam. Editors decided to publish these papers because of their import to the national debate on the war. Other newspapers quickly followed the *New York Times's* lead, and the government went to court to seek an injunction to prevent publication in advance. In a per curiam opinion the Court held that the government had not met the "heavy burden" of justifying prior restraint. The many opinions of the badly divided Court in this case (all nine justices wrote separate opinions) did not add up to an unequivocal victory for the First Amendment because many questions were left unanswered.

The second case, *Snepp v. U.S.* (444 U.S. 507, 1980), involved a former Central Intelligence Agency (CIA) agent who wrote a critical book about the CIA without agency clearance but did not use classified information. The Supreme Court ruled against Snepp on the grounds that a position of trust had been violated, causing harm to the interests of the United States. Although not advancing any new constitutional doctrine, *Snepp* does indicate the Court is willing to suspend First Amendment rights when it deems national security is at issue. Except for *Brandenburg v. Ohio,* which barely resurrected the "clear and present danger" test, the Supreme Court has avoided general standards in First Amendment disputes. The significance of *Schenk* is that today, nearly seventy years later, we continue to be troubled by its central question: How much can society limit the freedom of the few in order to preserve the community of the many? Justice Holmes's solution—that we should tilt the balance in favor of the few by means of a "clear and present danger" test—is still a vital part of this ongoing debate. Professor Hans Linde, now a justice of the Oregon Supreme Court, criticizes the "clear and present danger" test as unworkable for a number of specific reasons. The late Alexander Bickel, one of the most eminent constitutional scholars of the postwar generation, offers a more sanguine view of the commonsense properties of balancing tests and the First Amendment.

Yes: The Uninhibited, Robust, and Wide-Open First Amendment

Alexander M. Bickel

THERE would be considerably less of a problem with the First Amendment if we could distinguish with assurance between speech and conduct, as the late Justice Black and Justice Douglas have sometimes tried to persuade us that we can. Only conduct, their argument has run, can overthrow the government, be violent, hurt someone or something. Speech cannot. That, however, is unfortunately not so.

Very little conduct that involves more than one person is possible without speech. Speech leads to it, merges into it, is necessary to it. That is the point of Holmes's famous metaphor: "The most stringent protection of free speech would not protect a man in falsely shouting fire in a theater, and causing a panic." It was Holmes also, in the course of a truly fervent defense of free speech, in the dissent in the *Gitlow* case, who said: "Every idea is an incitement. It offers itself for belief and if believed it is acted on unless some other belief outweighs it or some failure of energy stifles the movement at its birth."

There are, then problems. . . . One is the problem of speech which is not discussion forming part of the political process, but which is aimed at dispensing with it, or at a disruption of it, a coercion of it by violence. Second, there is the problem of speech which is aimed at, or otherwise involves, the violation of a valid law or procedure, speech that has no general purpose to supplant the political process but that refuses to accept its operation or its outcome in a given instance. Here I have in mind counseling, or inciting to, disobedience of law—perfectly peaceable disobedience, but disobedience. I have in mind also speech or assembly that involves a breach of laws or procedures which safeguard the public peace and tranquility, or some other

Alexander Bickel, from "The 'Uninhibited, Robust, and Wide-Open' First Amendment," 54 *Commentary* (November 1972), pp. 61–67.

public interest: laws or procedures whose validity would not be questioned except as they are violated in the course of engaging in speech or assembly.

That aspect of the first problem—the problem with efforts to supplant or coerce the political process—which is embraced in the historic concept of seditious speech is dealt with and perhaps solved as well as may be, by the clear-and-present danger test that Holmes formulated better than half a century ago. The solution is in terms of a judgment as Holmes often liked to say, of proximity and degree: a pragmatic judgment, drawing a distinction between speech that carries a high risk of disruption, coercion, or violence, and speech that carries no, or less, risk. This judgment is generalized loosely into the clear-and-present danger formula, under which speech is protected unless it constitutes, in the circumstances an intentional incitement to imminent forbidden action. . . .

The clear-and-present danger test as originally formulated by Holmes also purported to solve the second of the problems I have mentioned—the problem of speech which does not incite to violence or any other coercion of the political process, but merely to the violation of an otherwise valid law or procedure. Our political process, however, is too dependent on registering intensity of feeling as well as majority wish, the former of which it cannot do through the ballot box; it has too many stages of decision-making before laws are ultimately held valid, and too many stages of law formation which often render law provisional only; and on the other hand it results by now in a very pervasive government and makes numerous laws and regulations of vastly differing orders of importance—the process is, in sum, too complex, diverse, and resourceful to subsume an unvarying duty to obey all laws. Simple application of the clear-and-present danger test to forbid all speech which constitutes an intentional incitement to break a law, or all speech which by itself or through its by-products, as in the form of assembly, or of marching, or of handing out leaflets, involves a breach of rules or procedures safeguarding an otherwise valid public interest, would be an anomalous and unrealistic result. It would rest on a snapshot of the political process that showed it as consisting of discussion and voting and nothing else. That is not the whole process, not nearly. It would not work if it were, it would not generate the necessary consent to government, and would not be stable. We cannot, therefore, as a society, be held to put that kind of store by the duty to obey.

Consequently, quite early, in *Whitney v. California,* Brandeis, with Holmes concurring, drew some further distinctions, and made occasion for additional judgments of proximity and degree. The fact that speech is likely to result in some violation of law was not enough, he said, to justify its suppression. "There must be the probability of serious injury to the state." And Brandeis gave a very interesting example, calling to mind an ancient and persistent form of civil disobedience: speech that creates an imminent danger of organized trespass on unenclosed, privately owned land. It would be unconstitutional, he suggested, to prohibit such speech, despite the imminent danger it presented, because the harm to society which the prohibition would seek to avert would be "relatively trivial."

Subsequent cases have required government to show not merely a rational, otherwise valid, interest in support of a law or procedure that is endangered, or actually violated by speech or by activity attending speech, but a "compelling interest." . . . Hence, the ultimate formulation of the clear-and-present-danger test, by Judge Learned Hand, is that the courts must ask "whether the gravity of the evil, discounted by its improbability justifies such invasion of free speech as is necessary to avoid the danger."

The nature and gravity of the evil, its gravity as well as its proximity, thus form part of the judicial judgment. One may ask by what warrant courts decide that some valid laws passed by a legislature are less important than other ones, and may be endangered or disobeyed. Someone must, however, unless each and every legitimate but utterly trivial public interest is to prevail over the interest in what Meiklejohn called those activities of communication by which we govern. Hence courts do so decide. And we have thus built into the system a kind of domesticated form of civil disobedience.

It is this aspect of the First Amendment that the *Pentagon Papers—New York Times* case of 1971 illustrated and developed. The case can be viewed in another light, as I shall show. And it had other features. It was a prior restraint case. Prior restraints are traditionally disfavored—and in circumstances such as those of the Pentagon Papers publication, with very good reason—even where an attempt might be allowed to regulate the same sort of speech through the *in terrorem* effect of a subsequent sanction. Again, the case involved a question of statutory construction and a problem of the separation of powers. Passing these features, the essence of the government's complaint was that publication of the Pentagon Papers violated a public interest in the confidentiality of government documents, an interest which the executive order establishing the classification system, and also, the government contended, the Espionage Act were intended to safeguard. The Espionage Act raised the question of statutory construction to which I have referred, and the attempt to apply the executive order concerning classification of documents, not internally within the executive branch of government, but externally to private persons and entities gave rise to the problem of separation of powers. Assuming, however, that the government had prevailed on either or both of these points—assuming, that is, acceptance of the government's argument that the public interest in confidentiality of government documents was embodied in valid and applicable law, either in the executive order or in the Espionage Act or both—there remained the issue whether the given injury to this public interest was in the circumstances grave enough to justify a restriction on speech, or too trivial to justify it.

Justice Harlan took the position that the weighing of the gravity of the injury was in this instance not for the judges to undertake, because when the injury is to the nation's foreign relations, as it was plausibly alleged to be, judges should, he thought, simply accept the President's assessment of its gravity. The government did not really contend for this much, and no other justice seemed prepared to concede it. Rather the government tried to persaude the judges themselves that the breach of confidentiality constituted, in the circumstances, a grave and not merely probable, but immediate injury. The injury was prolongation of the Vietnam war by providing the enemy with helpful information, and embarrassment to the United States in the conduct of diplomatic affairs.

Now, as to the war, there was a question of immediacy, and indeed of causal connection between publication and the feared injury. The discount for improbability was heavy. There was actually nothing more than a tendency, if that, and the bad-tendency test in seditious speech cases is precisely what the clear-and-present danger doctrine displayed, as its very formulation indicates. It required a high probability instead. As to the claim of embarrassment in the conduct of diplomatic affairs, however, an immediate causal connection was reasonably clear. Here the gravity of the injury was squarely in issue. And it was held insufficient. The predilection for in-system civil disobedience prevailed.

The clear-and-present danger doctrine, then, as it has evolved beyond its original formulation, makes room for what used to be called seditious speech, and for a measure of necessary in-system civil disobedience. It gives fair satisfaction, even though it places a bit more reliance in the discretion and prudence of judges that either voluptuaries of liberty or judicial conservatives find altogether comfortable. The underlying broad principle is that the First Amendment protects the political process, and a right of self-expression consistent with its requirements. But other, fundamental difficulties remain, which the clear-and-present-danger test rather tends to sweep under the rug. Obviously the political process is not what we pursue everywhere, for purposes of all decision-making, or always. There are times when we do not, and places where we do not, and times when the need for self-expression is also not a dominant interest. Equally obviously, not all the results that the political process might attain are acceptable. . . .

In approaching the other and greater difficulty—unacceptable results that the political process, with free speech as a principal component, might reach, or unacceptable acts that speech might counsel its hearers to engage in—one wants to be extremely careful not to be understood as following the teaching of Herbert Marcuse. But that does not mean that the problem shouldn't be stated and faced. Take, for example, the advocacy—not the intentional incitement, which the clear-and-present danger test does allow us to reach—but the advocacy of genocide. Or, to recall what is more familiar, suppose, more minimally, a speech as in *Beauharnais v. Illinois,* decided in 1952, which urged the segregation of Negroes on the ground that they are all given to rape, robbery, knives, guns, and marijuana. Or the speech in *Brandenburg v. Ohio,* decided in 1969: "I believe the nigger should be returned to Africa, the Jew returned to Israel." Or the speech in a case of the early 1950's, *Kunz v. New York:* "All the garbage that didn't believe in Christ should have been burnt in the incinerators. It's a shame they all weren't." Or Jerry Rubin urging the young to go home and kill their parents, or other talk looking with favor on murder, rape, fire, and destruction. . . .

Disastrously, unacceptably noxious doctrine can prevail, and can be made to prevail by the most innocent sort of advocacy. Holmes recognized as much in the passage in the *Gitlow* dissent in which he said that every idea is an incitement. He went on: "Eloquence may set fire to reason." In the *Gitlow* case itself he saw neither incitement nor eloquence, and no chance of a present conflagration, no clear and present danger. Yet he did admit that all ideas were an incitement and that they carried the seed of future dangers as well as benefits. His answer was this: "If in the long run the beliefs expressed in proletarian dictatorship are destined to be accepted by the dominant forces of the community, the only meaning of free speech [—*the only*—] is that they should be given their chance and have their way."

If in the long run the belief, let us say, in genocide is destined to be accepted by the dominant forces of the community, the only meaning of free speech is that it should be given its chance and have its way. Do we believe that? Do we accept it?

Even speech which advocates no idea can have its consequences. I may inflict injury by its very utterance, as the Court said a generation ago, in the *Chaplinsky* case, of lewd or profane or fighting words. More, and equally important, it may create a climate, an environment in which conduct and actions that were not possible before become possible. It is from this point of view that the decision in the *Watts* case, in which the Court passed off as political hyperbole an expressed intention to shoot the President, is perhaps dubious. We have been listening for years now—the level of it in the universities is happily on the decline—to countless apocalyptic pronouncements and to filthy and violent rhetoric, and have dealt with them as speech, as statements of a position, of one side of an issue, to which we may respond by disagreeing, while necessarily accepting by implication the legitimacy of the statement, the right of the speaker to make it.

To listen to something on the assumption of the speaker's right to say it is to legitimate it. There is a story—I cannot vouch for its accuracy, but I found it plausible—of a crowd gathered in front of the ROTC building at a university some years ago. At this university, as elsewhere in this time, some members of the faculty and administration had undertaken to discharge the function of cardinal legate to the barbarians, going without the walls, every so often, to negotiate the sack of the city. On this occasion, with the best of intentions, members of the faculty joined the crowd and participated in discussing the question whether or not to set fire to the building. The faculty, I gather, took the negative, and I assume that none of the students arguing the affirmative could have been deemed guilty of inciting the crowd. The matter was ultimately voted upon, and the affirmative lost—narrowly. But the negative taken by the faculty was only one side of a debate which the faculty rendered legitimate by engaging in it. Where nothing is unspeakable, nothing is undoable. . . .

The argument for resolving these problems by extending protection to speech except as the clear-and-present danger formula would authorize very limited suppression is stated by Holmes in the dissent in *Abrams v. New York:* "Persecution for the expression of opinions seems to me perfectly logical. If you have no doubt of your premises or your power and want a certain result with all your heart you naturally express your wishes in law and sweep away all opposition." To allow opposition by speech, Holmes continues, indicates either that you think the speech does not matter, or that you doubt your power or your premises. He goes on: "But when men have realized that time has upset many fighting faiths, they may come to believe even more than they believe the very foundations of their own conduct that the ultimate good desired is better reached by free trade in ideas—that the best test of truth is the power of the thought to get itself accepted in the competition of the market, and that truth is the only ground upon which their wishes safely can be carried out." This is the point at which one asks whether the best test of the idea of proletarian dictatorship, or segregation, or genocide is really the marketplace, whether our experience has not taught us that even such ideas can get themselves accepted there, and that a marketplace without rules of civil discourse is no marketplace of ideas, but a bullring. . . .

Actually, ambiguity and ambivalence, not the theory of the truth of the marketplace, as Holmes would have had us think, is, if not the theory, at any rate the condition of the First Amendment in the law of our Constitution. Nothing is more characteristic of the law of the First Amendment—not the rhetoric, but the actual law of it—than the Supreme Court's resourceful efforts to cushion rather than resolve clashes between the First Amendment and interests conflicting with it. The Court's chief concern has been with process, with procedural compromises (using the term in a large sense), and with accommodations that rely on the separation and diffusion of power. A great deal of freedom of speech can flourish in a democratic society which naturally shares, or accepts from its judges or other pastors, a minimal definition of the good, the beautiful, the true, and the properly civil. A great deal of freedom of speech can flourish as well, for a time, at any rate, in a society which accepts the proposition of bullring, or marketplace, truth. We are neither society. We have tended to resemble the latter, of late, and we have more freedom than the former might enjoy, and than we enjoyed in the 19th century, but we are actually more nearly the former: Freedom of speech, with us, is a compromise, an accommodation. There is nothing else it could be.

The devices of compromise and accommodation that are perhaps in commonest use go by the names of vagueness and overbreadth. The Court will not accept infringements on free speech by administrative or executive action, and if the infringement occurs pursuant to a statute, the Court will demand that the statute express the wish of the legislature in the clearest, most precise, and narrowest fashion possible. Essentially what the Court is exacting is assurance that the judgment that speech should be suppressed is that of the full, pluralist, open political process, not of someone down the line, representing only one or another particular segment of the society, and assurance that the judgment has been made closely and deliberately, with awareness of the consequences and with clear focus on the sort of speech that the legislature wished to suppress. . . .

Madison knew the secret of this disorderly system, indeed he invented it. The secret is the separation and balance of powers, men's ambition joined to the requirements of their office, so that they push those requirements to the limit, which in turn is set by the contrary requirements of another office, joined to the ambition of other men. This is not an arrangement whose justification is efficiency, logic, or clarity. Its justification is that it accommodates power to freedom and vice versa. It reconciles the irreconcilable. . . .

The upshot in our system is that a whole series of defensive procedural entrenchments and an obstacle course of the diffusion of powers and functions lie between the First Amendment and claims adverse to it. Hence the direct, ultimate confrontation is rare, and when it does occur, limited and manageable. We thus contrive to avoid most judgments that we do not know how to make.

No: Clear and Present Danger Reaxamined

Hans A. Linde

C LEAR and present danger" is no help with the constitutionality of laws directed against words. . . . If you proscribe particular revolutionary acts, or attempts or conspiracies to commit them, then words inciting to such acts may perhaps be punishable if the evidence shows that they create imminent serious danger. But stick to such proscriptions; if your bill presumes the danger and directly outlaws the words themselves, it proposes a law "abridging the freedom of speech" forbidden you by the First Amendment.

There are compelling reasons why this is the better answer if the First Amendment is seen as directed at the legislative process of "making a law" antecedent to its function of protecting particular private rights in the execution of a law.

First, It is too much to expect of legislators that they prevent genuinely felt and potentially serious danger, but still refrain from prohibiting verbal promotion of those dangers, if they are told that the First Amendment leaves it open to them to strike also against the words, subject only to later judicial determination whether individual rights have been infringed. On those terms, who can vote to outlaw revolutionary violence but not the advocacy of revolutionary violence?

The legislative impulse is quite the opposite, as the record shows. Laws directed only at preventing unlawful result or effects, and prohibiting acts, attempts, or conspiracies to accomplish them, are politically unsatisfactory because the evidence may never justify their actual enforcement. The impelling motive to make a law often results not from fear of the consequences of

Hans A. Linde, from "Clear and Present Danger Reexamined: Dissonance in the *Brandenburg Concerto*," 22 *Stanford Law Review* (1970), pp. 1179–1186. Copyright 1970 by the Board of Trustees of the Leland Stanford Junior University.

expression (whether revolutionary, obscene, or otherwise offensive) but from outrage with the expression. When a red flag becomes a "symbol of opposition to organized government," legislators are not satisfied with laws to protect government against anarchistic action; they strike a symbolic counterblow against the red flag and against individuals or groups who will not forswear holding or sharing a commitment to antisocial views. . . .

"Persecution for the expression of opinion seems to me perfectly logical," wrote Justice Holmes in his famous *Abrams* dissent. "To allow opposition by speech seems to indicate that you think the speech impotent . . . or that you do not care wholeheartedly for the result, or that you doubt either your power or your premises." When lawmakers face a demand for action against outrageously hostile, belligerent, obscene, or otherwise offensive forms of expression, they will not be permitted by their constituents to doubt their premises or to care less than wholeheartedly for the result. If they are to make no law abridging the freedom of speech, or of the press, constitutional law must make it unmistakable to their constituents as well as to them that they lack the power to do so.

Second. It is unrealistic to sustain laws directed in terms against expression on the basis of deference to a greater capacity of the legislative than the judicial process to assess the danger of the proscribed expression. Most laws are not a one-time solution to an immediate problem; most are, in terms, permanent. The most conscientious legislation is at best a diagnosis made today and a prescription for the indefinite future. True, in the rash of anti-Communist laws between 1950 and 1954, congressional committees could draw upon years of extensive investigation of Communisn both by themselves and by others. But unlike adjudication (by court or agency), the legislative process requires no obligatory link between the lawmakers' decision and the factual premises. . . . But even if the legislative findings which are given deference are the true premises of the legislative action, for what length of time can such findings provide the predicate of "danger," if that is constitutionally required? Are the laws that were sustained 10 years ago by deference to congressional findings of 20 years ago still constitutional today? And when we turn from Congress to state legislatures and city councils, the premise of superior capacity to predict future danger from the content of speech or press becomes even more attenuated.

Despite his eloquent defense of free speech, Justice Brandeis disagreed with the majority in *Whitney* only insofar as he thought the California legislature's implicit judgment of the danger of advocating criminal syndicalism must be open to reexamination in each concrete case. Yet the extrinsic premises of the legislative judgment in the days of the I.W.W. may bear no resemblance to a real or supposed extrinsic danger many years later, as the use of Ohio's 1919 Criminal Syndicalism Act against a 1967 Klan meeting illustrates. In judicial review of legislation not affected by the First Amendment, deference to the factual assumptions presumed to underlie the legislative prescription, no matter how fictitious or anachronistic those assumptions are, rightly reflects the constitutional allocation of power. But such conventions of limited judicial review are inappropriate to First Amendment cases. If present danger is to be a prerequisite to punishing speech, there is no room for deference to a past legislative assessment of danger. The *Brandenburg* decision was right, in overruling *Whitney*, to go beyond Brandeis and hold that the Act contravened the First Amendment independently of the extrinsic circumstances of Brandenburg's speech.

Third. Legislation against outrageous kinds of speech, once enacted, is hard to repeal. A theory of the First Amendment that would apply "clear and present danger" to the validity of such laws contributes to that difficulty. For consistent with the logic of that theory, legislation against undesirable forms of expression can safely be enacted and stored for the occasion when some public danger might warrant its enforcement. If suppression is not justified by the actual circumstances, the courts will apply the protection of the First Amendment as a direction to judges rather than to legislators.

Rarely is there any political incentive to initiate and carry out an effort to repeal repressive laws against unpopular and annoying forms of speech. It is a quixotic undertaking, thankless and very likely futile. Who would have bothered to try to repeal Ohio's Criminal Syndicalism Act in the decades since all danger from the Wobblies must have been forgotten? Who would propose legislation to "legalize" revolutionary propaganda, or obscenity, or other offensive expression? We have long ago come to rely on the courts to clean out the statute books when it no longer matters. . . .

Thus the legislative assessment of danger that is presumed to underlie the law is not likely ever to be reexamined in the political arena. The Court's deference to that presumed legislative judgment and the lawmakers' reliance on judicial surveillance of constitutional limits confront each other like Alphonse and Gaston.

Fourth. One function to be asked of a rule in constitutional law, as in any other body of law, is that it communicate an understandable standard. It is not enough if a doctrine explicates the difficult balance of competing considerations that lead the Justices of the United States Supreme Court to a particular decision, and often enough a split decision at that. Application of constitutional law takes place every day in lower state and federal courts. If those courts are all to apply the same constitutional law, it is sometimes more important how readily a rule can be administered than how felicitously it expresses a philosophy of judicial review. What is important in constitutional law as applied in litigation by judges is essential in a constitutional rule addressed, as is the First Amendment, to lawmakers, ranging now from Congressmen through state legislators to city councilmen and school board members. A clear rule that the First Amendment does not permit a law directed in terms against speech, irrespective of clear and present danger, will better serve the legislator's task. It is not too much to ask lawmakers, if they believe that hateful expression actually causes identifiable harm, to direct their laws against the causing of such harm (laws which speech, under the original use of "clear and present danger," may under some circumstances be sufficient to violate), rather than to vent the public indignation by outlawing the expression itself.

The first time someone causes a panic by shouting "Fire!" in a crowded theater, some lawmaker's impulse will be to make a law against shouting "Fire!" in crowded theaters, and to leave it to some future court to declare that it cannot constitutionally be applied to censor an actor's lines in a play. The First Amendment can tell him before enactment that the law had better be directed against causing panics or substantial risk of panics, under whatever conditions of intent, negligence, or probability may seem appropriate, and leave it to the court whether that law constitutionally applies to some particular shout of "Fire!"

The rule suggested by this Comment may tentatively be summarized as follows: The First Amendment invalidates any law directed in terms against some communicative content of speech or of the press, irrespective of extrinsic circumstances either at the time of enactment or at the time of enforcement, if the proscribed content is of a kind which falls under any circumstances within the meaning of the First Amendment.

4

Miller v. California: Should Public Morality Be Invoked to Limit Freedom of Expression?

Robert A. Poirier

THE issue concerning the extent to which the law can or should be used to bring about a socially approved behavior dates back to early political philosophy. That it is an eternal issue of politics is evidenced by the contemporary controversy over obscenity guidelines for the nation or for particular communities. On the one hand are arguments that support the control, if not strict censorship, of obscenity on moral grounds or because such materials are deleterious and/or offensive to many. On the other hand are views that question the harm of pornography, the right of the state to determine moral standards, and the right of majorities to impose matters of taste on all members of the community.

The case of *Miller v. California* (413 U.S. 15, 1973) represents the capstone of a tortuous history of constitutional litigation in this controversial First Amendment area. It, and its seminal forerunners, *Roth v. U.S.* and *Alberts v. California* (345 U.S. 476, 1957), are likely to be the controlling constitutional standard and focal point for conservative and liberal argumentation for the remainder of this century. *Miller* adheres to what Thomas I. Emerson calls a "two-level theory of free speech": that which is not in the category of "obscene" speech is protected, whereas that which falls in the category of "obscene" is not protected. Consistent with the core of the 1957 *Roth-Alberts* standard, *Miller* presumes before the fact that obscenity is harmful to wider community interests. As Emerson points out, "The most striking thing about the law of obscenity is that it is sui generis, not following most of the rules developed in other areas of the First Amendment."[1] Specifically, Emerson is referring to the extent to which the Supreme Court ignores standards common to other speech cases in favor of a rejected "bad tendency" standard. Having formulated a "two-level" approach to the First Amendment and a "presumption of harm" test in "obscene" speech, it became necessary for the Court to establish definitional guidelines on what is permissible (constitutionally protected) and what is harmless in sexual expression in the media and other art forms.[2]

Prior to *Roth-Alberts* there was no attempt by the Supreme Court to provide the needed yardstick. *Regina v. Hicklin* (1868), an English case, was the common standard at all jurisdictional levels. It relied heavily on a "presumption of harm" test and defined obscenity as material that might corrupt the "most susceptible" recipient, which presumably meant minors. The danger that such material might fall into the hands of a juvenile or other susceptible person was sufficient grounds for censorship. Judicial dissatisfaction with the test, particularly since it limited adult reading to what was safe for children, led to the celebrated *Ulysses* decision in 1933 (*U.S. v. One Book Entitled "Ulysses,"* 72 F.2d 525) in which Judge John Woolsey argued that the test for obscenity must at least consider the context of a work rather than isolated passages.

This refinement, however, seemed inadequate as the public's taste in both literature and film began to change in the 1950s. Adult audiences were demanding more sophisticated entertainment such as that found in European cinema, and U.S. producers were only too eager to appeal to that demand. The changes in mores and the Supreme Court's distress over the inadequacy of *Hicklin* generated a need for a more authoritative definition of obscenity.

That opportunity was presented the Court in 1957 in the *Roth-Alberts* cases. Intending to close the door on the trend toward sexual explicitness in film and literature, a 5–4 decision authored by Justice William Brennan answered the constitutional issue before the Court by saying that obscenity was not under the protection of the First Amendment. Obscenity, the majority ruled, is to be judged by its tendency to arouse sexual thoughts. This ruling therefore retained an essential feature of *Hicklin* and placed the Court in a position of adhering to a "bad tendency" doctrine. Borrowed from *Hicklin,* "bad tendency" grants power to prohibit any expression that *might* have a tendency to have a deleterious effect without waiting for actual harm to occur and without the necessity of an a priori proof of harm.

The Supreme Court indicated in *Roth-Alberts* its willingness to adhere to a priori assumptions about the harmful consequences of pornography, providing that a constitutional due process standard could be established that would permit the courts to distinguish permissible speech from nonpermissible speech. This new standard defined obscenity as any expression that "whether to the *average person,* applying *contemporary community standards,* the *dominant theme* of the material, *taken as a whole, appeals to prurient interest,"* and "goes substantially beyond the *customary limits of candor."* Additionally, to be judged obscene a work not only had to meet the above requirements but had to be "utterly without redeeming social importance." The unintended consequence of the Court's new constitutional policy was to elicit a host of litigation testing the meaning of the key phrases in the definition—a definition that lacked the crystal clarity one would expect in constitutional doctrine.

The pitfalls and legal traps were many. By advancing the "two-level" theory, the Court was continuously pressed to apply its definition to other obscenity litigation. If some speech is obscene and not protected and some speech is not obscene and protected, how can one clearly establish a difference that can withstand close judicial scrutiny? Ironically, the Court's deference to legislative wisdom in determining the harmful social consequences of obscenity transformed the Justices into the active role of categorizing speech. Also, by advancing the plausible notion that sex and obscenity are not synonymous and that the former need not be obscene because "obscene material is material which deals with sex in a manner appealing to prurient interest," the Court painted itself into a corner by becoming the arbiter of what is acceptable in matters of human sexuality.

This is especially so when one is reminded by the Court that in fact sex "is one of the vital problems of human interest and public concern," which should be afforded the liberty of public discussion. That concession on the Court's part was motivated by the concern for the excessively restrictive standard of the *Hicklin* test, which judged obscenity by the effect of isolated passages on the most susceptible person. The Court noted that such a standard "might well encompass material legitimately treating with sex, and so it must be rejected as unconstitutionally restrictive of the freedoms of speech and press."

The practical effect of that concession was to place the Court in almost total agreement with Alexander Meiklejohn's theory of the First Amendment. Although widely hailed as a liberal champion of First Amendment freedoms, Meiklejohn's views could easily be adopted by those favoring a more restrictive view of free speech. Meiklejohn argues that full and open discussion of public issues in a town hall manner is necessary for self-government and for arriving at the community consensus; hence, such discussion is protected by the First Amendment. The Fifth Amendment's Due Process Clause, on the other hand, grants a civil liberty of speech that can be limited by government. "This means," Meiklejohn professes, "that, under the Bill of Rights, there are two freedoms, or liberties, of speech, rather than only one. There is a 'freedom of speech' which the First Amendment declares to be nonabridgable. But there is also a 'liberty of speech' which the Fifth Amendment declares to be abridgable."[3] Thus, the Court is not willing to restrict freedom of speech for "material legitimately treating with sex" if that discussion were necessary to achieve some higher purpose. For example, consistent with Meiklejohn or *Roth,* the free speech of citizens to discuss the propriety of having an adult bookstore in the community is a nonabridgable liberty even for those who would advocate allowing such establishments to exist. Conceivably both supporters and opponents of the issue would be allowed, in order to make their point, to show samples of the type of literature or films available in the bookstore without violating obscenity statutes. The photographer who makes the film or the photo layout for the magazine, on the other hand, is subject to an abridgement of his or her speech with proper procedural and substantive due process guarantees. The Court attempted in *Roth-Alberts* to draw that distinction and to establish a due process standard for justifying limitations on a particular category of speech.

The dissenters expressed concern over the majority's willingness to censor speech not directly related to actual or potential antisocial conduct and, anticipating the Pandora's box of litigious issues raised by *Roth-Alberts,* declared the standard "too loose, too capricious, too destructive of freedom of expression to be squared with the First Amendment." With each succeeding obscenity case the Court found that its principles were becoming even more confusing. Finally, frustrated by the growing controversy and its unwanted role as arbiter of sexual taste, the Court ruled in *Redrup v. New York* (386 U.S. 767, 1967) that it would no longer uphold obscenity convictions unless the statute in question "reflected a specific and limited state concern for juveniles," or "individual privacy" had been assaulted, or materials were distributed in a "pandering" manner.

Ironically, the last major Warren-era obscenity case, *Stanley v. Georgia* (394 U.S. 557, 1969), stands out for the manner in which it rejects the premises of the *Roth* case and its progeny. Specifically *Stanley* turns on the question of the constitutionality of state laws that prohibit private possession of proscribed sexually explicit material. By granting the right of private possession in the home, the Court opened the door to an assault on the basic *Hicklin-Roth* contention that obscenity is inherently harmful and established a formidable legal dilemma that a citizen would have to violate other laws in order to exercise a right guaranteed by *Stanley.*

In hopes of resolving that quandary, cases before the Burger Court in the 1970s asked the Court to consider if the right to private possession did not also imply a right to introduce such material into the channels of commerce. In *U.S. v. Thirty-Seven Photographs* (402 U.S. 363, 1971), the Burger Court, unwilling to liberalize on this issue, firmly ruled against any such notion. In *Paris Adult Theater v. Slaton* (413 U.S. 49, 1973), the Court showed it was not disposed to allowing a *Stanley* privacy right to adults freely patronizing a theater clearly marked "For Adults Only."

By far the most controversial and far reaching of the Burger decisions is *Miller v. California* in 1973. Accepting the *Roth* "prurient interest" and "contemporary community standards" tests, Chief Justice Burger rejected the idea of "national community" and gave a green light to each local community (he did not define "local") to set its own standards for judging obscenity. Furthermore, Burger asserted that the Court was now providing "positive guidance to the federal and state courts alike" by rejecting the negative direction of the "utterly without redeeming social value" test and substituting the new test: "whether the work, taken as a whole, lacks serious literary, artistic, political, or scientific value."

For the moment, then, the Supreme Court has stated its unwillingness to place pornographic material under the protective umbrella of the First Amendment. We have also seen, however, the bizarre definitional difficulties that the same Court has had to address in seeking to regulate that which is pornographic. In the ensuing essays, Irving Kristol defends the attempts by communities to control or ban such material. Walter Gellhorn, on the other hand, asserts that the First Amendment protects all such speech and that controlling legislation that attempts to control such material does more harm than good.

Yes: Pornography, Obscenity, and the Case for Censorship

Irving Kristol

EING frustrated is disagreeable, but the real disasters in life begin
when you get what you want. For almost a century now, a great
many intelligent, well-meaning and articulate people—of a kind
generally called liberal or intellectual, or both—have argued eloquently
against any kind of censorship of art and/or entertainment. And within the
past 10 years, the courts and the legislatures of most Western nations have
found these arguments persuasive—so persuasive that hardly a man is now
alive who clearly remembers what the answers to these arguments were.
Today, in the United States and other democracies, censorship has to all
intents and purposes ceased to exist.

Is there a sense of triumphant exhilaration in the land? Hardly. There is,
on the contrary, a rapidly growing unease and disquiet. Somehow, things
have not worked out as they were supposed to, and many notable civil libertarians have gone on record as saying this was not what they meant at all.
They wanted a world in which "Desire Under the Elms" could be produced,
or "Ulysses" published, without interference by philistine busybodies holding
public office. They have got that, of course; but they have also got a world in
which homosexual rape takes place on the stage, in which the public flocks
during lunch hours to witness varieties of professional fornication, in which
Times Square has become little more than a hideous market for the sale and
distribution of printed filth that panders to all known (and some fanciful)
sexual perversions. . . .

The basic point that emerges is one that Prof. Walter Berns has powerfully argued: no society can be utterly indifferent to the ways its citizens publicly entertain themselves. Bearbaiting and cockfighting are prohibited only in

---

Irving Kristol, from "Pornography, Obscenity and the Case for Censorship," *New York Times
Magazine* (March 28, 1971), pp. 24–25; 112–114; 116. Reprinted with permission of the
author.

part out of compassion for the suffering animals: the main reason they were abolished was because it was felt that they debased and brutalized the citizenry who flocked to witness such spectacles. And the question we face with regard to pornography and obscenity is whether . . . they can or will brutalize and debase our citizenry. . . .

I say pornography *and* obscenity because, though they have different dictionary definitions and are frequently distinguishable as "artistic" genres, they are nevertheless in the end identical in effect. Pornography is not objectionable simply because it arouses sexual desire or lust or prurience in the mind of the reader or spectator; this is a silly Victorian notion. A great many non-pornographic works—including some parts of the Bible—excite sexual desire very successfully. What is distinctive about pornography is that, in the words of D.H. Lawrence, it attempts "to do dirt on [sex] . . . [It is an] insult to a vital human relationship."

In other words, pornography differs from erotic art in that its whole purpose is to treat human beings obscenely, to deprive human beings of their specifically human dimension. That is what obscenity is all about. It is light years removed from any kind of carefree sensuality—there is no continuum between Fielding's "Tom Jones" and the Marquis de Sade's "Justine." These works have quite opposite intentions.

It may well be that Western society, in the latter half of the 20th century, is experiencing a drastic change in sexual mores and sexual relationships. We have had many such "sexual revolutions" in the past—and the bourgeois family and bourgeois ideas of sexual propriety were themselves established in the course of a revolution against 18th century "licentiousness"—and we shall doubtless have others in the future. It is, however, highly improbable (to put it mildly) that what we are witnessing is the Final Revolution which will make sexual relationships utterly unproblematic, permit us to dispense with any kind of ordered relationships between the sexes, and allow us freely to redefine the human condition. And so long as humanity has not reached that utopia, obscenity will remain a problem.

One of the reasons it will remain a problem is that obscenity is not merely about sex, any more than science fiction is about science. Science fiction, as every student of the genre knows, is a peculiar vision of power: what it is really about is politics. And obscenity is a peculiar vision of humanity: what it is really about is ethics and metaphysics. . . .

Sex—like death—is an activity that is both animal and human. There are human sentiments and human ideals involved in this animal activity. But when sex is public, the viewer does not see—cannot see—the sentiments and the ideals. He can only see the animal coupling. And that is why, when men and women make love, as we say, they prefer to be alone—because it is only when you are alone that you can make love, as distinct from merely copulating in an animal and casual way. And that, too, is why those who are voyeurs, if they are not irredeemably sick, also feel ashamed at what they are witnessing. When sex is a public spectacle, a human relationship has been debased into a mere animal connection.

It is also worth noting that this making of sex into an oscenity is not a mutual and equal transaction, but is rather an act of exploitation by one of the partners—the male partner. I do not wish to get into the complicated question as to what, if any, are the essential differences—as distinct from conventional and cultural differences—between male and female. I do not claim to know the answer to that. But I do know—and I take it as a sign which has meaning—that pornography is, and always has been, a man's work; that women rarely write pornography; and that women tend to be indifferent consumers of pornography. My own guess, by way of explanation, is that a woman's sexual experience is ordinarily more suffused with human emotion than is man's, that men are more easily satisfied with auto-erotic activities, and that men can therefore more easily take a more "technocratic" view of sex and its pleasures. Perhaps this is not correct. But whatever the explanation, there can be no question that pornography is a form of "sexism," as the Women's Liberation Movement calls it, and that the instinct of Women's Lib has been unerring in perceiving that, when pornography is perpetrated, it is perpetrated against them, as part of a conspiracy to deprive them of their full humanity. . . .

The basic psychological fact about pornography and obscenity is that it appeals to and provokes a kind of sexual regression. The sexual pleasure one gets from pornography and obscenity is autoerotic and infantile; put bluntly, it is a masturbatory exercise of the imagination, when it is not masturbation pure and simple. . . .

It is true that, in our time, some quite brilliant minds have come to the conclusion that a reversion to infantile sexuality is the ultimate mission and secret destiny of the human race. I am thinking in particular of Norman O. Brown, for whose writings I have the deepest respect. One of the reasons I respect them so deeply is that Mr. Brown is a serious thinker who is unafraid to face up to the radical consequences of his radical theories. Thus, Mr. Brown knows and says that for his kind of salvation to be achieved, humanity must annul the civilization it has created—not merely the civilization we have today, but all civilization—so as to be able to make the long descent backwards into animal innocence.

What is at stake is civilization and humanity, nothing less. The idea that "everything is permitted," as Nietzsche put it, rests on the premise of nihilism and has nihilistic implications. I will not pretend that the case against nihilism and for civilization is an easy one to make. We are here confronting the most fundamental of philosophical questions on the deepest levels. But that is precisely my point that the matter of pornography and obscenity is not a trivial one, and that only superficial minds can take a bland and untroubled view of it. . . .

I am already touching upon a political aspect of pornography when I suggest that it is inherently and purposefully subversive of civilization and its institutions. But there is another and more specifically political aspect, which has to do with the relationship of pornography and/or obscenity to democracy, and especially to the quality of public life on which democratic government ultimately rests.

Though the phrase, "the quality of life," trips easily from so many lips these days, it tends to be one of those cliches with many trivial meanings and no large, serious one. Sometimes it merely refers to such externals as the enjoyment of cleaner air, cleaner water, cleaner streets. At other times it refers to the merely private enjoyment of music, painting or literature. Rarely does it have anything to do with the way the citizen in a democracy views himself—his obligations, his intentions, his ultimate self-definition.

Instead, what I would call the "managerial" conception of democracy is the predominant opinion among political scientists, sociologists and economists, and has, through the untiring efforts of these scholars, become the conventional journalistic opinion as well. The root idea behind this "managerial" conception is that democracy is a "political system" (as they say) which can be adequately defined in terms of—can be fully reduced to—its mechanical arrangements. Democracy is then seen as a set of rules and procedures, and *nothing but* a set of rules and procedures, whereby majority rule and minority rights are reconciled into a state of equilibrium. If everyone follows these rules and procedures, then a democracy is in working order. I think this is a fair description of the democratic idea that currently prevails in academia. One can also fairly say that it is now the liberal idea of democracy par excellence.

I cannot help but feel that there is something ridiculous about being this kind of a democrat, and I must further confess to having a sneaking sympathy for those of our young radicals who also find it ridiculous. The absurdity is the absurdity of idolatry—of taking the symbolic for the real, the means for the end. The purpose of democracy cannot possibly be the endless functioning of its own political machinery. The purpose of any political regime is to achieve some version of the good life and the good society. It is not at all difficult to imagine a perfectly functioning democracy which answers all questions except one—namely, why should anyone of intelligence and spirit care a fig for it?

There is, however, an older idea of democracy—one which was fairly common until about the beginning of this century—for which the conception of the quality of public life is absolutely crucial. This idea starts from the proposition that democracy is a form of self-government, and that if you want it to be a meritorious polity, you have to care about what kind of people govern it. Indeed, it puts the matter more strongly and declares that, if you want self-government, you are only entitled to it if that "self" is worthy of governing. There is no inherent right to self-government if it means that such government is vicious, mean, squalid, and debased. Only a dogmatist and a fanatic; an idolator of democratic machinery, could approve of self-government under such conditions.

And because the desirability of self-government depends on the character of the people who govern, the older idea of democracy was very solicitous of the condition of this character. It was solicitous of the individual self, and felt an obligation to educate it into what used to be called "republican virtue." And it was solicitous of that collective self which we call public opinion and which, in a democracy, governs us collectively. Perhaps in some respects it was nervously oversolicitous—that would not be surprising. But the main thing is that it cared, cared not merely about the machinery of democracy but about the quality of life that this machinery might generate.

And because it cared, this older idea of democracy had no problem in principle with pornography and/or obscenity. It censored them—and it did so with a perfect clarity of mind and a perfectly clear conscience. It was not about to permit people capriciously to corrupt themselves. Or, to put it more precisely: in this version of democracy, the people took some care not to let themselves be governed by the more infantile and irrational parts of themselves. They have, it may be noticed, uttered that dreadful word, "censorship." And I am not about to back away from it. If you think pornography and/or obscenity is a serious problem, you have to be for censorship. I'll go even further and say that if you want to prevent pornography and/or obscenity from becoming a problem, you have to be for censorship. And lest there be any misunderstanding as to what I am saying, I'll put it as bluntly as possible: if you care for the quality of life in our American democracy, then you have to be for censorship.

But can a liberal be for censorship? Unless one assumes that being a liberal *must* mean being indifferent to the quality of American life, then the answer has to be: yes, a liberal can be for censorship—but he ought to favor a liberal form of censorship.

Is that a contradiction in terms? I don't think so. We have no problem in contrasting *repressive* laws governing alcohol and drugs and tobacco with laws *regulating* (i.e., discouraging the sale of) alcohol and drugs and tobacco. Laws encouraging temperance are not the same thing as laws that have as their goal prohibition or abolition. We have not made the smoking of cigarettes a criminal offense. We have, however, and with good liberal conscience, prohibited cigarette advertising on television, and may yet, again with good liberal conscience, prohibit it in newspapers and magazines. The idea of restricting individual freedom, in a liberal way, is not at all unfamiliar to us.

I therefore see no reason why we should not be able to distinguish repressive censorship from liberal censorship of the written and spoken word. In Britain, until a few years ago, you could perform almost any play you wished—but certain plays, judged to be obscene, had to be performed in private theatrical clubs which were deemed to have a "serious" interest in theater. In the U.S., all of us who grew up using public libraries are familiar with the circumstances under which certain books could be circulated only to adults, while still other books had to be read in the library reading room, under the librarian's skeptical eye. In both cases, a small minority that was willing to make a serious effort to see an obscene play or read an obscene book could do so. But the impact of obscenity was circumscribed and the quality of artistic life was only marginally affected.

I am not saying it is easy in practice to sustain a distinction between liberal and repressive censorship, especially in the public realm of a democracy, where popular opinion is so vulnerable to demagoguery. Moreover, an acceptable system of liberal censorship is likely to be exceedingly difficult to devise in the United States today, because our educated classes, upon whose judgment a liberal censorship must rest, are so convinced that there is no such thing as a problem of obscenity, or even that there is no such thing as obscenity at all. But, to counterbalance this, there is the further, fortunate truth that the tolerable margin for error is quite large, and single mistakes or single injustices are not all that important. . . .

Just one last point which I dare not leave untouched. If we start censoring pornography or obscenity, shall we not inevitably end up censoring political opinion? A lot of people seem to think this would be the case—which only shows the power of doctrinaire thinking over reality. We had censorship of pornography and obscenity for 150 years, until almost yesterday, and I am not aware that freedom of opinion is this country was in any way diminished as a consequence of this fact. Fortunately for those of use who are liberal, freedom is not indivisible. If it were, the case for liberalism would be indistinguishable from the case for anarchy; and they are two very different things.

But I must repeat and emphasize: what kind of laws we pass governing pornography and obscenity, what kind of censorship—or, since we are still a Federal nation—what kinds of censorship we institute in our various localities may indeed be difficult matters to cope with; nevertheless the real issue is one of principle. I myself subscribe to a liberal view of the enforcement problem: I think that pornography should be illegal *and* available to anyone who wants it so badly as to make a pretty strenuous effort to get it. We have lived with under-the-counter pornography for centuries now, in a fairly comfortable way. But the issue of principle, of whether it should be over or under the counter, has to be settled before we can reflect on the advantages and disadvantages of alternative modes of censorship. I think the settlement we are living under now, in which obscenity and democracy are regarded as equals, is wrong; I believe it is inherently unstable; I think it will, in the long run, be incompatible with any authentic concern for the quality of life in our democracy.

No: Dirty Books, Disgusting Pictures, and Dreadful Laws

Walter Gellhorn

MY sentiments concerning the constitutionality of antiobscenity laws, . . . approach those of the minority rather than the majority of the Supreme Court. Objections to the Court's judgment are multiple.

First, the Court has persistently assumed that when the Constitution was adopted, obscenity (whatever it is) was already widely outlawed and was therefore not deemed to be among the kinds of expression meant to be safeguarded from governmental interference. This is untrue. A drunken Englishman who had cavorted in the nude on the balcony of a London tavern, whence he had thrown on the heads of passersby a number of bottles which he had filled with what the judge euphemistically called an "offensive liquor," had been convicted of obscenity in the seventeenth century. That was the common law beginning, and it plainly has little to do with words or graphics. Among the American colonies in pre-Revolutionary times only Massachusetts had adopted a law relating to obscenity, and it had to do with mockery of preaching or divine worship, rather than with sexual nervousness. What was indeed a commonplace in preconstitutional days was legislation which penalized blasphemy. Statutory reinforcement of the Biblical command not to take the name of the Lord in vain was, of course, meant to preserve the spiritual well-being of persons who might otherwise hear blasphemous or sacrilegious expressions. Nobody, so far as I know, argues today that the community can constitutionally be immunized against moral debilitation by suppressing words which our forefathers thought would endanger society.

Walter Gellhorn, from "Dirty Books, Disgusting Pictures, and Dreadful Laws," 8 *Georgia Law Review* (1974), pp. 291–312.

Second, I deplore the Court's insistence that depiction or description of sexual conduct can be suppressed unless it appears in a work which, taken as a whole, has serious literary, artistic, political, or scientific value. Many persons—the late President Kennedy was among them, and I am, too—like to relax with silly novels about spies and manhunts. In them the hero usually conceals in his trousers personal equipment resembling a twenty-shot repeating rifle, to be used against any female target; every girl whom the hero encounters is beautiful, pneumatic, horizontally gymnastic, and ready at a moment's notice to enjoy a roll in the hay. What harm is done by trash of this kind? The suspense novel deserves its name because readers temporarily suspend contact with reality. Sooner or later, however, most readers return to real life no worse for their bookish exposure to lust, larceny, and lifelessness. Who can pretend that a published study of Agent 007's bedroom athletics has enduring literary worth? Still, it may entertain—and that, too, is socially worthwhile.

You will no doubt remind me that the Supreme Court did not condemn sex and nudity as such, but only works which appeal to prurient interest and which are patently offensive. The words have a confident ring, but, plainly, they mean different things to different people in different circumstances. Our great grandfathers, if one can believe serious novels of the nineteenth century, were thrown into paroxysms of concupiscence when they glimpsed a prettily turned ankle. When I was a boy the sight of a girl's knee occasioned lewd thoughts, and *La Vie Parisienne,* a long dead precursor of *Penthouse* and similar magazines, drove young males mad with pictures a good deal less explicit than today's department store advertisements of brassieres and bikinis. Not until the 1960's did the motion picture industry dare to show a woman's navel. Today, as I understand, pubic hair is a generally respected tabu, and a showing of genitalia (the possession of which is thought to be fairly widespread and therefore unlikely to come as a complete surprise to a patron of the movies) is presumably a rather blatant "appeal to prurient interest." Some years ago college women were asked what had aroused their libidinous thoughts, if any. An overwhelming majority answered, simply, MEN—whose appeal to prurient interest one hopes will be allowed to continue.

Moreover, the process of judging whether or not particular matter is offensive to the community does not inspire confidence. What exactly is the community whose attitudes supposedly determine the labeling of material as inoffensively sex-oriented or, on the contrary, as objectionably pornographic? The Chief Justice has said that the community is not the nation as a whole; the country's makeup is too diverse to permit a nationwide norm. Maine, the Chief Justice observed, might have different standards from Las Vegas. Is the community, then, to be the state or the city—or even in the case of the larger metropolitan areas, a segment of the city? "Can a man be prosecuted for reading a dirty book in a plane occupying air-space over eastern

Kansas? What recourse will the publisher of Baudelaire have against the city council of Ogallala, Nebraska?" Must a California publisher or film producer gear himself to San Clemente or San Francisco? A prominent federal judge believes that "community" will come to be related to small geographical units, since nobody can determine the standards of an entire state which like California has a population of more than 18,000,000, "notoriously diverse in culture and life style." In short, he foresees not fifty standards, but thousands and thousands—and even then uncertainties will remain. "Is a college bookstore," he asks, "governed by the standards of the college community or of the town or county in which the college is located?"

No matter how the "community" may be defined, who knows it well enough to compute the average of the degrees of its sensitivity? The omniscient juror, of course. Approximately eighty-five percent of adult males and seventy percent of adult females in the United States, according to recent surveys, "have been exposed at some time during their lives to depictions of explicit sexual material in either visual or textual form"; most of the exposure occurred during adolescence, and yet the young people survived. Since this exposure had been chiefly voluntary and has been both extensive and intensive, one might reasonably assume that the material had not offended the community, since almost everybody supposes that he is different from, and very probably superior to, the rest of the human herd. In actuality, however, the determiners of offensiveness are unlikely to be jurors, anyway. Much more probably they will be judges, sitting in declaratory judgment or equity proceedings or engaging in de novo review of others' findings, for the Supreme Court, as the late Justice Harlan once complained, has tied itself to the "absurd business of perusing and viewing the miserable stuff that pours into the Court," an unedifying task the Court has recently declared its intention of continuing to perform.

All of these uncertainties and imperfections would be more readily acceptable if only the cause for being socially concerned were more solidly established. The reason for social concern about pornography is—what? Is it that pornography stimulates sexual fantasizing, impure thoughts, "genital commotion" (as a well known cleric phrased it)? Some who favor regulation do indeed seem to be concerned with what goes on in the mind and, consequently, in one's physiology. But a moment's reflection reassures us that lustful thoughts, which can be aroused in myriad ways, are beyond governmental control. Verbal or pictorial expression which simply stimulates *thoughts* about sexual activity cannot be suppressed, whether the expression be an advertisement for a provocatively named perfume or a book showing provocatively undraped humans, mailed in a plain brown wrapper. Thanks to the Constitution, Americans are free to have sex on their minds often, indeed constantly. They are allowed to think what they wish, and not merely what legislators regard as pure thoughts. As a corollary, expression which goes no farther than causing mental operations could not be penalized. The power to halt expression must rest on a finding that the mental operations which expression has stirred will lead in a straight line to conduct of a kind society may reasonably seek to forestall.

At this time the evidence of a nexus between pornography and antisocial acts is slim indeed. Numerous empirical studies have yielded no clear proof that reading or seeing has caused crimes, sexual aberrations, or other behavioral dislocations. To some extent, on the contrary, reading dirty books or looking at disgusting pictures seems to have had a sublimating effect, so that misconduct which might otherwise have occurred has been turned into subjective fantasies, without anyone's being hurt. The literature on the subject is vast. The available evidence is not persuasive of the harmfulness of pornography; equally, however, it fails to prove its harmlessness. If a legislature chooses to act on the intuitive judgment that pornography does jeopardize the public welfare by increasing the likelihood of undesirable behavior which would not have occurred but for the pornographic matter, courts should perhaps respect the legislative judgment. Man lives by his images of reality, not by reality alone. Belief that danger exists powerfully shapes judgment; and when a legislature cannot be shown to have acted arbitrarily in indulging that belief rather than another, courts must perhaps stand aside. Especially when the belief has been acted upon in essentially the same manner by a host of presumably reasonable legislators, judges may well hesitate to insist upon a contrary finding whose evidential underpinnings are only debatably firm. Be well aware, nevertheless, that widespread, persistent belief is not necessarily consonant with truth. The great Seventeenth Century common law judge Sir Matthew Hale, when sentencing two women to be hanged as witches, asserted to some doubters that "the reality of witchcraft" was indisputable, a conclusion he had reached at least partly because "the wisdom of all nations had provided laws against such persons, which is an argument of their confidence of such a crime."

My discussion thus far, with its focus upon the constitutionality of regulatory measures, falls into the mistake which characterizes much of the American political debate. Far too often we Americans leap to the conclusion that if a measure is constitutional, it must perforce be good. Of course this is palpably untrue. The Constitution sets boundaries beyond which a statute may not go, but it certainly does not imply that everything within the outer boundaries is socially desirable. In its most recent cases upholding measures aimed at pornography the Court itself has been at pains to remind that the States remain free to eliminate all controls if they choose to do so. In my opinion the legislature would be wise not to enact new laws (or to reaffirm old laws) which go as far as the Court now says would be constitutional, but, at the same time, the states should not abandon controls altogether.

First, the factual uncertainties about the impact of erotica on very young persons may justify efforts to reinforce parental restrictions on children's reading matter or movie-watching. A New York statute, widely copied in other states, prohibits commercially distributing to juveniles materials which stress nudity, sexual acts, or sadomasochistic abuse that is found to be harmful to minors. Harmfulness turns on a threefold test: the material must predominantly appeal to the prurient interest of minors *and* it must patently offend prevailing standards in the adult community concerning what is suitable material for minors *and* it must have no social importance for minors. The validity of this approach has been settled by the Supreme Court, and it has been widely copied by many of the other states, almost all of which have adopted statutes aimed particularly at distribution of erotica to the young. . . .

The second are of control is one about which I feel much more positively. I see no reason at all not to forbid imposition of sexual expression upon an unwilling audience. As to this branch of the matter, I would happily extend the doctrine of *Rowan v. Post Office Department* upholding a federal law which permits mail recipients to require removal of their names from the mailing lists of those who have dispatched material the recipient "believes to be erotically arousing or sexually provocative." This has the effect, obviously, of limiting the mailer's freedom of expression, but the limitation is permissible because the "right of every person 'to be let alone' must be placed in the scales with the right of others to communicate." The Constitution, the Court said, creates no "right to press even 'good ideas upon an unwilling recipient. . . .'"

Of course the same is true of conduct which, permissible in itself, becomes impermissible when it needlessly shocks the sensibilities of others. Laws against nudity on the highway seem to me to be explicable not on moral, but purely on aesthetic grounds. Humans rarely possess forms of unalloyed delight; to say that God created man in His own image sometimes borders on the defamatory. So the law seeks to safeguard the wayfarer against visual outrages, rather than against sexual arousal. The inadequate man who exposes his genitals in a public place engenders revulsion, not lust. The prohibition of exhibitionism of this kind is meant not to protect morality, but to protect unwilling viewers. Defecating in public is discouraged for similar reasons. So is public copulation. A live performance of a couple "locked in a sexual embrace at high noon in Times Square," Chief Justice Burger recently remarked, would not be constitutionally protected even if "they simultaneously engage in a valid political dialogue." By a parity of reasoning, display advertising which thrusts genitalia or genital contacts before the eyes of shocked passersby can be forbidden. As Justice Holmes once remarked, "[m]y right to swing my arm ends at the point at which your nose begins. . . ."

I cannot close without anticipating the questions—why should people of probity be disturbed by efforts to suppress the vulgarities which enrich pornographers? Writers have been able to produce successful books without possessing a vocabulary consisting chiefly of four letter words, and many a worthwhile motion picture has been produced without showing a penis in glorious technicolor. Why should we as concerned citizens have the slightest interest in protecting meretricious material which debases those who make it as well as those who consume it?

First, the threat or the actuality of law enforcement has a chilling effect upon expression which is in fact not meretricious at all, though some official might seek to stigmatize it. This is not an imagined danger. "The Changing Room," chosen as the best play of 1972–1973 season by the New York Drama Critics Circle, has had difficulty in arranging a national tour because theater owners in Los Angeles, San Francisco, Detroit, Philadelphia, and Boston have been afraid to book it. They fear being shut down because the performance involves occasional frontal nudity. Motion pictures which have been exhibited without major incident before general audiences in many cities find themselves the center of lawsuits in others, as has happened with the "Last Tango in Paris" and "Carnal Knowledge" among others. Because local standards multiply the threat of being found unacceptable, those who publish or produce or sell the work of writers and performers will, I think, halt well short of the line beyond which they may not step with impunity. Some of them will prudently hunt for the lowest common denominator. We lawyers are well aware that nobody likes to buy a law suit. Too much altogether legitimate expression will be stifled lest somebody's hypersensitivity be activated. This has happened already in the case of magazines, which have been driven from stores by zealous policemen or prosecutors whose threats have sufficed to discourage sales of such periodicals as *Playboy*.

Second, the First Amendment has too often been discussed as though it was meant only to protect speakers and writers. It was meant also, if indeed not mainly, to protect hearers' and viewers' freedom of choice. Our Constitution is designed to make for an unconstricted flow of spoken and written words or of pictures that take the place of words—and the flow is for the benefit of the consumer, not merely the producer of expression. We have made a constitutional commitment to a do-it-yourself system, in which each person is his own censor. So long as one remains free to read or not to read, to look or not to look, I think society would gain from leaving selection with the consumer. Like Justice Douglas, a person can go through life without being trapped into reading or seeing what offends him.

Third, selective law enforcement has hit especially hard at suppressing political communication which has appeared in publications with incidental sexual material. Underground newspapers and similarly irreverent publications have been harassed by prosecutors who found "pornography" a convenient peg upon which to hand proceedings brought for other purposes entirely.

How frequently courts will be able to examine closely into the merits of suspect cases is problematical.

Fourth, the burdens of enforcing laws pertaining to the quality of sexual words as distinct from acts weigh heavily but unrewardingly on police, prosecutors, and judges. Successful enforcement is not commonly achieved. So far as the laws do in fact operate as deterrents of undesired forms of expression, they do so not chiefly because the risk of punishment after legal proceedings is great, but because the risk of being involved in costly litigation is great. The possibilities of arbitrarily selective law enforcement, with attendant shakedowns and subversions of official rectitude, are apparent. And in any event, "Are police forces, prosecution resources, and court time being wastefully diverted from the central insecurities of our metropolitan life—robbery, burglary, rape, assault, and governmental corruption?"

Fifth and most important, the forces in our society which constantly seek to intensify concern about pornography seem fixated upon conceptions of sexual morality, as though moral values related to sex alone. What about the other human virtues? "No book has ever been suppressed on the ground that it promoted selfishness or dishonesty or cowardice." The daily press and the television newscasts provide numerous accounts of real life skullduggery, often leading to public eminence. . . . Americans would do well to consider the quality of life as a whole, and not merely sex life. Objecting to authoritarianism reflected in obscenity legislation which he links with this country's religious heritage, a professor of religion bitingly exclaims: "In so far as the God in whom we, as a nation, officially trust is thought to be more concerned about illicit sexual pleasure than about social justice or the use of napalm, it is inevitable that attention will be diverted from these issues and concentrated on the control of pornography." Like him, I favor a redirection of reformist energies toward an attack upon social evils more debilitating than erotica have been shown to be. . . .

5

New York Times v. Sullivan: Should Freedom of the Press Be Limited by Libel Laws?

Robert A. Poirier

LEXANDER Meiklejohn's impassioned defense of free speech and its relationship to self-government has frequently found judicial support in a number of Supreme Court opinions, both majority and dissenting, in the past three decades. No decision, however, completely enshrines Meiklejohn's views more than the great libel case of *New York Times v. Sullivan* (376 U.S. 255, 1964).

Writing for the Court, Justice Brennan's words that "debate on public issues should be uninhibited, robust, and wide open" would have given Meiklejohn great pleasure. Meiklejohn believed that the essence of democracy rests with the principle of self-government.[1] A procedural necessity to achieve this goal is the exercise of free speech on public matters. Democracy for Meiklejohn operates best when citizens are well informed. Only through open discussion without fear of retribution can citizens acquire the information needed to make informed decisions. Ancillary to the view of free speech as a procedural requirement, Meiklejohn argued forcefully for the right of citizens to hold public officials accountable for their actions on behalf of the public. Meiklejohn's theory of democracy, although not particularly novel, is distinguished by the almost absolutist role given to free speech.

There is, indeed, a public interest in a free and open exchange of information even if that exchange may involve attacking the views and decisions of a public official. Democracy necessitates and guarantees a right of confrontation with the state. The state, however, is an abstraction. It acts and speaks only through individuals who, although officials of the state, are citizens with the right to be secure from a destructive invasion of reputation. The theory of the First Amendment recognizes that everyone is entitled to some psychic space that should not be invaded by speech.

Realistically, however, those who are in positions of political power might wish to insulate themselves from public criticisms by gratuitously using the label of seditious libel against their opponents, thereby hoping to intimidate the opposition into silence. A concern for the "chilling effect" on the press in carrying out its responsibility to inform the public of the behavior of its officials led to the *New York Times* decision, a decision that disturbed 170 years of stability in U.S. libel law.

At issue was a full-page paid political advertisement in the *New York Times* that made allegations about the way Alabama police had dealt with black demonstrators. The advertisement, which contained hyperbole and inconsequential factual errors, mentioned public officials by function and not by name. Sullivan, the commissioner responsible for the police, sued to reclaim his reputation and won a $500,000 award from an Alabama jury. The Supreme Court unanimously, but for various reasons, overturned Sullivan's award and established the now-famous libel standard for "public officials."

Prior to *New York Times* the standards by which a "public official" could sue for libel were the same as those that applied to any private citizen. Juries, since the historic trial of John Peter Zenger in the eighteenth century, were empowered to infer malice in a defamation case on the basis of the evidence presented in court. Since *New York Times,* persons defined as "public officials" would have the burden of showing evidentiary proof that "actual malice" was intended by the disseminator of defamatory information. "Actual malice" was defined in *New York Times* as a known falsity printed with a reckless disregard for the truth. Placing this burden of proof on a "public official" acting as plaintiff amounted to, as some of the case's critics were quick to point out, an open season for the press to attack politicians because the standard of proof of malice would be difficult, if not impossible, to muster.

Additionally the Court effectively put aside the traditional standard of truth as a defense against libel and took comfort in the fact that the "public official" had the recourse of access to the media for rebuttal that the private citizen did not have. Acknowledging that the new standard of proving "actual malice" burdened a plaintiff and could open the door to press abuses, Justice Brennan's majority opinion argued that the needs of the press as a public watchdog were compelling enough to justify the risk. The Court reasoned that to place the burden of proof on the speaker would certainly lead to a "chilling effect" on the publication of sensitive information on public issues and government officials, especially if the spectre of expensive litigation was a constant threat. *New York Times* therefore was intended to relieve the press from the fear of libel used as a tool of political reprisal.

Ironically, libel litigation appears to be more of a threat to press freedom now than ever before. This is so because by incorporating Meiklejohn's theory of full discussion on public matters in the manner adopted in *New York Times,* the Court has opened the doors to many troublesome issues. Specifically, *New York Times* did not carefully address itself to a precise definition of "malice" or inform future plaintiffs of the exact scope of the "actual malice" standard's application. Furthermore, the Court did not provide procedural guidelines and safeguards for the use of the "malice" standard or the standard for differentiation "public" persons. It remained for subsequent decisions to tackle some of these issues.

The first of these decisions dealt with identifying the parameters of the "public official" category. If a "public official", unlike a private citizen, has the burden of proving "actual malice" in a libel action (as stated in *New York Times*), then the Supreme Court had to provide a yardstick to distinguish one category of persons from another. That yardstick was promulgated in *Rosenblatt v. Baer* (383 U.S. 75, 1966) when the Court ruled that the "public official" designation applied "at the very least to those among the hierarchy of government employees who have, or appear to the public to have, substantial responsibility for control over the conduct of governmental affairs." The Court did not define "substantial responsibility," but since the official in this case was an unelected county employee who supervised the county's recreation area, *Rosenblatt* seems to suggest that the "public official" designation would include most civil servants.

The next significant *New York Times* progeny were the companion cases of *Curtis Publishing Co. v. Butts* and *Associated Press v. Walker* (338 U.S. 130, 1967), which greatly expanded the class of "public officials." Henceforth, "public figures" would join "public officials" as a special class of plaintiffs who must demonstrate "actual malice" in a libel suit. The *Butts* case involved a football coach and athletic director at the University of Georgia who had been accused of plotting to fix a football game. The *Walker* case involved retired Major General Edwin Walker's alleged role in disorders at the University of Mississippi when the first black student, James Meredith, enrolled. Neither Butts nor Walker was a "public official", but the Court opined that "by reason of their fame, [they] shape events in the areas of concern to a society at large." Because of their status as "public figures," the Court argued that they have access to the same means of rebuttal available to "public officials." Thus, the "public figure" category could include persons from any occupation who by reason of fame and social status are "intimately involved in the resolution of important public questions."

Finally, *Rosenbloom v. Metromedia, Inc.* (403 U.S. 29, 1971) further expanded the *New York Times* doctrine by including private individuals involved in matters of "public or general concern." Rosenbloom, a publisher of nudist magazines, was accused by a radio station of being involved in the "smut literature racket." Although Rosenbloom was clearly not a "public official" or "public figure" by the standards of *New York Times* and *Butts,* the Court's decision effectively eliminated a balance of interest approach by arguing that "society's interest in protecting individual reputation often yields to other important social goals." *Rosenbloom* raised once again the prospect of press abuse, a risk the Court felt justified in taking in *New York Times.* Was the Court coming around to the Black-Douglas view expressed in *New York Times* that the First Amendment absolutely precludes libel law?

Three years later in *Gertz v. Robert Welch, Inc.* (418 U.S. 323, 1974), the Court began to slow the expansion of the *New York Times* doctrine. *Rosenbloom* had cast the Court into the difficult position of deciding on an ad hoc basis what issues were of "general or public interest," effectively making the Court a constitutional editorial board. Furthermore, as Justice Thurgood Marshall's dissent pointed out, the "public or general concern" test was a threat "to society's interest in protecting private individuals from being thrust into the public eye by the distorting light of defamation" because "all human events are arguably within the area of 'public or general concern.' " Marshall's concerns found their way into the *Gertz* majority.

This case involved a defamation suit by Gertz against the John Birch Society publication *American Opinion.* Gertz, a Chicago attorney, had been retained in a civil action against the Chicago police by the family of a youth who had been shot to death by a Chicago police officer. The officer, Richard Nuccio, was convicted of second-degree murder for the shooting. *American Opinion,* in an article entitled "Frame-Up: Richard Nuccio and the War on Police," suggested that the conviction of Nuccio was part of a nationwide Communist conspiracy to discredit local law enforcement authorities. Gertz was specifically named in the article and accused of having a criminal record and being a front for the Communist party. Gertz, a prominent Chicago-area personality because of his publications and frequent guest appearances on local talk shows, could have qualified for "public figure" status under *Butts.* Also the issue of public behavior and alleged attempts to discredit the police nationally would have qualified Gertz's libel action under the "public or general concern" test of *Rosenbloom.* In short, Gertz seemingly would have to prove "actual malice" to sustain an award for defamatory libel.

This was not to be the case because the Court, in a 5–4 decision, ruled that *New York Times* did not extend to falsehoods about an individual who is not a "public official" or a "public figure." Thus the Court signaled its unwillingness to continue its trend toward absolute protection for the press. The Court attempted to replace the "matter of general or public concern" test with a more narrow "public figure" category. Noting Gertz' prominence, the Court suggested that his was a general notoriety "for all purposes" and that Gertz therefore was not a public figure with respect to the "particular subject." Since Gertz was now a private individual by this standard, he was "more vulnerable to injury and the state's interest in protecting him is correspondingly greater."

In 1976 the Court applied the new *Gertz* rule in *Time v. Firestone* (424 U.S. 448), which turned on a *Time* magazine allegation that the divorce of tire millionaire Russell A. Firestone, Jr., involved adultery on Mrs.

Firestone's part. Mrs. Firestone sued for libel after the magazine refused to retract its allegations. *Time* argued she was a "public figure" and would have to prove "actual malice." The Court did not agree, and the majority opinion stated that Mrs. Firestone "did not assume any role of especial prominence in the affairs of society . . . and she did not thrust herself to the forefront of any public controversy in order to influence the resolution of the issues involved in it."

Whether *New York Times* and its progeny have been an asset to the First Amendment right of freedom of the press is arguable. The press itself is divided on this issue. It is evident that libel suits by "public officials" and "public figures" against the press and broadcast media are on the rise, with plaintiffs asking for large sums. Retired General William Westmoreland, for example, sought $120 million in damages from CBS. Although he eventually withdrew his complaint, the fear of such libel judgments and associated legal fees could well put smaller newspapers and television stations out of the investigative reporting business—precisely the "chilling effect" the Court hoped to avoid in *New York Times*. Furthermore, the case of former Israeli Defense Minister Ariel Sharon against *Time* magazine, which ended in no award because Sharon failed to prove "actual malice," raises the spectre of foreign "public officials" suing U.S. journalists in U.S. courts. *Gertz's* braking action indicates the Court's willingness to tighten standards, but it is evident that clarification should be exacted in future libel decisions.

Additional issues in the debate concerning libel and the First Amendment are addressed in the essays that follow. Law Professor Franklin Haiman contends that the remedy for defamation is not a limitation on speech as such but rather *more* speech principally in the form of right-to-reply statutes. David Hunsaker, an attorney specializing in communications law, argues in favor of libel and its importance to the credibility of the press.

Yes: Defamation Law and Media Credibility

David M. Hunsaker

OVER the past fifteen years the United States Supreme Court has worked great changes in the law of defamation (libel and slander) in what has been regarded as a balancing of interests between the rights and functions of a free press and the state's interest in protecting the reputation and privacy of its citizens. In the working out of this new balance, the rights of the communications media have usually prevailed. The continuing rationale of the Court has been the "profound national commitment to the principle that debate on public issues should be uninhibited, robust, and wide-open," a process that requires "breathing space."

During the same period, the trustworthiness of the press has been drawn increasingly into question, a result of a number of changing conditions, including increasing monopolization of ownership and power. Though not unmindful of increasing media power, the Supreme Court has done little to promote diversity of ideas and recently, in fact, has placed severe barriers in front of those voices seeking access to the mass media. The relationship between freedom and responsibility may have become too imbalanced. . . .

The Court was faced with supplying a broader rationale than the seditious libel analogy in order to justify giving First Amendment protection to criticism of public figures. For Justice John Marshall Harlan, author of the plurality opinion in *Curtis Publishing Co. v. Butts,* the epistemological premise underlying the "profound national commitment to . . . uninhibited, robust, and wide-open debate" was that "speech can rebut speech, propaganda will answer propaganda," with a closer approximation to the "truth" and wiser governmental policies as a result. Thus the preferred remedy for false speech was *more speech,* and one who has "sufficient access to the means of counter-argument to be able 'to expose through discussion the

David M. Hunsaker, from "Freedom and Responsibility in First Amendment Theory: Defamation Law and Media Credibility," 65 *Quarterly Journal of Speech* (1979), pp. 25–35.

falsehood and fallacies' of the defamatory statement" has less need of the state's protection for a damaged reputation.

The access rationale, however, has been criticized by other members of the Court. Justice William Brennan, who in 1971 advocated a public/private interest distinction instead of the public figure/private individual one discussed in *Butts*, discounted Justice Harlan's contention that public figures have greater access to the media. It may be true, he argued, that public figures have greater access to the press, but denials, retractions, and corrections are not "hot news" and rarely receive the prominence of the original story. Rather in most instances the ability of public officials or public figures to respond through the media will depend upon the same complex factor on which the ability of a private individual depends: "the unpredictable event of the media's continuing interest in the story . . . seems too insubstantial a reed on which to rest a constitutional distinction."

Justice Brennan then added the suggestion that if the states were concerned about the inability of their private citizens to respond to defamatory publicity about them, "the solution lies in the direction of ensuring their ability to respond, rather than in stifling public discussion of matters of public concern." He noted that several states had enacted retraction and right-of-reply statutes, and implied that such forms of limited guaranteed access would be consistent with the central meaning of the First Amendment.

It seems odd that Justice Brennan did not recognize the apparent contradiction in this recommendation. If retractions and the like are not hot news, and thus would not receive prominent coverage, the solution proposed by the Justice, by his own reasoning, would be ineffective. Moreover, traditional retraction statutes operate solely to mitigate the damages of the plaintiff and do not bar a defamation action itself. If the media defendant refused to print or otherwise "publish" the retraction, the libel suit would take its normal course, and to that extent public discussion of matters of public concern would be stifled. . . .

In an era of increasing concentration and power of mass communication, increasing sophistication of mechanisms of exploitation and manipulation of public opinion, and increasing wariness and cynicism by the public of the mass media, the need for some vehicle of *accountability* has become acute. We are beyond the point where industry self-regulation, even if it were accepted, would do much good in maintaining credibility. The National News Council, created in 1973 to handle citizen complaints against unfair treatment by national news sources, by its own admission has neither the resources, the scope, nor the support from the industry to do much more than make brief commentaries on press coverage—and lacks any power to demand retraction, correction, or apology.

Government regulation, on the other hand, while partially effective in protecting the public from false and misleading advertising, in achieving truth in packaging, and assuming full disclosure in the marketing of securities, has had little success in producing "fairness" in electronic journalism in the eyes of the public, and constantly runs the risk of inhibiting freedom of expression. Further, little has been done to break up large concentrations of ownership, either of broadcasting or newspaper outlets. The FCC rules on diversification of media ownership are frequently relaxed when a licensee has a good program record, and its current regulations on cross-media ownership do almost nothing about breaking up newspaper-broadcasting combinations. And, moreover, Congress has enacted protective legislation exempting newspapers from the full impact of anti-trust laws. But beyond the limitations on government-induced accountability lie all the dangers of censorship and suppression which the First Amendment was supposed to prevent.

Given such ineffective and self-limiting alternatives, should we not reexamine the law of defamation in a new light? It may very well be the most effective check on media irresponsibility and all that follows, and may be by far the greatest safeguard against loss of credibility in the press—with the least danger to the freedom of the press. Unlike press boards, government agencies, and even limited forms of government-required access (such as the "Equal Time" provision of the Communication Act and the "Fairness Doctrine" promulgated by the FCC), the defamation action is available to all citizens who believe and can prove their reputation has been damaged by a negligently (or recklessly or intentionally) published falsehood. The issue is tried in the person's own community by a jury of the plaintiffs [sic] peers, with the normal safeguards against an unjust verdict available to the defendant and new Supreme Court rules requiring proof of actual damages.

Although it may be that "the role of libel law in the system of freedom of expression has been relatively minor and essentially erratic," its role in perpetuating public trust in the media may be far more signifcant than anyone supposed. As noted by Lippman,

> [Each] of us tends to judge a newspaper, if we judge it at all, by its treatment of that part of the news in which we feel ourselves involved. The newspaper deals with a multitude of events beyond our experience. But it deals also with some events within our experience. And in its handling of those events we most frequently decide to like it or dislike it, to trust it or refuse to have the sheet in the house.

Knowing that the defamation suit exists as a check against falsehood and damaging inaccuracy, and knowing that other members of the community also know it, the private citizen is able to place more complete faith in the truthfulness of reports about which that citizen could not possibly have direct knowledge or experience. The existence of such a check relating to that part of the news which is within the knowledge and experience of the reader thus secures a public good in addition to a private remedy for a personal injury. Such a public good should not be taken lightly.

In constitutional confrontation between the press and citizen claiming injury from it, the rights of the press, over the last fifteen years, have usually been upheld and strengthened. In some respects the Court's decision in *Gertz v. Robert Welch, Inc.* may have tipped the scales too far in favor of press autonomy. By requiring the plaintiff to prove a measure of fault on the part of the media defendant, the Court eliminated the "vindication" right of a non-public official/figure to "set the record straight." Even though the defamation in such case was not a result of negligent or intentional wrongdoing, the innocent plaintiff still suffers harm to reputation, without the possibility of either recompense or correction. In the *Tornillo* case the court left open the question of the constitutionality of retraction statutes. A constitutionally permissible procedure might be to allow a vindication suit, one in which the plaintiff is required to prove all the elements of the tort of defamation except negligence, and the media defendant would be required to elect between defending the suit and paying the plaintiff's out-of-pocket damages or printing (or broadcasting) the correction necessary to vindicate the plaintiff's tarnished reputation.

It has been suggested, however, that in other respects *Gertz* does not go far enough in protecting the press's First Amendment freedoms. Critics have argued, for example, that the defamation action in the past has inhibited the press too much in its attempts to be a watchdog on government and society, and that the mere threat of the defamation suit brings with it self-censorship and the so-called "chilling effect" on the exercise of press freedom; therefore the press requires "breathing space" to engage in uninhibited debate on any subject deemed "newsworthy" or of "public interest." One should keep in mind, however, that the Supreme Court has never intimated that falsehoods should be protected by the First Amendment, or that there is any First Amendment purpose to be served by protecting falsehoods. Nor is all self-censorship an evil. We censor ourselves in thought, word, and action every day, and must do so if we are able to live in organized society.

What is to be avoided is the kind of self-censorship which results not from the exercise of caution, due care, and prudent restraint, but that from fear of unacceptable retaliation by powerful persons determined to keep hidden from public view their actions or influence in the way society is run. The constitutionalization of defamation law has gone a long way to prevent the latter.

Whether the fault requirement of *Gertz* will prove too insurmountable a barrier to the vindication of harms done the private citizenry remains to be seen. There is some indication in the *Firestone* case that the Court is willing and able to evolve a standard of due care for the news media which will ensure that the investigation, reporting, and dissemination of information will not be engaged in carelessly or recklessly.

Whether one speaks in Madisonian or more modern terminology, we live in a world of "factions" or "spheres of influence," each holding the other in check. The Supreme Court in the past has addressed some imbalances between the press and certain "factions" described as public officials and public figures. The fundamental rationale offered by the Court was that the public would be better served and protected from wrongdoing by those factions if the press were given greater power to bring their deeds to light without fear of reprisal. But it will not do to create an imbalance in the other direction. The mass media are just as much a faction as are public officials and public figures, and the public can be served poorly by any of them.

Although it would be extreme hyperbole to suggest that nothing stands between the current concern over media credibility and the collapse of the privately owned mass communication system except the law of defamation, it is not hyperbole to suggest that the need to maintain public faith in both government and media is critical, and that the availability of a private remedy against media abuses will play no small role in maintaining that faith. Such recognition compels me to view the role defamation plays in First Amendment theory in a new light, and to offer the above analysis as validation of the old saying to which we all pay lip service: "There can be no freedom without responsibility."

No: Defamation and Law
in a Free Society

Franklyn S. Haiman

T HE principle enunciated by Justice Brandeis that, where time permits, the proper remedy for false speech is more speech has gained
only partial acceptance in contemporary judicial doctrine concerning defamation. The Supreme Court, in noting that public officials and public
figures have greater access to the media of communication to answer false
accusations than do private persons, has indicated that, at least in the realm
of public affairs, it views replies as preferable to lawsuits. However, with
respect to private defamations, as well as to all other libels uttered with "actual malice," our society has continued looking to litigation as the remedy
rather than to providing greater access to the media for "more speech." This
is not because we are unaware of any mechanism to accomplish the latter
end, for the idea of a right of reply as an alternative to actions for defamation
has been known and advocated for a long time. . . .

These laws come in several varieties. German law has limited one's right
to reply to a correction of allegations of fact, whereas French law has allowed
also for an answer to expressions of opinion. While Mississippi's law provided for a limited right of reply only to alleged defamations, the law of
Florida required that any newspaper which attacked either the personal
character of offical record of any candidate for public office, irrespective of
the truth of the charges, was obligated, upon the candidate's request, to provide equivalent space for an answer to the attack.

It was this Florida law which provided the basis, in 1974, for the U.S.
Supreme Court's only confrontation to date with the right-to-reply issue. The
Miami Herald Publishing Company claimed that the state law requiring it to
print material it did not wish to publish was in violation of its freedom of the
press, and the Supreme Court unanimously agreed. The language of the

---

Franklyn S. Haiman, from *Speech and Law in a Free Society,* University of Chicago Press, 1981,
pp. 48–54.

Court's opinion was so sweeping in its condemnation of the idea of the government telling a newspaper to print something it might not want to that Justices William Brennan and William Rehnquist felt moved to report, in a one-sentence concurrence, their understanding that the decision did not invalidate statutes which compel publication of a retraction as a remedy in cases where a plaintiff has proven defamation in court.

Laws which might establish a right to reply to alleged defamations, as a *substitute* for libel actions in court, would be neither as narrow as those noted with apparent approval by Justices Brennan and Rehnquist nor need they be as broad as the condemned Florida statute, which went beyond defamation to include any political attack. Thus it is an open question whether or not they would pass constitutional muster in the eyes of the present justices. . . .

The argument which has been made against the concept of a right to reply to alleged defamations as an alternative to litigation are readily answered. The major objection, of course, is the one voiced by the Supreme Court in the *Miami Herald* case—that of compelling communicators to utter words or publish material they may not wish to. This problem can be met, in part at least, by framing the law in such a way as to provide those accused of defamation with the threefold choice of either retracting their statements, disseminating a reply, or contesting a potential libel or slander lawsuit. Thus, persons who feel so righteous or confident about what they have communicated that they are unwilling to participate in the distribution of a reply would have the option of refusing to do so and facing, as they already do under present law, the risk of having to defend themselves in court. If, on the other hand, they agreed to a retraction or to disseminate a reply, at their own expense of course, through the same medium and with an equivalent degree of prominence and length, the law would immunize them from any further liability.

Another argument offered against the right to reply as a remedy for defamation is that an answer never completely catches up with the original charges and, even if it does, may not succeed entirely in wiping out the doubts that have been planted in people's minds. The same thing can be said, of course, about the verdict in a lawsuit for defamation. There is no assurance that the court's finding that a plaintiff has been defamed will receive any greater publicity than would a reply. To be sure, the plaintiff may be compensated financially for the harm that has been done, and there also may be a deterrent effect on future would-be defamers. But as far as public opinion about the reputation of that particular defamed person is concerned, a successful lawsuit many months or even years after the original charges have been circulated may actually be less effective than a more immediate reply that is guaranteed distribution through the same medium of communication.

Furthermore, there is a glaring inconsistency between our dependence on the courts to set the public's thinking straight about a person's reputation and our sharply contrasting reliance on the competition of the marketplace of ideas to counteract fallacious political or religious propositions. If the public could be educated to respond to personal attacks upon individuals with the same degree of skepticism and suspended judgment with which they ideally should react to the advocacy of social doctrines, replies to alleged defamations could be a sufficiently effective way to deal with that problem. Because we know that many people do not listen as critically as they should to the false political and religious prophets to whom they are exposed, we do not therefore assign to our courts the task of cleansing their minds. We trust that in the long run the truth will somehow emerge. Perhaps that same trust is in order with respect to personal defamations.

Implicit in the foregoing line of thought is the answer to another of criticisms that have been made of right-to-reply laws as a remedy for defamatory speech. That criticism is that a reply from an individual who has been defamed, because it is obviously an expression springing from self-interest, will not have as much credibility as a pronouncement by an impartial court that the charges which were made are false. It may very well be that the public, *if* they hear about it, might be more inclined to believe a court verdict that a statement about an individual is untrue than a response from that individual. But that again is a more authoritarian than democratic way of dealing with the problem. We do not look to our courts to tell us what is true or false in the realm of public affairs, but have to figure it out for ourselves on the basis of the competing messages available to us. As a part of that process we must learn to assess the relative credibility of the various messengers. There is no reason that we should not be expected to make the same kinds of judgments in the realm of personal attacks and counterattacks, with the assistance of an "impartial tribunal." We do it all the time in the intimate circles of our families, friendships, and work groups, and are thus not without experience in figuring out who is lying and who is telling the truth.

A final argument that has been made against a statutory right-to-reply scheme is that such laws will have a chilling effect on the willingness of the media of communication to report personal charges which the public ought to hear. The reasoning offered in support of this contention is that publishers or broadcasters, in order to avoid the possibility of having to give free space or time to people who demand their right to reply to allegedly defamatory statements, will simply refrain from communicating any material that is the least bit risky. This criticism assumes the kind of right-to-reply which requires granting a reply request without the option of refusing that request and taking the risk of a lawsuit. Even if that were the case, however, it is difficult to conceive how a right to reply would be any greater a deterrent to potentially defamatory statements than the danger of a libel suit. At least with a right-to-reply law, publishers and broadcasters would know precisely what the limits of their liability could be—that is, the provision of space or time equivalent to that involved in the original charges. Given the probable infrequency of reporting allegedly defamatory statements, that could hardly be a prohibitively costly matter for any medium of communication other than one that specializes in personal attacks. Libel suits, on the other hand, are much more unpredictable, both with respect to when they may occur and the kinds of damages that might be awarded. Only one thing about them is certain and that is the lawyers' fees that the media have to pay in defending themselves.

Although one becomes convinced that the right-to-reply remedy proposed here is neither unconstitutional, ineffective, nor unacceptably inhibitory, further persuasion may be needed to win agreement to the limitation on defamation actions which the reply option would create. For that purpose we must explore the advantages and disadvantages of defamation law itself.

Perhaps the most frequently voiced argument on behalf of prohibitions against slander and libel is that, in the absence of such restrictions, people who are defamed will take the law into their own hands and strike out violently against their defamers. It is a philosophy of frontier justice which suggests that no red-blooded man is going to take defamation lying down and that, if the law does not provide retribution, fists, swords, or guns will. . . .

The problem with this argument, of course, is that it presumes a kind of primitive society in which self-restraint in response to offensive symbolic conduct is considered to be either impossible or unlikely. The validity of that premise in contemporary America is open to serious question. Indeed, the sexist nature of the proposition about "red-blooded men" suggests something of its outdatedness, or at least of its parochialism. Not all persons, male or female, are unable to control themselves in the face of symbolic provocations by others, and it ought to be a goal of a democratic society to help people learn to handle their disputes in nonviolent ways. By that standard it must be admitted that defamation litigation was an advance over duels, but perhaps we are now ready to graduate to an even less revengeful substitute.

A second argument that has been offered in support of defamation laws is that without them the credibility of the press would suffer so seriously that it could no longer effectively serve its vital watchdog function. The theory here is that the public, knowing that the press is free to indulge in irresponsible journalism without fear of punishment, would feel no assurance that what is communicated is true and would therefore become distrustful of everything that is said. Since, according to this line of thought, the press has a hard enough time even now in maintaining the confidence of the public, its problem of credibility would be multiplied if everyone knew that it was not legally accountable for any defamatory statements it might circulate.

If the press is having problems in maintaining its credibility in the minds of the public, the existence of the defamation remedy is a thin reed on which to lean as even a partial solution. The reasoning seems analogous to a proposition that the only way people can trust other human beings not to cheat, rob, or murder them is in the knowledge that any potential assailant is taking the risk of being caught, convicted, and punished. If that were the only basis, or even the primary basis, for interpersonal trust in our society, we would either have to have far more policemen, courts, and jails than can be imagined, or we would all have to be on our guard every moment of our lives.

Newspapers and broadcasters win or lose the confidence of their readers or listeners on the basis of many variables, only one of which may be the awareness that they can be sued for making libelous statements. It is hard to believe that a restriction on that possibility would have anything more than a minimal negative impact on the credibility of the press. On the other hand, it might have the salutary effect of placing greater responsibility on the consumer of communication to become a more careful and critical listener or reader.

A third and bottom-line justification for the law of defamation is that even if the news about a vindication in court does not reach all who heard and may have believed the original charges, at least the victim may be provided with some monetary compensation for the injuries suffered, and the punishment meted out to the defamer may serve as an example and deterrent to other potential offenders. These are irrefutable benefits of our present system and must simply be weighed against the disadvantages which also inhere in that system. We turn to those considerations now. . . .

If it is acknowledged that the law of defamation serves as a deterrent to some willfully irresponsible communication, it follows that it must also have a chilling effect on the expression of those who are not sure whether charges they feel impelled to voice could be proven to the satisfaction of a court if suit were brought. Although it can be argued that such comments, unless verifiable, are best kept to oneself, the rationale of the *New York Times v. Sullivan* decision was that, in the realm of public affairs, it is better if suspicions of wrongdoing are expressed rather than inhibited, even if eventually they are shown to be untrue and then, presumably, rejected. The Supreme Court's reluctance to extend that same permissiveness beyond the realm of public affairs appears to draw its inspiration from the old Meiklejohnian concept that discussion of matters related to the process of self-government warrants a higher degree of First Amendment protection than "mere" private discourse—a concept which the Court has never admitted to embracing, although some justices have occasionally flirted with the idea.

If Zechariah Chafee was right . . . in rejecting as invalid and unworkable Meiklejohn's distinction between "public" and "private" speech, then the Supreme Court has mistakenly deviated from its general adherence to the Chafee view in its not-altogether-predictable efforts with respect to libel to draw a line between private and public affairs. If it is important for a citizen who suspects the city treasurer of stealing the taxpayer's money to speak up and say so, it would seem just as important that similar suspicions be aired about a merchant who may be fleecing customers, an auto mechanic making unsafe car repairs, a doctor giving harmful advice to patients, or a father sexually molesting his daughter.

As if the mere existence of defamation law were not sufficient to cast a chilling effect on potentially valuable communication, the use of the law as a tool of harassment by plaintiffs with dubious cases seriously compounds the problem. Publishers and broadcasters with large corporate assets are tempting targets for the adventurer who sees the possibility, at best, of winning a sizable judgment for a libel that a jury can be convinced has been committed or, at worst, of getting paid off in the out-of-court settlement which may be far less costly to the defendant than fighting the case through to even a victorious conclusion. At the other end of the harassment spectrum is the wealthy plaintiff who can well afford the costs of litigation, and a defendant of modest means (such as the leader of a protest movement or the publisher of a cause journal) who is dragged into court and put to the expense of a legal defense for having dared to criticize the plaintiff. Examples of both kinds of lawsuits abound.

Just as there are many libel actions in which the plaintiff may have no real justification for suing, so there are countless situations in which a genuinely defamed individual does not sue. It is costly to engage attorneys for a lawsuit, and the possibility of success is so unpredictable as to make it an uncertain investment. Also, there is the discouraging example of people like John Henry Faulk, a McCarthy-era radio personality who was blacklisted from employment as a result of being labeled a "subversive" in a publication called *Red Channels*. Faulk won a handsome damage award in a libel suit against the publication's author but was never able to collect a cent from the defendant who had become impoverished.

Furthermore, there is the emotional turmoil that going through a trial entails, for plaintiff as much as defendant, as well as the possibility that news coverage of that event may give the alleged defamation even wider circulation than the original charges received. Thus, as a practical matter, for many people legal action as a remedy for defamation is not an attractive course of action.

Another serious disadvantage of defamation law is the hole it opens in the already difficult line of defense the press has been trying to maintain to protect the confidentiality of its sources of information and of its editorial processes. Just as the Supreme Court has ruled that the First Amendment does not give a journalist the right to refuse to divulge to a grand jury confidentially obtained information about a possible criminal act, so our courts have held that the plaintiff in a libel suit is entitled to discover not only the confidential source of allegedly defamatory remarks reported by the press but even to explore the thought processes of those making the editorial decisions.

6

Zurcher v. Stanford Daily: Does the First Amendment Award Special Privileges to the Press?

Robert A. Poirier

ZURCHER *v. Stanford Daily* (436 U.S. 547, 1978), although not a First Amendment case, raises important questions germane to the Free Press Clause. A campus demonstration at Stanford University resulted in several assaults against the police. It was believed that the *Stanford Daily,* a student newspaper, had in its possession photographic evidence that would identify the perpetrators of the assaults. Neither the newspaper nor its reporters were suspects, but the police sought and won a "third-party" search warrant on a judge's determination of probable cause. Empowered by the authority of the search warrant, the police made an unannounced search of the *Stanford Daily's* files seeking the evidence they hoped would help them make an arrest. The newspaper protested that the police action was a violation of the constitutional safeguards of both the First and Fourth amendments and pursued its case to the Supreme Court.

Justice Byron White's majority opinion focused on the "reasonable search" requirement of the Fourth Amendment and maintained that the police, in searching the property of a nonsuspect, had not violated the *Stanford Daily's* rights. The newspaper complained that such searches would impose a "chilling effect" on the press by threatening the news-gathering process. Who, for example, would talk to the press if that institution were perceived as an information sieve? This complaint was dismissed by the Court's decision that a properly administered search warrant "which must be applied with particular exactitude when First Amendment interests would be endangered by the search, are adequate safeguards against the interference with the press's ability to gather, analyze, and disseminate news that respondents claim would ensue from use of warrants for third-party searches of newspaper offices."

The decision was not well received by the news media because it was feared that it would jeopardize the confidentiality of news sources, especially if police could rifle a newspaper's files with a search warrant. Under intense lobbying from the news media and other professional groups, such as doctors and lawyers, concerned with the confidentiality of records, Congress passed the Privacy Protection Act of 1980 to counter the effects of *Stanford Daily*. The act requires the use of the less intrusive subpoena process, instead of search warrants, when evidence is being sought from organizations working in the First Amendment area who are not under suspicion of direct involvement in a crime.

The salient issue raised by the *Stanford Daily* case is whether the press, as an *institution,* is entitled to First Amendment privileges beyond those granted to ordinary citizens. In other words, does the wording of the First Amendment, which separately mentions freedom "of speech" and "of the press," imply a distinction between the two? Does "of the press" grant a special *corporate* right to the press? In addressing these issues, one needs to focus first on the intent of the Framers; second on the interpretations of the Press Clause in contemporary decisions; and third on the policy implications of granting a corporate privilege to the press.

The reason the First Amendment speaks in terms of freedom "of speech" and "of the press" is more a matter of conjecture than certainty. Constitutional historians have proposed contrary explanations ranging from a specific intent to grant distinct privileges to the working press to the argument that *speech* and *press* were synonymous to the Framers. Given the economy of words found in the Constitution and its studied imprecision, it is unlikely that the Framers would be so redundant as to use two phrases to mean the same thing. It is safer to speculate that *speech* referred to oral communication, whereas *press* was meant to protect written expression. What is certain is that the Supreme Court is not compelled to see the original understanding of the Framers as controlling; instead, these phrases are subject to interpretation according to the circumstances of the time.

The words of the First Amendment with regard to the press have been interpreted in various ways; however, there is no specific case that establishes once and for all that the Press Clause implies separate guarantees merely because it exists apart from the Speech Clause. Although several justices have sought to address the problem in dissenting or concurring opinions, the issue was first seriously broached by Justice Potter Stewart in a 1974 speech at Yale Law School. Stewart's thesis, reprinted here, argues that the Framers intended for the working press to receive specific protection and that the "primary purpose of the constitutional guarantee of a free press" is "to create a fourth institution outside the Government as an additional check on the three official branches."

Chief Justice Burger, on the other hand, holds an opposing view, which he expressed in *First National Bank v. Belotti* (435 U.S. 765, 1978). Not a free press case per se, *Belotti* provided Burger the opportunity to condemn the notion that the institutional press has been granted special privileges by the Constitution. His concurring opinion emphasized that his reading of the historical evidence concluded that the Framers used *speech* and *press* synonymously.

The potential conflict between the freedom of the press and an accused's right to a fair trial has also offered the Court an opportunity to think out loud on the matter of institutional press privilege. In *Sheppard v. Maxwell* (384 U.S. 333, 1966), the most famous of the free press versus fair trial cases, the Court granted Dr. Sheppard's request for a new trial because the trial judge had failed to protect him from prejudicial publicity. Although scolding the press for its abuses in this case, the Court did express a concern for protecting the unique role of the press in society. Concentrating on the meaning of the Press Clause, Justice Clark's majority opinion hinted that *speech* and *press* were not synonymous but might be in conflict. *Sheppard* is noteworthy because it suggests that in the conduct of a criminal trial, the role of the press is to disseminate information. The media, Clark argued, should be free to publish what they can learn of a trial; the judge's responsibility is to regulate the speech of principals involved in the trial.

Notwithstanding this hint at a special press privilege in covering criminal trials, the problem of protecting the confidentiality of news sources when dealing with criminal matters raises an interesting question: Does the constitutional right of freedom of the press imply a freedom to gather news? News gathering is an activity that seemingly would belong only to press and not speech. Although Justice White recognized that "news gathering is not without its First Amendment protections," the Court has been reluctant to extend that concept to include a reporter's right to protect the confidentiality of sources, a practice deemed by many journalists essential for gathering news.

The issue was brought before the Court in three cases in 1972. *Branzburg v. Hayes, In re Pappas,* and *United States v. Caldwell* (408 U.S. 665, 1972) involved reporters who had refused to testify before grand juries on matters relating to criminal activities made known to them in their news-gathering activities. Although troubled over this issue because of the conviction that "without some protection for seeking out the news, freedom of the press could be eviscerated, the Court ruled that reporters did *not* have any constitutional right to refuse to give testimony before a grand jury. The minority of four believed strongly that news gathering was an important corollary to the freedom to publish the news. Stewart, consistent with his views expressed later in the Yale speech, charged that the majority opinion "reflects a disturbing insensitivity to the critical role of an independent press in our society."

The extent of the press's special constitutional privileges seems also to depend on the type of media. Two cases involving access to the media are illustrative of this point. First, the landmark *Red Lion Broadcasting v. Federal*

Communications Commission (395 U.S. 367, 1969) involved radio, a medium utilizing the regulated and publicly owned airways. The Court upheld the right of the FCC to require licensees to provide free time for reply to individuals whose honesty and integrity were attacked over the air during discussion of public issues. "It is the right of the viewers and listeners," noted the Court, "not the right of broadcasters, which is paramount."

The second case, *Miami Herald Publishing Co. v. Tornillo* (418 U.S. 241, 1974), probably went as far as the Court is likely to go in acknowledging some special privilege for the institutional press. The decision overturned a Florida statute that required a "right to reply" to political candidates attacked by newspapers. The law effectively granted the state the power to tell a newspaper what it must print. Amounting to "compulsory access," which was presumed to be as invalid as prior restraint, the Florida law infused the state with "the functions of editors in choosing what materials they wish to print." The decision has not laid to rest the access issue nor has it established the rights of the institutional press. *Miami Herald* does, however, grant institutional protection to the autonomy of the press at least in the area of what the Court refers to as the "function of editors." By denying compulsory access to newspapers, the Court has rejected the notion that the press is a provider of a marketplace of ideas because that conception of the press's role is contrary to the function of taking positions on public issues. Thus, *Miami Herald* establishes a Court endorsement of the view that the role of the press is to provide an adversarial check on government and to be more than an instrument to provide balanced or responsible coverage.

Miami Herald stops short of endorsing Stewart's position. Whether the Court will ever come around to adopting that position fully is problematical. The press does not unanimously endorse a corporate constitutional privilege for itself. It is also unlikely that the public will support special press rights above other constitutional values. In the absence of strong popular support and in view of the division within the interest group to be affected, it is unlikely that the Court in this century will promulgate constitutional doctrine that would satisfy the Stewart position.

The division within the press community itself raises questions about the wisdom of granting the press special privileges. As the following article by Anthony Lewis suggests, problems abound over the definition of "press" and how to delineate the constitutional rights of other "truth seekers" (such as academics) not so classified. The grant of special privilege inevitably is accompanied by requirements of strict accountability and responsible behavior. Ironically, the press may have to answer to a licensing authority or regulatory agency, as the broadcast media must do with the FCC. This would bring about the very condition the Framers hoped to avoid.

On balance the Court has been generous in extending constitutional protection to the *role* of the press even while denying protection to the *institu-*

tion. N.Y. Times v. Sullivan (376 U.S. 255, 1964) and its progeny—*N.Y. Times v. United States* (403 U.S. 713, 1971), *Miami Herald,* and *Landmark Communication, Inc. v. Virginia* (435 U.S. 829, 1978)—are examples of important press gains. However, as in other constitutional freedoms, the Court has attempted to balance press rights with other societal interests.

Portions of Potter Stewart's famous speech urging recognition of special freedoms for the press follow. Anthony Lewis, journalist and author of the highly regarded *Gideon's Trumpet,* responds with some constitutional and practical concerns relative to Stewart's position.

Yes: Or of the Press

Potter Stewart

I T was less than a decade ago—during the Vietnam years—that the people of our country began to become aware of the twin phenomena on a national scale of so-called investigative reporting and an adversary press—that is, a press adversary to the Executive Branch of the Federal Government. And only in the two short years that culminated last summer [1973] in the resignation of a President did we fully realize the enormous power that an investigative and adversary press can exert.

The public opinion polls that I have seen indicate that some Americans firmly believe that the former Vice President and former President of the United States were hounded out of office by an arrogant and irresponsible press that had outrageously usurped dictatorial power. And it seems clear that many more Americans, while appreciating and even applauding the service performed by the press in exposing official wrongdoing at the highest levels of our national government, are nonetheless deeply disturbed by what they consider to be the illegitimate power of the organized press in the political structure of our society. It is my thesis . . . that, on the contrary, the established American press in the past ten years, and particularly in the past two years, has performed precisely the function it was intended to perform by those who wrote the First Amendment of our Constitution. I further submit that this thesis is supported by the relevant decisions of the Supreme Court.

Surprisingly, despite the importance of newspapers in the political and social life of our country the Supreme Court has not until very recently been called upon to delineate their constitutional role in our structure of government.

Our history is filled with struggles over the rights and prerogatives of the press, but these disputes rarely found their way to the Supreme Court. The early years of the Republic witnessed controversy over the constitutional

Potter Stewart, from "Or of the Press," 26 *Hastings Law Journal* (1975), pp. 631–637.

validity of the short-lived Alien and Sedition Act, but the controversy never reached the Court. In the next half century there was nationwide turmoil over the right of the organized press to advocate the then subversive view that slavery should be abolished. In Illinois a publisher was killed for publishing abolitionist views. But none of this history made First Amendment law because the Court had earlier held that the Bill of Rights applied only against the Federal Government, not against the individual states.

With the passage of the Fourteenth Amendment, the constitutional framework was modified, and by the 1920's the Court had established that the protections of the First Amendment extend against all government—federal, state, and local.

The next fifty years witnessed a great outpouring of First Amendment litigation, all of which inspired books and articles beyond number. But, with few exceptions, neither these First Amendment cases nor their commentators squarely considered the Constitution's guarantee of a Free Press. Instead, the focus was on its guarantee of free speech. The Court's decisions dealt with the rights of isolated individuals, or of unpopular minority groups, to stand up against governmental power representing an angry or frightened majority. The cases that came to the Court during those years involved the rights of the soapbox orator, the nonconformist pamphleteer, the religious evangelist. The Court was seldom asked to define the rights and privileges, or the responsibilities, of the organized press.

In very recent years cases involving the established press finally have begun to reach the Supreme Court, and they have presented a variety of problems, sometimes arising in complicated factual settings.

In a series of cases, the Court has been called upon to consider the limits imposed by the free press guarantee upon a state's common or statutory law of libel. As a result of those cases, a public figure cannot successfully sue a publisher for libel unless he can show that the publisher maliciously printed a damaging untruth.

The Court has also been called upon to decide whether a newspaper reporter has a First Amendment privilege to refuse to disclose his confidential sources to a grand jury. By a divided vote, the Court found no such privilege to exist in the circumstances of the cases before it.

In another noteworthy case, the Court was asked by the Justice Department to restrain publication by the *New York Times* and other newspapers of the so-called Pentagon Papers. The Court declined to do so.

In yet another case, the question to be decided was whether political groups have a First Amendment or statutory right of access to the federally regulated broadcast channels of radio and television. The Court held there was no such right of access.

Last Term the Court confronted a Florida statute that required newspapers to grant a "right of reply" to political candidates they had criticized.

The Court unanimously held this statute to be inconsistent with the guarantees of a free press.

It seems to me that the Court's approach to all these cases has uniformly reflected its understanding that the Free Press guarantee is, in essence, a *structural* provision of the Constitution. Most of the other provisions in the Bill of Rights protect specific liberties or specific rights of individuals: freedom of speech, freedom of worship, the right to counsel, the privilege against compulsory self-incrimination, to name a few. In contrast, the Free Press Clause extends protection to an institution. The publishing business is, in short, the only organized private business that is given explicit constitutional protection.

This basic understanding is essential, I think, to avoid an elementary error of constitutional law. It is tempting to suggest that freedom of the press means only that newspaper publishers are guaranteed freedom of expression. They *are* guaranteed that freedom, to be sure, but so are we all, because of the Free Speech Clause. If the Free Press guarantee meant no more than freedom of expression, it would be a constitutional redundancy. Between 1776 and the drafting of our Constitution, many of the state constitutions contained clauses protecting freedom of the press while at the same time recognizing no general freedom of speech. By including both guarantees in the First Amendment, the Founders quite clearly recognized the distinction between the two.

It is also a mistake to suppose that the only purpose of the constitutional guarantee of a free press is to insure that a newspaper will serve as a neutral forum for debate, a "market place for ideas," a kind of Hyde Park corner for the community. A related theory sees the press as a neutral conduit of information between the people and their elected leaders. These theories, in my view, again give insufficient weight to the institutional autonomy of the press that it was the purpose of the Constitution to guarantee.

In setting up the three branches of the Federal Government, the Founders deliberately created an internally competitive system. As Mr. Justice Brandeis once wrote:

> The [Founders'] purpose was, not to avoid friction, but, by means of the inevitable friction incident to the distribution of the governmental powers among three departments, to save the people from autocracy.

The primary purpose of the constitutional guarantee of a free press was a similar one: to create a fourth institution outside the Government as an additional check on the three official branches. Consider the opening words of the Free Press Clause of the Massachusetts Constitution, drafted by John Adams:

> The liberty of the press is essential to the security of the state.

The relevant metaphor, I think, is the metaphor of the Fourth Estate. What Thomas Carlyle wrote about the British Government a century ago has a curiously contemporary ring:

> Burke said there were Three Estates in Parliament; but, in the Reporters' Gallery yonder, there sat a Fourth Estate more important far than they all. It is not a figure of speech or witty saying; it is a literal fact—very momentus to us in these times.

For centuries before our Revolution, the press in England had been licensed, censored, and bedeviled by prosecutions for seditious libel. The British Crown knew that a free press was not just a neutral vehicle for the balanced discussion of diverse ideas. Instead, the free press meant organized, expert scrutiny of government. The press was a conspiracy of the intellect, with the courage of numbers. This formidable check on official power was what the British Crown had feared—and what the American Founders decided to risk.

It is this constitutional understanding, I think, that provides the unifying principle underlying the Supreme Court's recent decisions dealing with the organized press.

Consider first the libel cases. Officials within the three governmental branches are, for all practical purposes, immune from libel and slander suits for statements that they make in the line of duty. This immunity, which has both constitutional and common law origins, aims to insure bold and vigorous prosecution of the public's business. The same basic reasoning applies to the press. By contrast, the Court has never suggested that the constitutional right of free *speech* gives an *individual* any immunity from liability for either libel or slander.

In the cases involving the newspaper reporters' claims that they had a constitutional privilege not to disclose their confidential news sources to a grand jury, the Court rejected the claims by a vote of five to four, or, considering Mr. Justice Powell's concurring opinion, perhaps by a vote of four and a half to four and a half. But if freedom of the press means simply freedom of speech for reporters, this question of a reporter's asserted right to withhold information would have answered itself. None of us—as individuals—has a "free speech" right to refuse to tell a grand jury the identity of someone who has given us information relevant to the grand jury's legitimate inquiry. Only if a reporter is a representative of a protected *institution* does the question become a different one. The members of the Court disagreed in answering the question, but the question did not answer itself.

The cases involving the so-called "right of access" to the press raised the issue whether the First Amendment allows government, or indeed *requires* government, to regulate the press so as to make it a genuinely fair and open "market place for ideas." The Court's answer was "no" to both questions. If a newspaper wants to serve as a neutral market place for debate, that is an objective which it is free to choose. And, within limits, that choice is probably necessary to commercially successful journalism. But it is a choice that government cannot constitutionally impose.

Finally the Pentagon Papers case involved the line between secrecy and openness in the affairs of Government. The question, or at least one question, was whether that line is drawn by the Constitution itself. The Justice Department asked the court to find in the Constitution a basis for prohibiting the publication of allegedly stolen government documents. The Court could find no such prohibition. So far as the Constitution goes, the autonomous press may publish what it knows, and may seek to learn what it can.

But this autonomy cuts both ways. The Press is free to do battle against secrecy and deception in government. But the press cannot expect from the Constitution any guarantee that it will succeed. There is no constitutional right to have access to particular government information, or to require openness from the bureaucracy. The public's interest in knowing about its government is protected by the guarantee of Free Press, but the protection is indirect. The Constitution itself is neither a Freedom of Information Act nor an Official Secrets Act.

The Constitution, in other words, establishes the contest, not its resolution. Congress may provide a resolution, at least in some instances, through carefully drawn legislation. For the rest, we must rely, as so often in our system we must, on the tug and pull of the political forces in American society.

Newspapers, television networks, and magazines have sometimes been outrageously abusive, untruthful, arrogant, and hypocritical. But it hardly follows that elimination of a strong and independent press is the way to eliminate abusiveness, untruth, arrogance, or hypocrisy from government itself.

It is quite possible to conceive of the survival of our Republic without an autonomous press. For openness and honesty in government, for an adequate flow of information between the people and their representatives, for a sufficient check on autocracy and despotism, the traditional competition between the three branches of government, supplemented by vigorous political activity, might be enough.

The press could be relegated to the status of public utility. The guarantee of free speech would presumably put some limitation on the regulation to which the press could be subjected. But if there were no guarantee of free press, government could convert the communications media into a neutral "market place of ideas." Newspapers and television networks could then be required to promote contemporary government policy or current notions of social justice.

Such a constitution is possible; it might work reasonably well. But it is not the Constitution the Founders wrote. It is not the Constitution that has carried us through nearly two centuries of national life. Perhaps our liberties might survive without an independent established press. But the Founders doubted it, and . . . I think we can all be thankful for their doubts.

No: A Preferred Position for Journalism?

Anthony Lewis

C ONGRESS shall make no law . . . abridging the freedom of speech, or of the *news media*. That was the clarified version of the First Amendment proposed by Justice Stewart in his memorable 1974 address at the Yale Law School, *Or of the Press*. Most parts of the Bill of Rights, he said, protect liberties whoever exercises them; but the press clause of the First Amendment is "a *structural* provision" protecting a particular institution: "the organized press," which Justice Stewart defined as "the daily newspapers and other established news media." Journalism, in short, has a special constitutional status, with rights not available to others.

The Yale speech broke important new ground. The Supreme Court had never really addressed the question posed by Justice Stewart—whether the press clause has an independent purpose and meaning—much less given his bold answer. The press clause, he said, did not merely join with the speech clause to guarantee freedom of expression to all; that would make it "a constitutional redundancy." Rather, the "primary purpose" of those who framed it was "to create a fourth institution outside the Government as an additional check on the three official branches." That purpose, Justice Stewart said, informed recent Supreme Court decisions on the right of the press.

The media welcomed the message. In recent years, news organizations, both print and broadcast, have become increasingly sensitive to perceived legal threats and increasingly determined to define their rights in the courts. The more aggressive mood no doubt stems in part from the experience of Vietnam and Watergate, which weakened the old premise of shared beliefs and mutual respect between press and government. A growing sense of pro-

Anthony Lewis, from "A Preferred Position for Journalism?" 7 *Hofstra Law Review* (1979), pp. 595–627.

fessionalism, fed by journalism schools and journalism reviews and press councils, also adds to journalism's pride of place. The news business in this country is now quick to use the law as both sword and shield. The last two terms of the Supreme Court alone have seen battles about access to news, searches of news premises, protection of confidential sources, and the confidentiality of the editorial process. I think Justice Stewart's speech contributed to the determination of news organizations to fight those cases, and to the legal doctrines advanced by their lawyers. . . .

But in the end the Stewart thesis of press exceptionalism—of a preferred status for journalists—will succeed or fail in the marketplace of constitutional ideas. It should be tested there by three standards: its roots in history, its basis in the decided cases, and its wisdom in principle. By those tests I find it unconvincing.

"For centuries before our Revolution," Justice Stewart said in his Yale speech, "the press in England had been licensed, censored, and bedeviled by prosecutions for seditious libel. The . . . free press meant organized, expert scrutiny of government. The press was a conspiracy of the intellect, with the courage of numbers. This formidable check on official power was what the British Crown had feared—and what the American Founders decided to risk."

Those words are an admirable tribute to the romance of journalism and to its high duty. But as history designed to prove that the first amendment gave special status to the news media, the passage is less convincing. For "the press" that was licensed and bedeviled in England was not newspapers alone. Those who called for "freedom of the press" in the seventeenth and eighteenth centuries had in mind books and pamphlets and all kinds of occasional literature as much as newspapers. Indeed, some were not thinking of newspapers at all.

The most famous statement on behalf of press freedom in that period was John Milton's *Areopagitica*. Published in 1644, it was an attack on the requirement that any printed work be read and licensed by official censors before publication—a requirement first established by the Crown in 1538 and reimposed by Parliament in a statute of June 14, 1643, after the Puritan Revolution. Milton argued that "regulating the Press" could be accomplished by means less onerous than the licensing system. By "the Press" he meant any product of a printing press; at one point, for example, he ironically sympathized with the conscientious censor who must be "the perpetual reader of unchosen books and pamphlets, oftimes huge volumes. . . ."

Justice Stewart's suggestion, rather, is that the concept was applied exclusively to newspapers. No historian of whom I am aware has produced any evidence to support that proposition.

The precise motives of those who drafted the speech and press clauses of the first amendment are unlikely to be discovered now, if indeed they were ever ascertainable. Madison sponsored in the House what became the first amendment, and another amendment that would have prohibited *state* abridgment of press and other freedoms; the latter was killed in the Senate. Committee changes, unexplained in the material left to us, reduced the language to its final compelling simplicity: "Congress shall make no law . . . abridging the freedom of speech, or of the press."

The most natural explanation seems the most probable: The framers wanted to protect expression whether in unprinted or printed form. Freedom of the press was more often mentioned in colonial and state bills of rights than freedom of speech; at the time of the first amendment ten state constitutions protected the former while only two the latter. Very likely, as Chief Justice Burger has said, press freedom "merited special mention simply because it had been more often the object of official restraints." But the two phrases were used interchangeably, then as now to mean freedom of expression. And there is evidence suggesting that eighteenth-century Americans, when they thought about the rights of speech and press, regarded them as aspects of the same fundamental personal freedom. George Mason began drafting the Virginia Declaration of Rights, which included a striking assertion of the need for freedom of the press, just two days after Dixon and Hunter's *Virginia Gazette* of May 18, 1776 carried the following on its front page:

> [The liberty of the press is inviolably connected with the liberty of the subject. . . [.] The *use* of *speech* is a *natural right,* which must have been reserved when men gave up their natural rights for the benefit of society. PRINTING is a more extensive and improved kind of speech.

In sum, the Stewart thesis of a preferred position for the news media finds no support in history. Those who wrote the first amendment were familiar with newspapers. But there is no evidence that they meant to limit the freedom of "the press" to newspapers, excluding books and other publications, or that they intended to afford newspapers a higher standard of protection than other forms of expression. . . .

The practical consequences of the Stewart thesis, if it became accepted constitutional doctrine, would not be as beneficial to journalists as many of them believe. And the thesis is against the real interest of the press, and of society, for deeper reasons of principle.

The whole idea of treating the press as an "institution" arouses uneasy feelings. In the American system, institutions are usually subject to external check. The press has operated as a freebooter, outside the system. The more formally it is treated as a fourth branch of government, the more pressing will be demands that it be made formally accountable. Moreover, as Robert M. Kaus has suggested, the institutional view of the first amendment envisages a corporate organization of society, with groups assigned different roles and corresponding legal rights. The traditional American vision has been universal, positing a society of individuals with equal rights and responsibilities: Justice Brennan's citizen-critics.

If a majority of the Supreme Court accepted the proposition that freedom of "the press" in the first amendment gives special status to the news media, the next question would be: Who is "the press"? Would the definition be limited to Justice Stewart's "established" newspapers, magazines, and broadcasters? Could it exclude underground papers? Journals of sexual exploitation? A sheet of viciously racist tone, like the news weekly at issue in *Near v. Minnesota*? In the age of the electronic copier, what about the citizen moved by outrage at some local development to circulate his or her views among neighbors? Or what of a specialty publication such as a Wall Street tip sheet: Could the Securities and Exchange Commission regulate it without violating the freedom of "the press"? . . .

The danger of exclusivity was demonstrated when Justice Stewart applied his thesis in literal terms to a case before the Court. The case was *Zurcher v. Stanford Daily*. A majority held that authorities could search a newspaper office under warrant—that is, without notice or a prior adversary hearing—for documentary evidence of a crime committed by other parties. Justice Stevens dissented on the ground that notice should ordinarily be required before such a search of any third party: one not suspected of crime. Justice Stewart, in an opinion joined by Justice Marshall, dissented on the ground that the search violated the freedom of the press. He wrote:

> Perhaps as a matter of abstract policy a newspaper office should receive no more protection from unannounced police searches than, say, the office of a doctor or the office of a bank. But we are here to uphold a Constitution. And our Constitution does not explicitly protect the practice of medicine or the business of banking from all abridgment by government. It does explicitly protect the freedom of the press.

In Justice Stewart's view, then, the Constitution forbids the unannounced search of a newspaper office for photographs of a felony; but it allows the police, without notice, to search a psychiatrist's files, or Ralph Nader's. I think such a concept of the Constitution would be quite unacceptable to most Americans. The Constitution protects values, not particular classes of people. And the values are not limited to those listed by name in the Constitution; if the significance of that eighteenth-century document were limited by such literalism, it would long since have become a museum piece. . . .

The idea that the news media are constitutionally unique may also encourage hubris, the excessive pride that goes before a fall. Powerful newspapers and networks are not universally beloved as it is; there is talk about the arrogance of the media. Ordinary citizens may find it hard to understand why the press should have rights denied to them. And in the long run, rights depend on public understanding and support. Professor Bork has put it succinctly: "To the degree that the press is alone in the enjoyment of freedom, to that degree is its freedom imperiled. . . ."

Justice Stewart is hardly to be held responsible if the press is sometimes strident in its own cause, sounding as if its own rights were central to freedom and all others peripheral. But on the question of confidential sources, which is more troubling to reporters and editors than any other legal issue, his opinions have embraced the press' cause. His dissent in *Zurcher* has been noted. Dissenting in *Branzburg,* he sounded a major press theme when he said, "A corollary of the right to publish must be the right to gather news. . . . News must not be necessarily cut off at its source, for without freedom to acquire information the right to publish would be impermissibly compromised. Accordingly, a right to gather news, of some dimensions, must exist."

But Justice Stewart's argument that a testimonial privilege arises from a first amendment "right to gather news" presents a paradox. For, two years after *Branzburg,* Justice Stewart wrote the opinion of the Court in *Pell v. Procunier,* holding that the press has no greater right than the public at large to gather news in a prison. He relied on the majority's statement in *Branzburg* that "'the First Amendment does not guarantee the press a constitutional right of special access to information not available to the public general.'" Toward the end of his Yale speech he made the point again, in words not so welcome to the press: "There is no constitutional right to have access to particular government information, or to require openness from the bureaucracy. . . . The Constitution itself is neither a Freedom of Information Act nor an Official Secrets Act." Then, in *Houchins v. KQED, Inc.,* Justice Stewart indicated that goverment could completely exclude both press and public from jails and other public facilities: "The First and Fourteenth Amendments do not guarantee the public a right of access to information generated or controlled by government, nor do they guarantee the press any basic right of access superior to that of the public generally."

How can a judge say in one case that the First Amendment affords a "right to gather news," and in another that the amendment does not give anyone "a right of access to information generated or controlled by government"? How can he tell journalists in one breath that the Constitution treats them differently from everyone else, and in the next that they have no more rights than the public? . . .

Blackstone, recording the successful outcome of the long English struggle against press censorship, wrote: "Every freeman has an undoubted right to lay what sentiments he pleases before the public; to forbid this is to destroy the freedom of the press. . . ." Every freeman, that is, not just those organized or institutionalized as "the press." Freedom of the press arose historically as an individual liberty. Eighteenth-century Americans saw it in those terms, and the same view is reflected in Supreme Court Decisions; freedom of speech and of the press, Chief Justice Hughes said, are "fundamental personal rights." To depart from that principle—to adopt a corporate view of the freedom of the press, applying the press clause of the First Amendment on special terms to the "institution" of the news media—would be a drastic unwelcome change in American constitutional premises. It would read the Constitution as protecting a particular class rather than a common set of values. And we have come to understand, after much struggle, that the Constitution "neither knows nor tolerates classes among citizens."

The press is not a separate estate in the American system. Its great function is to act for the public in keeping government accountable to the public. And it would be a poor bargain, for the press and the country, if a special status for journalism were accompanied by greater latitude for government to avoid accountability by closing its proceedings.

Justice Stewart's idea of a preferred constitutional position for the orgaized press was inevitably appealing to journalists, but it would hurt their real interests if it became accepted doctrine. It would separate the professional press from the public it represents, and increase the risk of arrogance. In our complex democracy, newspapers and magazines and broadcasters usually vindicate the "'social interest in the attainment of truth.'" They are at the cutting edge. But others play their part: scholars and conscience-stricken officials and citizen-critics. The First Amendment was written for them, too, and freedom is indivisible. The safety of the American press does not lie in exclusivity.

7
Miranda v. Arizona:
Is the Privilege
against Self-Incrimination
an Unreasonable Burden
on Public Order?

Glenn A. Phelps

IRANDA *v. Arizona* (384 U.S. 436, 1966) has become one of the Supreme Court's most controversial decisions. It has also become one of the Court's most visible decisions. Who, for example, has not seen dozens of arrests by Officer Belker, Lieutenant Kojak, or any number of other TV cops conclude with the reading of the suspect's *Miranda* rights: "You have the right to remain silent . . ." Few Supreme Court decisions are as well known by name as *Miranda*. Yet public understanding of the circumstances, principles, and constitutional issues involved in *Miranda* is not nearly so widespread.

The incident that led to the arrest and conviction of Ernesto Miranda occurred on the night of March 2, 1963, in the desert surrounding Phoenix, Arizona. A young woman had just gotten off the bus coming home from her job at a movie theater. A man emerged from a nearby parked car and forced her into the vehicle. He drove into the desert and raped her in the back seat of the car. After the rape, he drove the woman back to town and released her several blocks from her home.

After some investigation Ernesto Miranda emerged as the prime suspect. Not only did he match the physical description of the attacker, but his record also made the detectives suspicious. Miranda had been in and out of reform school and jail for various offenses since he was fourteen. One of those convictions was for rape and assault. Miranda was brought to the station house and identified by both the rape victim and a woman who had been robbed several months earlier by a man fitting a similar description. Two police officers then removed Miranda to interrogation room 2 and began questioning him about his involvement in the crimes. Miranda soon made the following confession:

Seen a girl walking up street stopped a little ahead of her got out of car walked towards her grabbed her by arm and asked her to get in car. Got in car without force tied hands and ankles. Drove away for a few miles. Stopped asked to take clothes off. Did not, asked me to take her back home. I started to take clothes off her without force, and with cooperation. Could not get penis into vagina got about ½ (half) inch in. Told her to get clothes back on. Drove her home. I couldn't say I was sorry for what I had done. But asked her to say a prayer for me.[1]

At his trial Miranda was represented by a court-appointed attorney. When the state sought to introduce his confession, an extremely damning piece of evidence, his lawyer objected. The lawyer claimed that his client's Fifth and Sixth Amendment rights had been violated and that the confession should be inadmissible in court. The judge disagreed, and Miranda eventually was convicted. Along with several other similar cases, Miranda's appeal reached the Supreme Court of the United States.

The Fifth Amendment stipulates that "no person . . . shall be compelled in any criminal case to be a witness against himself." Like many of the due process rights stipulated in the Bill of Rights, the Fifth Amendment has its genesis in the traditions of English common law. The case of John Lilburne is often cited as a principal source for the privilege against self-incrimination. In 1637 he had been brought before the Star Chamber, a particularly odious mechanism of government repression, to answer charges of sedition. Lilburne, however, refused to take the oath or to answer any questions put to him. Such behavior exasperated the Chamber; if they were unable to compel his testimony, then certain offenses would surely go "undiscovered and unpunished."[2] To punish such contempt, the Star Chamber ordered that Lilburne be whipped and pilloried as an example to others who might wish to remain silent before the power of the state. A few years later, Lilburne petitioned Parliament for a redress of this grievance. Parliament agreed that compelling a man to respond under oath as to his guilt or innocence was a violation of the liberties of a free man and awarded a large indemnity to Lilburne.

At first glance, John Lilburne's case seems to have very little to do with Ernesto Miranda. Lilburne's case established that an accused person ought not to be compelled to testify against himself in a court hearing. In fact, Miranda was never asked to testify *in court* in his trial for rape and kidnapping. Thus, if the Fifth Amendment meant only this, then Miranda's rights were not violated by the state of Arizona. Two phrases in this amendment, however, *"compelled"* and *"in any criminal case"*, are particularly ambiguous. First, what does *"compelled"* mean? Does it apply to physical coercion and threats? Does it apply to psychological persuasion and trickery? Second, what is a "criminal case"? Does it mean that an accused need not testify during trial proceedings? Or does a "criminal case" begin before the trial? If so, do criminal proceedings begin with the grand jury? At the station house? At the time of arrest? In the investigation phase?

Confessions have long played a significant role in establishing the guilt or innocence of the accused in U.S. courts. Whether motivated by remorse, fear, the weight of evidence, or some other factor, the confession and its cousin, plea bargaining, account for the vast majority of guilty verdicts. The Fifth Amendment does not preclude such admissions of guilt by the accused. What it *does* preclude is an extraction of incriminatory statements against the defendant's will.

For many years the Bill of Rights was deemed to limit only the powers of the national government. Indeed, *Twining v. New Jersey* (211 U.S. 78, 1908) made it quite clear that the specific wording of the Fifth Amendment did not apply to the states. The Fourteenth Amendment, however, does say that no state shall "deprive any person of life, liberty, or property, without due process of law." The question of what was required by due process occupied much of the Court's energy in the forty years prior to *Miranda*. For much of this period, a majority of the Court was inclined to accept Justice Felix Frankfurter's criteria for determining what would be *"incorporated"* under the due process clause. These criteria stated that only those procedures that were indispensable to a "system of ordered liberty" or essential for "fundamental fairness" were to be incorporated.

Thus, although an absolute privilege against self-incrimination *was not* indispensable to a "system of ordered liberty," the right of an accused person to be protected against "third-degree" methods of interrogation *was* essential for "fundamental fairness." This principle was made clear in *Brown v. Mississippi* (297 U.S. 278, 1936). Local police had brutalized and tortured a suspect, eventually eliciting a confession. The Supreme Court declared that although states did not have to follow the specific procedural guidelines of the Fifth and Sixth Amendments, "the rack and torture chamber may not be substituted for the witness stand." Brown's confession was declared inadmissible, as would any future confession obtained by physical coercion. But could any other actions be categorized as "compelling" a suspect to be a witness against himself? In *Ashcraft v. Tennessee* (322 U.S. 143, 1944), the Supreme Court examined the question of whether psychological coercion also was a violation of "fundamental fairness." The circumstances of the case could have been taken from the scripts of dozens of Hollywood gangster movies of the 1930s. Ashcraft was not beaten or blackjacked or threatened with torture. He had, however, been subjected to thirty-six hours of continuous questioning from a phalanx of police officers. He sat "under the lights" throughout this period, cut off from any outside contact. At last he confessed to a murder. In overturning his conviction, the Supreme Court noted the "inherent coerciveness" of the environment.

Gradually the prohibitions against physical and psychological coercion evolved into the "voluntariness rule". Under this rule whenever a prosecutor sought to enter a confession into evidence, it became his or her burden to demonstrate that the defendant had made the statements voluntarily. Miranda's attorney argued that his client's confession had been made under duress. Because there was no indication of misconduct or undue coercion by the interrogating officers, the trial judge denied the motion to suppress. But Miranda's lawyer raised another point. Miranda was assigned an attorney paid for by the state at his trial but not at the interrogation stage when the confession was made. Miranda's lawyer argued that it would do little good to provide an attorney to safeguard an individual's due process rights at the trial if those same rights had been ignored at the station house. Statements made to the police without access to legal counsel at this early stage in the legal process, he argued, were inherently coercive. Again, the judge denied the motion.

When *Miranda* finally reached the Supreme Court, the criminal due process revolution of the Warren Court had been underway for more than five years. Miranda's conviction was overturned because his Fifth (and Sixth) Amendment rights had been violated. His confession was inadmissible because he had been compelled to be a witness against himself. The decision surprised few but angered many. Police chiefs, prosecutors, and public officials expressed outrage at the decision. Some stated that the Supreme Court was coddling criminals while putting law enforcement in a straitjacket. Richard Nixon would soon campaign for president on a promise to strengthen the "forces of peace" that the Supreme Court had weakened.

Whatever the merits of these criticisms, *Miranda* was not nearly the radical transformation of police practices that some thought. In fact, *Miranda* was little more than a summary of precedents announced in the previous four years. It created very little new law as the holding in *Miranda* reveals. The essence of the Court's decision was stated by Chief Justice Earl Warren:

> We are satisfied that all the principles embodied in the privilege apply to informal compulsion exerted by law-enforcement officials during in-custody questioning. An individual swept from familiar surroundings into police custody, surrounded by antagonistic forces, and subjected to the techniques of persuasion described above cannot be otherwise than under compulsion to speak. As a practical matter, the compulsion to speak in the isolated setting of the police station may well be greater than in courts . . . where there are often impartial observers to guard against intimidation or trickery.

In short, the Fifth Amendment privilege against self-incrimination now extended to the moment of arrest or formal custody. Much of the opinion was skeptical of the degree of respect that local police departments had for due process rights. So that there would be no confusion as to how these constitutional principles should be applied, the majority stipulated a set of specific practices to be adopted throughout the states. Whenever an arrest was made, it would henceforth be the responsibility of the police to inform the suspect of his or her rights under the Fifth and Sixth Amendments. Specifically, suspects must be told that (1) they have the right to remain silent, (2) anything they say can be used against them in court, (3) they have the right to consult with counsel prior to answering any questions, and (4) if they cannot afford counsel, one will be appointed.

An examination of each of these *Miranda* warnings shows their derivative nature. *Malloy v. Hogan* (378 U.S. 1, 1964) had already overturned *Twining* and extended the right to remain silent to the states. *Gideon v. Wainwright* (372 U.S. 335, 1963) had guaranteed counsel to indigents accused of serious crimes. And *Escobedo v. Illinois* (378 U.S. 478, 1964) had asserted that these protections extended beyond the courtroom to the station house. Indeed, *Miranda* offered new insights only in its view that (1) unless the suspect intelligently waived these rights, any statements he or she made were presumed to be involuntary and its bold assertion that (2) the Court could stipulate specific police field practices to ensure the implementation of these rights.

Miranda's confession, then, because it was extracted without the benefit of an attorney, was presumed to be involuntary and therefore inadmissible. Arizona was ordered to grant Miranda a new trial. Two final ironies remain. Miranda was found guilty of both offenses at his second trial. (Indeed, the public perception of convicted murderers and rapists unloosed upon an innocent citizenry was more myth than reality.) Finally, on January 31, 1976, Ernesto Miranda was stabbed to death in a barroom fight in Phoenix. Suspects questioned about his killing were informed of their "Miranda rights."

In the essays that follow, Robert M. Kaus, columnist and editor of the *Washington Monthly,* not only criticizes the *Miranda* decision but also offers some provocative thoughts on the value of the Fifth Amendment in contemporary times. George Edwards defends *Miranda* in the light of his own dealings with the police establishment as a judge.

Yes: Abolish the 5th Amendment

Robert M. Kaus

THE Fifth Amendment was cobbled up in 1789 by James Madison from similar provisions in state constitutions, and it passed during the first United States Congress with virtually no debate. As a result, we don't know much about what the Founding Fathers themselves thought they were doing. But it traditionally is pointed out that the rule against self-incrimination originally grew out of the unpleasant practices of the ecclesiastical courts in early seventeenth-century England—particularly the infamous Star Chamber. Three aspects of the Star Chamber's method of operation are generally cited as especially repugnant. First, rather than accuse people of specific crimes and then bring them to trial, it frequently summoned citizens and asked them to confess to whatever crimes they happen to have committed—sort of a "What have you done wrong lately?" approach. Second, the criminals it prosecuted tended to be religious heretics and political dissidents, and the "crimes" to which they were expected to confess were crimes of belief, conscience, and association. Third, if they didn't confess, they were often tortured until they did. . . .

That's enough history. The problem, as you might suspect, is with the logic. Because the Fifth Amendment isn't, and wasn't, in any way necessary to outlaw the Star Chamber abuses it is said to protect us against. If we want to ban torture—as surely we do—then we need a provision that bans torture, and perhaps sets severe penalties for any government official caught in the act. To prevent government probes into our political and religious associations, we need an amendment banning that—as the First Amendment, we may hope, already has. Another amendment (the Sixth) already takes care of the right of a defendant to know the specific charges against him and to confront his accusers.

Robert M. Kaus, from "Abolish the Fifth Amendment," *The Washington Monthly* (December 1980), pp. 12–19. Reprinted with permission from *The Washington Monthly.* Copyright by The Washington Monthly Co., 1711 Connecticut Avenue, N.W., Washington, DC 20009. (202) 462–0128.

The Fifth Amendment goes beyond these rights and creates a far more dubious privilege: a right of ordinary criminals to conceal their crimes. The Amendment is used most frequently in cases . . . where it prevents a suspect from being asked in a civilized manner to tell about his actions, in a courtroom in which he will be afforded every other procedural protection known to the Anglo-Saxon legal mind. Can you find a Star Chamber in that picture? The accused is not being persecuted for his beliefs. He is not threatened with torture. He knows the charges against him. . . .

This realization has set lawyers scrambling to find other rationales that might justify the Amendment. One theory that was in fashion at the Supreme Court during the late 1950s held that "the privilege, while sometimes a shelter to the guilty, is often a protection to the innocent." The problem with this statement was that it is false. Law professors, racking their brains, have come up with only two basic "hypothetical situations" in which someone who is guilty of no crime nevertheless has a reason to hide behind the Fifth. First, they tell us, he may fear that his testimony will somehow lead to his unjust conviction—either because a bullying prosecutor will force him into trivial-yet-embarrassing contradictions, or because his testimony will fuel some sort of legalized lynching. But the professors have never explained why the solution to this first problem isn't simply to clamp down on overaggressive prosecutors, flimsy convictions, and biased juries. In the second "hypothetical," our hero takes the Fifth to hide some conduct that was merely disgraceful, rather than criminal (classically, he "was in the arms of his best friend's wife")—to which the obvious response is that it's his own rotten luck if he has to reveal his own disreputable conduct.

In the daily grind of the criminal justice system, both these hypotheticals are 10,000-to-one shots. The Amendment is much more likely to *harm* the innocent, when a guiltless suspect is unable to clear himself because the real culprit hides behind the Fifth.

The "protect the innocent" theory is so out of touch with reality that even the Supreme Court abandoned it, announcing in 1966 a second theory: "The basic purposes behind the privilege against self-incrimination do not relate to protecting the innocent," said Justice Stewart, "but rather to preserving the integrity of a judicial system in which even the guilty are not to be convicted unless the prosecution 'shoulder the entire load.' " According to Justice Fortas, the Amendment insured that a trial would be an occasion of "equals meeting in battle."

These are the sort of statements judges could never get away with if they were required to hold press conferences where follow-up questions were allowed. *Why* must the prosecution "shoulder the entire load?" A criminal trial isn't a horse race in which we require that one contestant carry more weight to make him prove his mettle, or a basketball game where we even up the sides beforehand to produce a close outcome. It is an attempt to determine the truth and punish the guilty. Many of its rules (the "reasonable doubt" rule, for one) make life harder for the prosecutor, but we have those rules to prevent an *innocent* man being convicted. If a defendant is *guilty*—and remember, that's what the Court is assuming here—what possible reason is there for making the prosecutor's job harder than necessary? Conservatives often accuse civil-libertarians of indiscriminantly rooting for the defendant even if he is guilty; this looks like one case where they are right.

What little the Justices have written in defense of this theory consists of abstract revelations that might embarrass Timothy Leary. According to Fortas, the Fifth Amendment "reflects the limits of the individual's attornment to the state and in a philosophical sense insists upon the equality of the individual and the state." Justice Douglas, elaborating on the "psychological insight" embodied in the rule, noted that it is designed "to ensure the total victory of the Life Instinct over its omnipresent antagonist."

There are two other theories that have been offered up for the Amendment. One recent favorite says it is necessary to preserve "the right of each individual to a private enclave where he may lead a private life." The idea seems to be that the state is rudely prying into an individual's affairs when it makes him take the stand to answer questions. But if this is true, why not allow *all* witnesses to refuse to testify, instead of only those whose testimony "would tend to incriminate them?" Is it more of an invasion of privacy to ask a suspected bank robber about his affairs than it is to ask an innocent customer who happened to be standing in the bank when it was robbed? As a guarantee of privacy, the Fifth Amendment is doubly perverse: it protects only the privacy of those (e.g. criminals) who least deserve it, and it protects most strongly the information (e.g. incriminating information) that is most needed by the courts if they are to do their job.

Eventually, when all else fails, lawyers will fall back on their final argument, which evokes the sheer human cruelty of putting a [person] on the witness stand and asking him for his side of the story. The courts call this "our unwillingness to subject those suspected of a crime to the cruel trilemma of self-accusation, perjury, [or punishment for refusing to answer]." Since we are assuming that the witness is not going to be tortured, the Justices will concede that the cruelty they are talking about is "intangible, it is true; but so is liberty, and so is man's immortal soul."

This "intangible" argument at least has the virtue of honesty, since it admits that those who make use of the Fifth Amendment are in fact guilty. (Otherwise there would be no "cruel trilemma"—they could escape by simply telling the truth.) What it says, in effect, is that a guilty man asked to testify is placed between a rock and a hard place. So he is. But isn't this exactly where we want him? He has, by hypothesis, done something criminal, and if this gets him tangled up with the law—well, isn't that what is supposed to happen? Why should the Constitution reach down and extricate him from the trap he has gotten himself into?

When judges begin babbling about "man's immortal soul," they are getting desperate. It's a feeling familiar to the first-year law students who are asked in class to state the reasons for the Fifth Amendment, and who suddenly realize there aren't any. But most students quickly learn to stop worrying and accept the Amendment, perhaps sensing that it is one of the many mysteries of the law they can turn to profit later on. . . .

The McCarthy years, of course, helped cement the Fifth Amendment more securely in place. A handy device for resisting red-hunting congressional committees, it quickly became part of the intellectual baggage that liberals were expected to carry as a badge of conscience. Respectable conservative lawyers also felt compelled to defend it against right-wing critics, although the most respectable of those lawyers, former Harvard Law School dean Erwin Griswold, later recanted, pointing out what should have been obvious all along: there is a world of difference between opposing a McCarthyesque attack on "those who are guilty only of heretical and unpopular beliefs" and endorsing the role of the Amendment in a murder case. . . .

But the most important application of the Fifth Amendment has been to criminal confessions. You would expect judges to treat voluntary confessions as something to be desired for both moral and pragmatic reasons. And that was generally the impression the courts gave for the first half of this century. Confessions to the police were judged by a simple standard: If a confession were coerced, by physical or mental torture, bribery, etc., the prosecution couldn't use it at a trial. Otherwise, the confession would be admitted into evidence, and it was up to the defendant to explain it away.

But, reading through the Court's more recent pronouncements, you feel as if you had wandered into a house of mirrors, in which morality has been turned upside down and the guilty transposed with the innocent. Even when there is no hint of coercion, we find the Court scolding the police for "deliberately and designedly setting out to elicit information" from a murder suspect. When the killer foolishly but freely admits his guilt, the Court—instead of breathing a sigh of relief—can be seen wringing its hands at the "skillful and effective" questioning by the police. . . .

As a result, in *Miranda* the Fifth Amendment became the basis for a ruling that required the police to warn anyone they arrested that he had "the right to remain silent." From then on, confessions could not be used in court unless the police could prove, not that the suspect's statements were voluntary, but that he had first "knowingly and intelligently" given up his right to keep silent. The "right," and not the confession, became the focus of concern, and perfectly spontaneous admissions of guilt were thrown out because police had failed to give the ritual *Miranda* warnings. . . .

By now, judges have created a web of procedures that even they have trouble figuring out, but that seem to have as their hidden purpose the maximizing of the number of times when the Fifth Amendment will be employed by the guilty to frustrate the police. When a suspect is on the verge of confessing, the police must warn him not to. At all times, he is to be whisked as quickly as possible under the protective wing of a lawyer who will try to prevent him from opening his mouth. Finally, the police may not (heaven forbid) make an "appeal to [his] conscience" if he appears "peculiarly susceptible" to one. Such an appeal is a Fifth Amendment no-no . . . because it is "reasonably likely to elicit an incriminating response"—in other words, because it might work.

But these attitudes came together most vividly . . . when the Supreme Court heard the appeal of an Iowa man named Robert Williams. It's worth retelling the facts of the case, because they help to restore some perspective to the house of mirrors.

The story begins on Christmas Eve, 1968, when a 10-year-old named Pamela Powers visited the Des Moines YMCA to watch a wrestling tournament in which her brother was competing. She made a trip to the washroom, and did not return. Shortly thereafter, Williams, an escaped mental patient, was seen carrying a large bundle across the YMCA lobby. He placed the bundle in the front seat of his car, and a boy who had helped him open the car door saw two legs inside that were "skinny and white." Williams's abandoned car was found on Christmas Day, 160 miles away in Davenport, Iowa.

On December 26, Williams telephoned an attorney, and decided to surrender to the Davenport police. The police read him his *Miranda* warnings. Over the phone, the attorney told Williams not to talk to the police until Williams had talked with the attorney back in Des Moines. Williams's lawyer then struck a deal with the police by which they agreed not to "question" Williams during the drive from Davenport to Des Moines.

At the beginning of the drive, however, Williams started a "wide-ranging conversation covering a variety of topics, including religion," with one of the detectives in the car. Since the kidnapping had occurred only two days earlier, there was still some hope that the Powers girl was alive—although the weather outside was freezing and sleeting. The detective, hoping, he later said, "to find out where that little girl was," made a brief "speech" to Williams. "I want to give you something to think about while we're traveling down the road," the detective began. "They are predicting several inches of snow tonight, and I feel that you yourself are the only person that knows where this little girl's body is . . . and if you get a snow on top of it you yourself may be unable to find it . . . I feel that we could stop and locate the body, that the parents of this little girl should be entitled to a Christian burial for the little girl who was snatched away from them on Christmas Eve." The detective added, "I do not want you to answer me, I don't want to discuss it any further. Just think about it as we're riding down the road."

Williams repeated several times that he would tell the police the entire story when they got to Des Moines. But over an hour later, still 100 miles away, Williams asked whether the police had found the victim's shoes. When the police said no, Williams directed the car to a nearby gas station, where he said he had hidden the shoes. They were not there. As the car turned back to Des Moines, Williams next asked if the police had found the blanket, and then led them to a rest area where he said he had disposed of it. The blanket couldn't be found either. Finally, as the car headed once again to Des Moines, Williams said he would show the police where the body of Pamela Powers was. This time a search found what the detective was looking for.

Williams's statements and actions in the car were recounted at his trial, where he was convicted of first degree murder. Outside the hall of mirrors, it's hard to see any particular injustice in this. Clearly, Williams had voluntarily steered police to the body. He had done so after his attorney had expressly warned him not to—but it had been his decision, in response to a statement by the detective that appealed to his religion and his ordinary feelings of guilt. To be sure, the detective was less concerned that the Powers child receive a "Christian burial" than he was to discover her whereabouts, and he bluffed Williams by pretending to know that she was already dead. But perhaps he was thinking less of the possible interpretations of the *Miranda* ruling than about the time being lost while Williams followed his attorney's careful stage instructions.

In 1976, however, over eight years after the murder, the Williams case reached the Supreme Court. The Court's reasoning, in its opinion setting aside Williams's conviction, was familiar. His tacit confession, the Court declared, should not have been admitted into evidence, because the government had not met "its heavy burden of showing a knowing and intelligent waiver" by Williams of his "right to legal representation." Justice Thurgood Marshall was particularly scathing in his denunciation of the detectives who had "knowingly isolated Williams from the protection of his lawyers and during that period . . . intentionally 'persuaded' him to give incriminating evidence."

When we think of the Fifth Amendment, instead of recalling the Star chamber or Joe McCarthy, it would be more accurate to think of Robert Williams. . . . It is [he], along with assorted Mafiosi, drug smugglers, tax cheats, and labor racketeers, who make up the Amendment's natural constituency. For the rest of us, the Fifth Amendment offers nothing. It may have been a powerful weapon against oppression for our ancestors back in 1640, but they didn't choose their weapons with much precision. Over the last 200 years it has acquired a thick crust of traditions and rationalization. But we shouldn't let that prevent us from seeing that it is, at bottom, a fallacy—a constitutional mistake whose elimination would make life more difficult for the guilty, but would sacrifice none of our true freedoms.

┌ *Is the Privilege against Self-* ┐
│ *Incrimination an Unreason-* │
│ *able Burden on Public* │
└ *Order?* ┘

No: Some Views on *Miranda v. Arizona*

George Edwards

T HE most significant feature of the *Miranda* decision is that it marks the end of incommunicado interrogation of accused persons. Since the founding of this country, police power to arrest and to question in private, and without any legal representative or friend of the accused present, has been undisputed. The past arguments have concerned whether or not this power has been used so as physically, as in *Brown,* or psychologically as in *Spano,* to deprive the prisoner of the exercise of free will in determining whether or not he would confess. This case holds that incommunicado interrogation is inherently coercive and that police who employ it to secure a confession bear the burden of proof of proper warnings and waivers of counsel and the right of silence. . . .

[T]he Constitution seems plainly to vest power over its interpretation in the United States Supreme Court. The majority of that Court, exercising the judicial power, has spoken. It has spoken clearly and in an area where it has the power of decision. But, crime and police problems do not vanish with a court decision. And practical questions of great moment remain to be faced.

First, was there, predating *Miranda,* a serious threat to individual liberty in existing police interrogation practices in the various states? My own observation and knowledge compels an affirmative answer. I neither advocated nor predicted the Court's holding that there is a constitutional right to have a lawyer present at all police interrogation. Further, contrary to the situation relating to many other cases, I believe this case will have a real effect on law enforcement.

In some cases it will make identification and conviction more difficult. Further, the police in their daily confrontation with violent crime both need

George Edwards, from "Some Views on Miranda v. Arizona," 35 *Fordham Law Review* (1966), pp. 184–192.

and deserve the support of the public and the legal profession. And, finally, I am certain that in recent years police practices in interrogation of criminal suspects have markedly improved, as the police authorities in this country universally proclaim.

But, all of that being said does not lead me to join the public dissent to *Miranda*. I profoundly doubt that all physical abuse has been removed from all police interrogation rooms in the 50 states. I am sure that all psychological compulsion to confess has not ended. And I find it impossible to dispute the majority opinion in *Miranda* when it points to the inherently coercive nature of incommunicado interrogation.

I may be the only federal judge who has ever seen the third degree. Of course, to paraphrase T.S. Eliot, it was a long time ago, and in another state, and besides, the people involved are probably dead. But the memory lingers.

As a boy I worked in the summers in my father's law office. I accompanied him to court, to the records building, and on this occasion to see a client in jail. We were admitted through a steel-barred door to a large room off the jail office where my father began interviewing his client through the bars. Shortly, my interest in that interview was abruptly ended by blows and screams and groans coming from a small room partitioned off in a corner of the lockup room where we were. A few moments earlier I had seen several men lead a redheaded prisoner, whose arms were handcuffed behind his back into that room.

Several times in the next few moments someone went into or came out of the small room. And when the door was open, the scene in the room was unforgettable. The redheaded prisoner was spread-eagled over the end of a heavy table. His ankles were shackled to the table legs so that his legs were spread apart. One man stood behind him with a length of a rubber hose in his hand. A man on each side of the table had each of his arms twisted so that the prisoner was bent forward over the table. The prisoner was stripped to the waist and red welts criss-crossed the white skin of his back. Then the door would close and the blows and moans would start again.

The most macabre memory of all was seeing the jail personnel and other prisoners going about their routine jobs without ever looking in the direction of this human anguish.

There is more—but perhaps nothing more which bears polite description. What remains with me is a distinct and terrible doubt. Stubborn, as in franker moments I acknowledge that I am, I doubt that I could stand the torture I saw routinely administered to that redheaded prisoner without my "confessing," if that's the right word, anything the interrogator desired.

My father was stubborn too. He, and I with him, went promptly to the grand jury. I told the grand jury just what I have told you. I was asked whether I knew the names of the men in the little room. I said I did not. The foreman of the grand jury patted me on the head, said I was a fine boy, and gave me an apple. Then the grand jury voted a "No Bill."

If this bit of testimony from a now 40-year-old memory seems too old to be relevant, perhaps I should relate what I believe to be the facts about a case which I heard in trial board proceedings as Police Commissioner of Detroit not so long ago.

Several Detroit officers were informed by a complainant that a man named Daniels had threatened her with a gun. She said he had run off when she called the police. At the Daniels' house, his wife denied he was there and invited the officers in to establish that fact. In sworn testimony she subsequently acknowledged the invitation. Several of the officers proceeded to accept the invitation and found Daniels hiding in a coal cellar. They arrested and handcuffed him. So far, so good!

What happened next, however, was not far different from the story I have just related. Five officers surrounded Daniels in his own basement and proceeded to seek to extract from him information as to what he had done with the gun. Daniels denied stubbornly that he had ever had one.

The testimony I heard convinced me that Daniels was punched in the stomach somewhere between six and a dozen times, with questioning about the gun interspersed between the blows. At one point one officer picked up a baseball bat and put it on Daniels'- head, saying, "Now, Willie, where's the gun?"

No such episode was ever again reported during my tenure as Police Commissioner. But I had good reason to know that there were many of the older officers in my department who felt that I was most unsympathetic with what they believed to be "practical" law enforcement.

All in all, my experiences as Police Commissioner in my own department and elsewhere did not convince me that the third degree was completely dead. The episode just related was in the relatively enlightened city of Detroit, in the relatively civilized state of Michigan in the spring of 1962.

But it is also clear that the Supreme Court in *Miranda* was concerned with more than the problem of physical torture. If *Miranda* is a monument to anyone, perhaps it is to Fred Inbau. For years police have listened to this Northwestern University law professor in his national police institutes and gone away with what they thought was legal sanction for some fascinating interrogation practices.

The Mutt and Jeff technique which his text advocated was widely adopted. Jeff, the quiet, friendly officer, who is interrogating is interrupted by Mutt, his giant-sized partner who demands in a lion's-sized voice: "When are you going to turn that little punk over to me?" Several such interruptions, with variations on the theme of Mutt's impatience, I have been assured produce results if they do not correspond with exactness to the Fifth Amendment to the United States Constitution and our expanded concept of due process. Thus, I cannot share the dissenting opinion's objection to the reliance upon the quotations from Inbau and Reid found in the majority opinion in *Miranda*.

One other justification for the basic rules in *Miranda* deserves mention. There is no doubt that the full rights granted the poor and the ignorant by *Miranda* have been exercised to the fullest by our most affluent and arrogant criminals. The classic expectation in police circles concerning the arrest of a figure in organized crime is that the lawyer will beat his client to the police station. The Mafia trains its young that silence is not just a right but a duty to the mob. For them the Fifth Amendment warnings of *Miranda* are a duty enforceable by death.

Miranda also adds nothing of practical moment to the constitutional practices of the affluent and the educated. Those who fell into the toils of the law possessed of money, position in the community, and knowledge of their rights generally had little difficulty in securing them. . . .

The English have long had a strong tradition of local law enforcement also. They are as aware as we of the problems which would be created by a national police force. They have nonetheless striven with much more vigor than we for some solutions to the problems of lack of coordination, lack of training, and lack of adherence to national standards of due process which are inherent in any system of purely local police control.

Basically, they have employed two measures. The first is the enactment of what has been called "The Judges' Rules." These are direct orders governing police practices which are laid down by the judges of the Queen's Bench and made administratively effective as to the police forces of England through their enactment by the Home Secretary and their transmittal by him to every chief constable in England.

The second mechanism which the English have used is the coordination of local police policies and practices through the office of the Home Secretary. Since 1888 Parliament has appropriated 50 per cent of the total budget of all local police forces. And since that date there has, of course, been some participation on the part of the national government through the Home Secretary in establishing standards for police service.

It is obvious that the administrative counterparts of the English effort are to date completely lacking in the United States.

As I have suggested, the judicial controls set forth in *Miranda,* and preceding cases of recent years, may well indicate an inclination on the part of the Supreme Court to emulate the example set by the Judges' Rules.

The first rule to be found in *Miranda* is that the defendant be warned of his rights. But, when must the warning be given? I think the answer is "at the earliest practical moment." Certainly the warning should be given at the point of arrest. . . .

I do not seek to minimize the impact of such a warning. It will shut some mouths. There will, however, continue to be many voluntary statements after full warning with full waiver of counsel. For the most part, these will come from the obviously guilty who can be proved to be such anyhow. But, if the statement made after warning and waiver is thought likely to have any value, evidence as to how the warning was given and the waiver was accomplished should be preserved. There may be many better devices developed for this purpose, but at this point these occur to me.

In smaller police jurisdictions, the warning and waiver could be recorded on a dictaphone sleeve and properly marked and placed in the case file. In larger jurisdictions, I would think that television recordation of the whole process would be practical and valuable.

While the decision was "not intended to hamper the traditional function of police officers in investigating crime," and considerable out-of-custody questioning is still allowed, the police must, in my opinion, face the fact that *Miranda* means fewer confessions. Hence, the police must rely more on other sorts of evidence. In-custody interrogation has at least in some instances made for lazy police work. Detective staffing of crime investigations, particularly of murders and holdups, will need to be considerably increased.

Interestingly enough, since *Escobedo* there is good evidence in many jurisdictions that prosecutions without confessions have considerably increased and that the number of cases where a confession was thought to be essential has markedly decreased.

I certainly believe that higher quality of law enforcement—such as that mandated by the ideals of our Constitution as set forth in *Miranda*—does demand new practical measures of support for law enforcement.

Our city police officers are the front line of defense of law enforcement. Generally we have lampooned them, paid them badly, assigned them a relatively low social status, and appreciated them only when faced with an individual emergency. With this kind of attitude and the new demands for higher standards of police performance, our police may not be able to do an acceptable job. Something else must be added. . . .

For the next decades acceptable standards of law enforcement will require: (1) higher status for police officers; (2) more police officers; (3) higher pay for police officers; (4) better training for police officers; (5) more public support for law enforcement; (6) greater coordination between the agencies of our government concerned with law enforcement.

The great majority of police officers want no part of any abusive practices. They want and will support higher standards of training, of pay, and of performance in their profession. We should look forward to the day when our streets are policed by men recruited, trained and paid at the professional levels now maintained by the Federal Bureau of Investigation.

If it is said that law enforcement cannot be handled within constitutional limits, this is nonsense! In the two and a half years that I have been a federal appellate judge, I cannot remember one single case which came before us where the FBI agents were even charged with any physical abuse of the defendant who had been convicted in that case.

That is quite a record, because I certainly can't say that in relation to state court appellate review in past years. I do not need to be reminded that these FBI results are in large part a product of a very much lower case load than we currently require our metropolitan police to carry. But my point is that the standards of professionalization and manpower which the Federal Bureau of Investigation brings to its work are standards which we should seek to apply at local law enforcement levels. . . .

Now, a word on *Miranda's* place in history. Justice Frankfurter called the right to due process of law "the most majestic concept in our whole constitutional system."

Time has enshrined the great due process decisions of the past as monuments to the progress of mankind. But we should never forget that each of them was born of bitter controversy and was reviled by its detractors in its own day.

I suggest to you that the *Miranda* decision will prove to be one of the great due process documents of our time. And that the Court which delivered it will be honored for it in our nation's history.

8

Mapp v. Ohio:
Does the Fourth Amendment
Mandate an Exclusionary Rule?

Glenn A. Phelps

I N the spring of 1957 Cleveland police received an anonymous tip that a suspect in a bombing extortion racket was hiding in the home of Dollree (Dolly) Mapp, a twenty-nine-year-old black woman. Mapp was already known to the police. While never in serious trouble, she was one of those people whose lives seem to hover in the twilight of illegality. She was occasionally seen in the company of known numbers racketeers. For the police, then, the information from the informant was plausible. It seemed a good opportunity to search Mapp's home not just for the extortion suspect but also for paraphernalia related to the numbers racket.

Shortly after 1:00 P.M., three police officers arrived at the home. From her second-floor window, Mapp asked them what they wanted. The police demanded entry. Mapp, after a quick telephone call to her lawyer, stated that she had been advised not to let them in unless they had a search warrant. Three hours later several more officers appeared at the Mapp home. Testimony differs as to the specific number; police records suggest seven policemen were present; Mapp claimed that there were more than a dozen. They burst into the house and were met on the stairs by Mapp, who demanded to see the search warrant. An officer waved a piece of paper in front of her. When he refused to let her see it, she grabbed the paper from his hand and stuffed it down the front of her blouse. Police were momentarily dumbfounded, but they soon reacted. One officer determinedly stated, "I'm going after it." This was confirmed by Mapp's attorney who had been attempting to enter the house to assist his client but was being prevented from doing so by the police on the scene. (Indeed, he was never allowed to enter during the entire incident and was never shown the warrant.) While standing outside the door, though, the lawyer heard Mapp scream, "Take your hand out of my dress!" After a vigorous scuffle (Justice Clark's opinion would accuse the police of "running roughshod" over Mapp), Mapp was handcuffed and subdued.

The "warrant" having now been retrieved, the police thoroughly searched the Mapp home. They found no extortion suspect. They found no numbers paraphernalia. They did not, however, leave empty-handed. A locked trunk was opened, and the contents of a brown paper bag within it were examined by one of the officers. Despite warnings from Mapp that he ought not to look at the contents because "that might excite you," the officer nevertheless removed several paperback books from the bag. He examined them and deemed them—*The Affairs of the Troubadour, London Stage Affairs, Little Darlings,* and *Memories of a Hotel Man*—to be obscene.

For having possession of those four books, Dolly Mapp was found guilty of violating Ohio's antiobscenity statute. She was given an indeterminant sentence of between one and seven years in the women's reformatory. Her attorney appealed the conviction on several grounds, one of which was that the search that obtained the incriminating evidence was illegal. He contended, therefore, that the fruits of that search should be excluded from the trial.

This contention precipitated one of the most controversial criminal justice rulings of the Warren Court. The Court found itself confronted with a classic "what if?" problem. The Fourth Amendment merely states that "the right of the people to be secure . . . against unreasonable searches and seizures, shall not be violated." It does not, however, say what would happen if an unreasonable search were to occur. As Leonard Levy has pointed out,

> The amendment does not include sanctions for its violation, leaving the issue in doubt. It does not state that a court must suppress illegally obtained evidence, or allow a suit for damages against the offending police officers, or permit their prosecution, or provide some other remedy.[1]

The Fourth Amendment seems to say that persons are entitled to a degree of privacy against intrusions of the government. But unlike the unequivocal and absolute pronouncements of the First Amendment ("Congress shall make no law . . ."), the Fourth is couched in ambiguity (no *unreasonable* searches and seizures and the need to show *probable* cause).

This ambiguity is in part a reflection of the concerns of the Revolutionary generation. Two practices that were particularly onerous to colonists were writs of assistance and general warrants. As colonial resistance to such revenue-raising measures as the Townshend Acts and Stamp Act grew, agents of the Crown found it necessary to utilize more extreme measures to ensure compliance. One of the most hated of these was the writ of assistance, a kind of "John Doe" warrant that could be used by a customs agent to break into any home or business to search for evidence of tax violations. Colonial customs agents were occasionally quite aggressive in exercising their authority under these writs. Citizen indignation mounted, as exemplified by the following petition from a Boston town meeting in 1772: "Our houses and even our bed chambers are exposed to be ransaked, our boxes, chests, and trunks broke open, ravaged and plundered by wretches, whom no prudent man would venture to employ even as menial servants."[2]

Perhaps some of the resistance to these search and seizure practices was self-interested or the rhetoric of Revolutionary fever. But when the Revolution was over and the victors now faced the task of constructing their own constitutions and governments, the concerns for privacy and the need to control abuses of power did not vanish. At least three states forbade unreasonable searches and seizures in their constitutions. Five states specifically denied the authority of general warrants that did not specify the person, place, or purpose of a search. Other states found that the principles of the common law provided protection against abuses. It is not surprising, then, that the proposed Fourth Amendment generated little disagreement or debate within Congress or the ratifying states. It would provide one more check against the abuse of power by the *federal* government.

But the Amendment did not address the "what if?" question. This would become a thorny problem of interpretation for the Supreme Court. It was first addressed in *Boyd v. U.S.* (116 U.S. 616, 1886). Congress, in an 1874 law, authorized federal courts to require that defendants in customs cases produce in court any "private books, invoices, and papers," that might be requested by the government. If the defendant refused to produce the documents, the court was entitled to accept the assertions of the prosecution as indisputably true. The Court noted the catch-22 nature of the law ("Gimme the evidence—and if you don't, you're guilty!") and recognized its implications for the Fourth Amendment. Justice Joseph P. Bradley, for a unanimous court, pointed out that placing a defendant in such a dilemma compromised the adversarial system of justice. If the state could compel a suspect to turn over any incriminating materials without having to resort to a search warrant, then the Fourth Amendment would be so many empty promises. The Court asserted that the 1874 law compelled a defendant to be a witness against himself and thus violated the Fifth Amendment's prohibition against compulsory self-incrimination. The 1874 law was overturned, but more important, for the first time a court argued that there was a link between the Fourth and Fifth Amendments.

The full impact of this linkage was not appreciated until almost thirty years later, in *Weeks v. U.S.* (232 U.S. 383, 1914). Federal officers suspected Weeks and several others of selling illegal lottery coupons. Agents arrested Weeks (without a warrant) at Union Station in Kansas City. At the same time other officers converged on his home (also without a search warrant). Unable to obtain entry, they went to a neighbor who gave them the key that Weeks had left for safekeeping. They searched the home and discovered several documents and other items, which they turned over to a U.S. marshal. The marshal, convinced that the Weeks's home could produce even more materials, sent officers back for a more thorough search. Still without a warrant, they obtained entry a second time in the same way, this time with the assistance of a befuddled and frightened boarder.

The question—what if the police did conduct an unreasonable search?—was now directly joined. In another unanimous opinion, Justice William Day pointed out the implications of the problem. If letters and papers could be seized by police officers without a warrant and then used as evidence to obtain a conviction, then "the protection of the Fourth Amendment . . . might as well be stricken from the Constitution." The logic of *Boyd* in linking the Fourth Amendment to the Fifth was now carried to its conclusion: evidence obtained by an unreasonable search and seizure amounted to compulsory self-incrimination and should therefore be excluded.

For Dolly Mapp, though, the protections of this exclusionary rule were more illusory than real because the Bill of Rights and its specific due process guarantees were deemed for a long time applicable only to the federal government, not to the states. The Fourteenth Amendment did ordain that no state could deny due process of law to any person. But what did this mean? Did this Due Process Clause require that the Fourth and Fifth Amendments mean the same thing (the Exclusionary Rule) in the states that it meant in the federal courts?

The Supreme Court's answer to these concerns was, sometimes yes, sometimes no. This ambiguous position is illustrated in *Wolf v. Colorado* (338 U.S. 25, 1949). Unwilling to declare for a complete incorporation of the Bill of Rights, the Court instead determined that only those practices that were "essential to a system of ordered liberty" or required for "fundamental fairness" were obligatory on the states. Justice Felix Frankfurter at first went to great lengths to demonstrate that the principles of the Fourth Amendment were "essential to a system of ordered liberty" and therefore binding on the states through the Due Process Clause of the Fourteenth Amendment. Having offered this ringing endorsement of privacy and the principles of the Fourth Amendment, Frankfurter proceeded to uphold Wolf's conviction by refusing to apply the exclusionary rule to the states. In doing so he argued that the exclusionary rule was only one remedy to an illegal search or seizure. State legislatures and state courts were to be encouraged to seek their own solutions (for example, through civil suits and disciplinary actions) to the problem.

Thus, when *Mapp v. Ohio* (367 U.S. 643, 1961) reached the Supreme Court twelve years later, the decision was to come as a surprise not only to experienced court observers but also to Dolly Mapp. With almost perverse delight, Justice Clark used the bizarre circumstances of Mapp's arrest and search to spring into a broad attack on the problem of illegal searches and seizures in the states. *Wolf* had established that states were forbidden to engage in unreasonable searches and seizures but had declined to insist on the exclusionary rule universally, instead urging states to seek their own solutions. Clark now noted "that such other remedies have been worthless and futile is buttressed by the experience of other states." More and more states were recognizing that the exclusionary rule was the only effective protection for Fourth Amendment rights. He noted that unless the rule were applied uniformly in all jurisdictions, then the temptation of federal officials to share illegally obtained evidence with states (that did not exclude such evidence) would prove too attractive. Governments would engage in unseemly conspiracies to violate the Constitution. This led to Clark's last and most stinging point: failure to respect and enforce the Constitution could imperil the integrity of the judicial system.

> The criminal goes free if he must, but it is the law that sets him free. Nothing can destroy a government more quickly than its failure to observe its laws, or worse, its disregard of the charter of its own existence. . . . The ignoble shortcut to conviction left open to the State tends to destroy the entire system of constitutional restraints on which the liberties of the people rest.

Dolly Mapp was to go free. The debate over the merits of the exclusionary rule, however, did not end with Mapp's case. Several justices who were not on the *Mapp* court have expressed grave reservations about the exclusionary rule. They have asserted that the deterrence of illegal police practices is minimal, while the cost to society and the victims of crime is significant. Chief Justice Burger has been most outspoken in his dissent in *Bivens v. Six Unknown Federal Narcotics Agents* (403 U.S. 388, 1971) and his majority decision in *U.S. v. Calandra* (414 U.S. 338, 1974) refusing to extend the rule to grand jury proceedings. Many observers believe that there are now four solid votes on the Court (Burger, William Rehnquist, Sandra Day O'Connor, and White) to overturn *Mapp* and the exclusionary rule.

The two articles that follow address the principal arguments in the debate over the exclusionary rule. Harvey Wingo, Jr., a professor of law at Southern Methodist University, focuses on numerous shortcomings of the exclusionary rule. The late Sam Ervin, Jr., was a former judge and U.S. Senator from North Carolina. He offers a spirited defense of the rule.

Yes: The Exclusionary Rule:
An Essential Ingredient
of the Fourth Amendment

Sam J. Ervin, Jr.

ESPITE honest beliefs of sincere persons to the contrary, the exclusionary rule is an essential ingredient of the Fourth Amendment. Apart from it, the Amendment's guaranty against unreasonable searches and seizures is worse than solemn mockery, and the Amendment might well be expunged from the Constitution as a meaningless expression of a merely pious hope. . . .

The indispensable nature of the exclusionary rule was revealed in cases past numbering in state courts before the landmark decision in *Mapp v. Ohio,* where the Supreme Court held that the Fourth Amendment is made binding on the states by the Due Process Clause of the Fourteenth Amendment. Prior to *Mapp,* the courts of many states admitted in criminal prosecutions evidence obtained by the states in violation of their constitutions outlawing general warrants and prohibiting unreasonable searches and seizures, and thus converted solemn constitutional guaranties into dead letters. The exclusionary rule is, in reality, the only breakwater against conviction-prone courts and overzealous law enforcement officers. Those who maintain the contrary are like the comforters of Job: they multiply words without knowledge. . . .

Some judges, prosecutors, law enforcement officers, politicians, and others dislike the exclusionary rule and demand that it be abolished or substantially modified. The reasons for their dislike and demand are stated most ably by the most famous of them, Chief Justice Warren Burger, in his dissenting opinion in *Bivens v. Six Unknown Federal Narcotics Agents,* and his concurring opinion in *Stone v. Powell.* Let us analyze these reasons and ascertain their validity.

Sam J. Ervin, Jr., from "The Exclusionary Rule: An Essential Ingredient of the Fourth Amendment," 1983 *Supreme Court Review,* pp. 286–299. Published by the University of Chicago Press.

For their convenient consideration, I state the arguments of the opponents of the exclusionary rule in Chief Justice Burger's words and in this numerical fashion:

[1.] The rule is a judge-made rule without support in the Constitution. The function of the rule is to exclude "truth from the factfinding process" in criminal prosecutions. Unlike the Fifth Amendment's ban of self-incrimination, the rule excludes reliable rather than dubious evidence. "The direct beneficiaries of the rule can be none but persons guilty of crimes," and the rule results in a "bizarre miscarriage of justice" because it prevents the conviction of the guilty. . . .

[2.] The rule "rests upon its purported tendency to deter police" violation of the Fourth Amendment. The rule does "nothing to punish the wrongdoing official," frees "the wrong-doing defendant," "deprives society of its remedy against one lawbreaker because he is pursued by another," and "offers no relief whatever to victims of overzealous police work who never appear in court." "Despite its avowed deterrent objective, proof is lacking that the exclusionary rule . . . serves the purpose of deterrence. Notwithstanding Herculean efforts, no empirical study has been able to demonstrate that the rule does in fact have any deterrent effect. . . . To vindicate the continued existence of this . . . rule, it is incumbent on those who seek its retention . . . to demonstrate that it serves its declared deterrent purpose and to show that the results outweigh the rule's heavy costs to rational enforcement of the criminal law."

[3.] "The rule has long been applied to wholly good-faith mistakes and to purely technical deficiencies in warrants." The English and Canadian legal systems, which are highly regarded, have not adopted the rule.

The assertion that the courts of England and Canada have not adopted the exclusionary rule is wholly irrelevant. Unlike the United States, neither of them has a written constitution containing a Fourth Amendment and constituting its supreme law. The arguments of the opponents of the rule otherwise lack validity and indicate that they do not understand the rule or its origin or objective. The Chief Justice argues in his concurring opinion in the *Stone* case that the exclusionary rule is "a judge-made rule" without support in the Constitution, "a Draconian discredited device," and "a judicially contrived doctrine. . . ."

There are two absolute and incontrovertible answers to these and all other arguments offered in support of the proposition that the Supreme Court ought to divorce the exclusionary rule from the Fourth Amendment. Such arguments are totally repugnant to the Constitution in general and to the Fourth Amendment in particular. The Supreme Court is obligated to support the Constitution in its entirety and is destitute of power to alter the meaning of a single syllable of it.

The exclusionary rule is implicit and inherent in the Fourth Amendment itself. When they are interpreted aright, the words of the Amendment incorporate the exclusionary rule as a permanent and inseparable element, and by so doing make the Fourth Amendment a living constitutional guaranty that the right of the people to be secure in their persons, houses, papers, and effects against unreasonable searches and seizures shall not be violated by government. What the Fourth Amendment joins together Supreme Court Justices cannot put asunder. This conclusion is in full accord with the applicable Supreme Court decisions.

The function of the rule is not to exclude truth from the fact-finding process in criminal prosecutions. On the contrary, its objective is most laudatory. The recognition and enforcement of the rule is necessary to make the Fourth Amendment's guaranty against unreasonable searches and seizures effective and thus enable Americans to enjoy personal privacy, personal security, and private property free from arbitrary and Gestapo-like governmental invasions. . . .

Inasmuch as the Fourth Amendment is indispensable to the enjoyment of personal privacy, personal security, and private property, there is no merit in the argument that no persons are its direct beneficiaries except those guilty of criminal offenses. All human beings within the borders of our land are its direct beneficiaries because it enables them to enjoy their persons, their houses, their papers, and effects free from arbitrary and Gestapo-like searches and seizures by government.

Opponents of the exclusionary rule cannot resist the temptation to quote Judge Benjamin N. Cardozo's catchy aphorism: "The criminal is to go free because the constable has blundered." Unfortunately, Judge Cardozo's aphorism does not display his customary illuminating power, and many opponents of the exclusionary rule accept it as a substitute for thought on the subject. Judge Cardozo ought to have said, "The accused goes free because government, acting through a blundering constable, denied him his constitutional right to be exempt from an unreasonable search or seizure." The arguments which harp on the circumstance that judicial enforcement of the exclusionary rule sometimes permits guilty persons to escape conviction and punishment shed no light on the questions of the constitutionality or objective of the rule.

These questions are answered with unmistakable clarity by the emphatic declaration of the Fourth Amendment that "the right of the people to be secure in their persons, houses, papers, and effects, against unreasonable searches and seizures, shall not be violated." By these words, the Fourth Amendment emulates the impartiality of the rains of heaven, which fall on the just and unjust alike, and clearly extends to all men the protection of its guaranty against unreasonable searches and seizures irrespective of whether they be innocent or guilty. As the inevitable consequence, the Fourth Amendment condemns every search or seizure that is unreasonable and protects those suspected or known to be offenders as well as the innocent. Under the

Amendment, a search is constitutional or unconstitutional at its inception, and does not change its character by what it brings to light. . . .

My three-score years at the bar have taught me that some judges, lawyers, and laymen call every law or constitutional principle they dislike "a legal technicality." Criminal prosecutions reveal that the exclusionary rule is successfully invoked because of deficiencies in applications and warrants in cases where the application fails to establish probable cause for the search or seizure or the warrants fail to describe the place to be searched or the person or thing to be seized. These deficiencies are not legal technicalities. They are of constitutional dimensions.

The argument that the exclusionary rule should be discontinued unless those who accept its validity demonstrate that "it serves its declared deterrent purpose and that the results outweigh the rule's heavy costs to rational enforcement of the criminal law" is most intriguing. The exclusionary rule is an essential ingredient of the Fourth Amendment. An express or implied command of the Constitution, I submit, does not become inoperative because those who accept it as such do not demonstrate that in its operation the constitutional command produces results pleasing to those who dislike it. I note without comment that a violation of the Fourth Amendment by a judicial or executive officer of the government is not a rational way to enforce the criminal law.

The argument that the rule "does nothing to punish the wrongdoing official" is completely beside the mark. The rule is designed to prevent unreasonable governmental searches and seizures and not to punish the officers making them for their individual misconduct. For this reason, the Supreme Court declared in the *Weeks* case, "What remedies the defendant may have against [the wrongdoing officials] we need not inquire."

I revere the Constitution because it creates for America the soundest system of government the earth has ever known, and because it establishes for Americans basic constitutional rights which must be respected by the government it creates if America is to endure as the land of the free. For these reasons, I have the temerity to make some additional unvarnished comments respecting the views of those who seek to abolish or modify the exclusionary rule. After all, they seek to twist awry the guaranty of the Constitution of my country that America shall not be converted from a land of liberty into a police state.

When a Supreme Court Justice succumbs to the temptation to nullify or modify the handiwork of the Founding Fathers, he impairs his capacity to see such handiwork steady and whole. Chief Justice Burger asserts that the exclusionary rule is unlike the implied constitutional rules that reject involuntary confessions violative of due process and compelled testimony violative of the Self-Incriminating Clause; that evidence obtained in violation of the Fourth Amendment is always true, whereas involuntary confessions and compelled testimony violative of the Self-Incrimination Clause are false at worst and dubious at best; and that the Constitution requires Courts to exclude involuntary confessions and compelled testimony violative of the Self-Incrimination Clause simply because of their false or dubious nature.

The Chief Justice is in error. Many involuntary confessions and much compelled testimony violative of the Self-Incrimination Clause are true. The Constitution is not concerned with the truth or the falsity of this evidence or the evidence obtained in violation of the Fourth Amendment. On the contrary, the Constitution forbids the government to use such evidence in criminal prosecutions against persons aggrieved because it obtains the evidence by tyrannous practices that the Constitution outlaws.

The arguments of the opponents of the rule justify a final comment. The Chief Justice makes this assertion in his concurring opinion in the *Stone* case:

> A more clumsy, less direct means of imposing sanctions is difficult to imagine, particularly since the issue whether the police did indeed run afoul of the Fourth Amendment is often not resolved until after the event. The "sanction" is particularly indirect when . . . the police go before a magistrate, who issues a warrant. Once the warrant issues, there is literally nothing more the policeman can do in seeking to comply with the law. Imposing an admittedly indirect "sanction" on the police officer in that instance is nothing less than sophisticated nonsense.

The Chief Justice misses the entire point of the matter. The Court is not imposing a sanction on a policeman. It is enforcing the second clause of the Fourth Amendment, which declares in plain words that "no warrants shall issue, but upon probable cause, supported by oath or affirmation, and particularly describing the place to be searched, and the person or things to be seized." Surely it is never "sophisticated nonsense" for a judicial tribunal to enforce a guaranty which was embodied in the Constitution to make America the land of the free.

Opponents of the exclusionary rule urge that it be abolished and that alternatives be established to take its place. There is, in reality, no alternative for the rule. This is true because the only effective way to make the Fourth Amendment effective is to deny government the power to use evidence obtained by its violation of the rule.

Nevertheless, some who dislike the rule have proposed that the rule be abolished in its entirety and that civil and criminal sanctions against offending officers be substituted for it. The lawbooks already declare that an officer who makes an unreasonable arrest, search, or seizure is subject to both criminal and civil liability for his unconstitutional act. But his lawbook liability is fictitious rather than pragmatic. Because they work in close collaboration and are dependent on each other, prosecutors simply do not bring criminal prosecutions against officers of the law whose zeal or ignorance prompt them to overstep Fourth Amendment bounds. And because the injuries of the persons aggrieved are largely emotional rather than pecuniary, juries in civil cases are not prone to award them substantial damages against officers of the law, whose wrongs are motivated by well-meaning overzealousness or ignorance of law rather than by malice. And even if the damages awarded be substantial in amount, they are usually uncollectible because of the indigency of the officer. For these reasons, the bench and bar know that as practical deterrents to Fourth Amendment violations the lawbook liabilities of offending officers are illusory and futile. . . .

There is a repugnancy between the Fourth Amendment and the proposal that the exclusionary rule be modified to permit government to use evidence obtained in violation of the Fourth Amendment in criminal prosecutions against a person whose Fourth Amendment rights are violated if the police officer committing the violation acted in the good-faith belief that his conduct comported with existing law and he had reasonable grounds for his belief. This is true because the Fourth Amendment outlaws without exception or limitation all unreasonable searches and seizures. Besides, the adoption of the proposal would create an absurdity in our legal system. Ignorance of the law would not excuse the accused's commission of a crime, but ignorance of the Constitution would excuse the police officer's violation of it. If the United States is to be a free republic, the constitutional protections and rights of its people must be determined by the words of the Constitution and not by the understanding or lack of understanding of police officers respecting them. . . .

$\begin{bmatrix} \textit{Does the Fourth Amend-} \\ \textit{ment Mandate an Exclu-} \\ \textit{sionary Rule?} \end{bmatrix}$

No: Disillusionment with the Exclusionary Rule

Harvey Wingo, Jr.

THE Supreme Court's enchantment with the exclusionary rule in Fourth Amendment cases has been largely dependent upon two hastily drawn conclusions: (1) that the rule will act as a deterrent against illegal arrests, searches, and seizures, and (2) that there are no other "effectively available" means of enforcing the Amendment. One of the objectionable features of both *Weeks* and *Mapp* is that in neither case did the Court really inquire into the validity of either of these two theses.

Judge Friendly has noted that the use of the word "deter" in describing the purpose of the exclusionary rule "suggests" an analogy with the purpose of punishment in the criminal process. That purpose is often said to be two-fold: (1) the direct deterrence of future criminal acts by the convicted offender, and (2) a general deterrence of similar acts by others in the community who observe that punishment is imposed for commission of the particular offense. Can this same theory be applied to the effect of the exclusionary rule on the police? Will an individual policeman, observing that evidence secured by him illegally has been excluded at trial, be deterred from similar illegal conduct in the future? Will police in general be deterred from making unlawful arrests and searches because of the exclusion of evidence that was improperly obtained by other police officers?

An obvious flaw in the analogy is that a convicted offender is punished personally, while the exclusionary rule operates directly only against the prosecutor who is thwarted in his attempt to have the evidence admitted but who rarely, if ever, has any control over the persons responsible for the illegal conduct. Considered in a broader context, the prosecutor represents the people, who in turn are obliged to accept less than the truth in the case and,

Harvey Wingo, Jr., from "Growing Disillusionment with the Exclusionary Rule," 25 *South-western Law Journal* (1971), pp. 575–86. Copyright 1971 by Southern Methodist University. Reprinted with permission from Southwestern Law Journal.

therefore, are also "punished" by the rule. Those left unpunished are the obviously guilty defendant and the police officer who conducted the illegal search. Indeed, the rule has often been criticized as providing protection *only* for the guilty. Of course, as Professor LaFave has pointed out, if there is a deterrent effect, the police will be restrained from engaging in illegal conduct that is directed at innocent as well as guilty individuals. On the other hand, once the illegal invasion has been accomplished, it is the guilty who will profit by application of the exclusionary rule—evidence that proves guilt or clearly tends to do so must not be considered. As for the erring policeman, one might expect at least a reprimand or other form of disciplinary action, if only as punishment for damaging the state's case. It is more likely that general police response will be disdain for the court's action and complete sympathy with the individual policeman's position.

Another stumbling block to deterrence is that the police are often not so much concerned with convictions as with arrests and case clearances. At the time the search is conducted the trial is only a distant possibility; the immediate goal is to apprehend the offender and secure the evidence which proves that he is the offender. This will result in "clearance" of the case. In many instances there is never even any thought of seeking a prosecution. This is particularly true in cases involving gambling, liquor, narcotics, and drug offenses. The purpose of a search and seizure here may be harassment of the offenders or the removal of contraband items, such as narcotics, from circulation. This type of police action has the desired effect of demonstrating to the public that efforts are under way to control these criminal activities. The exclusionary rule can obviously play no role whatsoever in these cases, nor in instances in which the police are acting only to control a potentially dangerous situation, since no trial is even contemplated.

Finally, consider the numerous cases in which the police have simply made an honest and understandable error in judgment. It is likely that a substantial percentage of illegal police searches and seizures would fall within this category. There has been no intentional undercutting of Fourth Amendment requirements. To the police officer acting under the pressures of the moment the search appeared to be entirely reasonable, and there was very little time to ponder the question. The United States Supreme Court may consider the case for months before making its decision, and even then is apt to be divided in its determination of the issue. In fact, Supreme Court case law governing arrests, search, and seizure has been badly blurred by shifting sands. . . . As LaFave has emphasized, if a rule of conduct cannot be made clear to the person who must follow it, any deterrent effect it may otherwise have had is likely to be neutralized entirely.

It is probably impossible to reach a truly reliable empirical determination concerning the success of the exclusionary rule in deterring illegal searches and seizures. However, the most recent attempt, by Professor Dallin H. Oaks of the University of Chicago Law School, yielded findings of which the following is a sample. (1) In Chicago in 1969 motions to suppress evidence were "the dispositive event" in forty-five percent of the gambling cases and in thirty-three percent of the narcotics cases. These rates "seem considerably higher than would be necessary if the Chicago police were really serious about observing the search and seizure rules." (2) Police officers have long felt that their duty to recover stolen property overrides adherence to Fourth Amendment requirements. The study failed to show any correlation between adoption of the exclusionary rule and a decrease in recovery of stolen property. This indicates that the exclusionary rule probably does not induce greater conformity with Fourth Amendment rules. (3) The police do not look upon the exclusionary rule as a protective device for the citizenry, but see it as a "hindrance" in fighting crime and are willing to manufacture probable cause or violate the rules governing search and seizure when they feel it is important to do so in solving crime. In this regard, the police tend to "rely on departmental rather than legal norms of behavior."

Despite the gathering of "the largest fund of information yet assembled on the effect of the exclusionary rule," Professor Oaks was compelled to conclude that the information was insufficient either to sustain or refute the deterrence theory. However, his own personal conclusions were more decisive:

> As a devise for directly deterring illegal searches and seizures by the police, the exclusionary rule is a failure. There is no reason to expect the rule to have any direct effect on the overwhelming majority of police conduct that is not meant to result in prosecutions, and there is hardly any evidence that the rule exerts any deterrent effect on the small fraction of law enforcement activity that is aimed at prosecution.

While it is probably true that there is no presently effective means of enforcing the Fourth Amendment, there are enforcement tools available which could be made effective. In truth, adoption of the exclusionary rule in search and seizure cases may have impeded development and refinement of far better alternatives. . . .

There are two needs in connection with enforcement of the Fourth Amendment. One is the deterrence of police violations; the other is compensation for those whose Fourth Amendment rights have been infringed and who have suffered some injury. It is submitted that a combination of the civilian review board and the proposed new civil proceeding against the government would provide the most effective framework for meeting these two needs. The policeman would be deterred by a real prospect of disciplinary action, and the victim of illegal activities would be in a much more favorable position for recovery of adequate damages. Significantly, unlike the exclusionary rule, both procedures would provide a forum for consideration of cases involving innocent victims of police misconduct when no criminal proceedings result.

Even if the two theses discussed above are accepted as valid, imposition of the exclusionary rule as a constitutional requirement in search and seizure cases is still extremely difficult to justify. It is an inflexible rule requiring judicial suppression of reliable evidence regardless of the gravity of the police illegality and with dubious constitutional authority.

The most troublesome aspect of the rule is its direct suppression of the truth. In this connection, application of the rule in cases involving illegally obtained confessions should be contrasted. The rule's operation there can be supported on the ground that confessions are inherently suspect, and, when the confession has been obtained illegally, the courts are justified in treating it as unreliable evidence. Of course, the unreliability rationale has not been the primary basis for the Supreme Court's adoption of the exclusionary rule in the confession cases, but it does provide significant support for the rule in those cases. This is also true of the exclusion of courtroom identifications which have been shown to be dependent upon a pretrial confrontation between the witness and the accused conducted in an unnecessarily suggestive manner or without according the accused his Sixth Amendment right to counsel. Again, the rule may be considered appropriate to assure the exclusion of evidence—*i.e.,* identification testimony—reasonably believed to be unreliable. With illegally seized evidence, however, the only possible issues of reliability are: (a) whether the evidence was in fact found in the place alleged, and (b) if so, to what extent does it connect the defendant to the offense. The legality or illegality of the search has no bearing on these issues and, thus, can in no way affect the determination of whether the offered items constitute reliable evidence of guilt. In most cases the evidence is actual proof of guilt, and "[t]he criminal is to go free because the constable has blundered."

The discharge of obviously guilty persons is the most serious and direct result of the exclusionary rule, but there are also unfortunate side effects. One is that many criminal trials will suffer unnecessary and distracting delay while arguments are made on the motion to suppress evidence and the judge ponders his decision on this complex and crucial issue. The focus of the proceedings shifts abruptly from the question of guilt or innocence of the defendant to the question of the legality of police activities. This, of course, is not the purpose of a criminal trial. One critic of the rule has properly reminded us that not only is the determination of guilt or innocence of the defendant the "most important function" of the criminal trial, "it is its only function." To allow the criminal proceedings to be transformed into a court of inquiry concerning the alleged police illegality is nothing less than evasion by the courts of their responsibility in the case.

Another disturbing outgrowth of these cases is a loss of public confidence in our system of justice. Ironically, a strong argument against admissibility of illegally seized evidence has been that it allows the government to profit by its own lawbreaking and, thus, "breeds contempt for law." Indeed, the public's confidence in its *police force* may be undermined by repeated showings of police misconduct. But respect for and confidence in our *judicial system* would seem to be much more dangerously threatened by the continued refusal of the courts to consider perfectly reliable evidence that proves the guilt of the accused. To set the defendant free as a result of the exclusion of illegally seized evidence is certain to be looked upon as acquittal on a "technicality," a complaint that is heard so frequently from the general public. Another method of controlling police behavior—even one that has heretofore been unfavorably regarded by a large segment of the community—would undoubtedly be more acceptable to the public than this truth suppression device.

The exclusionary rule in search cases not only compels suppression of the truth, but does so indiscriminately, without regard for degrees of police illegality. Consider case one: A police officer has an unfounded suspicion that X committed a certain robbery. He breaks and enters X's house without a warrant, causes considerable damage to the premises during a general ransacking of the place, and finally succeeds in uncovering items which had been taken during the robbery in question. This leads to an arrest of X on the robbery charge. Compare case two: Two police officers, without a warrant, but having probable cause to believe that Y has committed a robbery, go to Y's house and arrest him on the front porch. Not wanting to risk removal of evidence from the house by a member of Y's family or a confederate, one of the officers enters the house and looks summarily through several rooms, discovering stolen items in an upstairs bedroom.

The searches in both of the above cases are illegal under the Fourth Amendment as currently interpreted by the United States Supreme Court. The search in case one is patently objectionable. In case two there is probable cause for the arrest, and the prosecutor may argue that the search is incident to a lawful arrest and, thus, covered by an exception to the requirement for a search warrant. However, the Supreme Court presently requires that a search incident to arrest must be limited to the area within the arrested person's immediate control. The interior of the house here is clearly not within Y's immediate control, yet the illegality of this search obviously cannot compare with the gross violation of Fourth Amendment rules in the first case. Nevertheless, the result in each case will be exclusion of the evidence seized. Chief Justice Burger has referred to this inflexibility as "universal 'capital punishment'" for illegally obtained evidence and has likened it to "a police order authorizing 'shoot-to-kill' with respect to every fugitive."

The exclusionary rule in its Fourth Amendment application is far too absolute in scope. There is no way to modify the harsh effect of the rule in appropriate cases. As Barrett has said: "there will always be a substantial number of cases in which the defendant will go free, however clear his guilt may be and however much more serious his crime may be than the policeman's error." Honest errors of judgment are treated as harshly as willful and malicious misconduct, and this alone makes the rule unreasonable in a large proportion of the cases to which it is applied.

In view of the serious objections to exclusion of reliable but illegally seized evidence, it might be expected that a clear constitutional mandate could be shown in support of the requirement. The Fourth Amendment prohibits unreasonable searches and seizures and requires that warrants be issued only upon a showing of probable cause, but there is no statement concerning enforcement of these guarantees. It is certainly reasonable to assume that had the Fourth Amendment been designed to require exclusion of evidence seized in violation of its provisions, it would have been drafted so as to make this purpose explicit. There is no question that the Supreme Court could impose the requirement in federal cases in the exercise of its supervisory authority over the federal court system. In addition, Congress might see fit to establish the rule as an implementing device; and it probably could do so even for state criminal proceedings, since it is expressly given the authority to enact "appropriate legislation" for the enforcement of the Fourteenth Amendment's command of due process. However, there is much to be said for the position that the Supreme Court has overstepped its authority by writing into the Fourth Amendment a constitutional requirement that is simply not there. This is not to advocate such a restrictive approach as to prevent the Court from interpreting the Constitution in light of present-day realities, for there is a significant difference between a liberal interpretation of constitutional language and the outright addition of language to the Constitution. . . .

9

Gregg v. Georgia:
Is the Death Penalty
"Cruel and Unusual Punishment"?

Glenn A. Phelps

E XECUTIONS are not pretty. As recently as the Elizabethan era, people were routinely burned at the stake, drawn and quartered, beheaded (though not always with the first blow), and subjected to various forms of mutilation and torture for "reasons of state." Over the years, societies developed methods for carrying out executions that sought to alleviate some of the inherent cruelty and barbarity of the act. In the United States, hanging and shooting became the preferred methods in the early years of the Republic, methods certainly less barbarous than older ones. Still, hanging depended on some technical skill in tying the noose and was often agonizingly slow. The phrase *dancing at the end of a rope* was a macabre reality more often than one would like to think. Shooting generally dispatched the victim more quickly but only when the firing squad members were accurate.

Twentieth-century methods of execution have proved no less ugly. When Dr. Alfred Southwick, a dentist, suggested using electrical current as a means of execution, New York and, later, many other states adopted it as a more humane and sure method. It *has* proved to be quite effective, although in one rather notorious incident, a subject was electrocuted *twice*. Insufficient current was generated to kill him on the appointed execution day. After appeals that eventually reached the Supreme Court (*Louisiana ex rel Francis v. Resweber,* 329 U.S. 459, 1946), the defendant was again electrocuted, this time successfully.[1]

Despite its effectiveness, many are critical of claims that electrocution is humane. Eyewitness descriptions of electric chair deaths are as lurid as anything to be found in pulp fiction: the victim writhes uncontrollably, often snapping arms or legs in the process, his skin swells and pops, he urinates and defecates involuntarily, on occasion eyeballs come out of their sockets, and steam rises from the body as the superheated flesh quite literally cooks. The electric chair is certainly a modern method of execution, but many believe it is no less cruel than the crucifixions of two thousand years past. Even death by gas chamber and lethal injection (the most recent development in official execution) have detractors.

Grisly as executions may be, the question remains: What has any of this to do with the Constitution and civil liberties? War, to reiterate the oft-quoted phrase, is hell; but it is not unconstitutional. Indeed, the Constitution speaks at some length on the legitimacy of arming for, declaring, and fighting wars. Terrorism and private murder are at least as heinous as government-sponsored executions, yet the Constitution is silent on these matters.

The Eighth Amendment, though, includes a provision that "cruel and unusual punishments" shall not be inflicted. What are "cruel and unusual punishments"? Is the death penalty such a punishment? The words of the Eighth Amendment shed little light on the question. Like numerous other strictures in the Bill of Rights, it expresses a limit beyond which the power of the federal government cannot extend but offers no boundaries to define that limit.

The Eighth Amendment is not, however, totally devoid of meaning. The authors of the clause were part of a philosophic tradition that embraced the concept of natural rights. The existence of such rights was seen as a limitation on the coercive powers of government. An essential element of this natural rights tradition was that human beings are endowed with inherent dignity. No government, therefore, can treat persons *in*humanly. Punishments that treat human beings as mere things or as examples of official displeasure violate these natural rights. Most of the Founding Fathers were well acquainted with the traditions of English common law. The notorious case of William Prynne was part of that tradition. Prynne was an outspoken Puritan whose pious criticisms of the government and clergy constantly irritated the Stuarts. He had stated in one of his tracts that any woman who appeared in a stage play could be presumed to be of bad character. This proved too much for Charles I because his wife, the queen, had acted in several court plays. Prynne was summoned to the Star Chamber and charged with libel. He was convicted and sentenced to stand in the pillory, have both his ears lopped off, pay a fine of five thousand pounds (an astronomical sum at a time when a good wage was ten pounds per year), and then be imprisoned for as long as the king wished. Prynne's treatment enraged many Englishmen and propelled the common law over time to a prohibition on excessive, barbaric, and "inhumane" punishments. The excesses of the infamous Salem witch trials were also known to many of the Founders. It is not surprising, then, that these concerns found their way into the Bill of Rights.

But did this Amendment ban the death penalty as a cruel and unusual punishment? Was it excessive, barbaric, and inhumane in the eyes of the Framers? If the morals and values of those who sponsored the Eighth Amendment were frozen permanently into the Constitution for all succeeding generations, then the answer to both questions would be an unequivocal no. Every state in the new Union had capital punishment on its statute books, and it was imposed without qualm. Several other provisions in the Constitution imply tacit authority for the death penalty. Article I grants Congress the power to establish penalties for violations of federal law. It later denies to Congress the authority to utilize bills of attainder and ex post facto laws, but it does *not* mention capital punishment as a forbidden sanction. Further, the Fifth Amendment recognizes the existence (and apparent propriety) of the death penalty in three places. It states that no one can be held to answer for a *capital* crime except by a presentment of indictment, that no one's *life* may be placed in jeopardy twice, and that no one may be deprived of *life,* liberty, or property without due process of law. In short, to the Founding Fathers the death penalty was neither cruel nor unusual.

Why, then, was the Supreme Court so deeply troubled in *Furman v. Georgia* (408 U.S. 238, 1972) and *Gregg v. Georgia* (428 U.S. 153, 1976) with the question of whether the death penalty was unconstitutional? The answer lies partly in the findings of the *Weems* case (*Weems v. U.S.,* 217 U.S. 349, 1910). Weems had been convicted of falsifying a public document. Under the provisions of Philippine law (he was an officer of the U.S. government there) he was sentenced to fifteen years of *cadena temporal.* This punishment, of Spanish origin, required the prisoner to spend his entire sentence at hard labor bound by heavy chains about his wrists and ankles. All of his civil rights were forfeited during his sentence, and he was subject to perpetual surveillance after his release. The Supreme Court declared that the sentence violated the Eighth Amendment. In doing so, the justices reflected on the meaning of "cruel and unusual punishment." The Framers, according to the Court, were less concerned with a specific, unalterable definition of what was cruel and unusual, but rather wanted to confine punishments within "contemporary standards of decency." Justice Joseph McKenna stated that "the clause . . . may be therefore progressive, and is not fastened to the obsolete but may acquire meaning as public opinion becomes enlightened by a humane justice."

Thus, while capital punishment had a long history of acceptance in the United States, the *Weems* standard suggested that as society's standards of decency evolve, punishments acceptable for one generation might become "cruel and unusual" to another. Indeed, some of the states, as well as many European democracies, abolished the death penalty in the sixty years between *Weems* and *Furman.*

When *Furman* and its companion cases reached the Court in 1972, the justices were faced for the first time with deciding whether the death penalty offended these evolving "standards of decency" and was therefore unconstitutional. At oral argument it became clear that lawyers for the accused men were going to make a full-scale frontal assault on capital punishment. Anthony Amsterdam, an impassioned and articulate abolitionist professor of law, led the attack and offered three central propositions in support of his position. First, the death penalty was cruel and unusual because it was capricious and arbitrary. Who lived and who died, among those convicted of capital crimes, was based on a kind of blind draw. Similar crimes were not treated similarly. Death under these circumstances was "cruel" *because* it was "unusual." Moreover, this capriciousness, Amsterdam contended, allowed the sentencing process to reflect the prejudices of society. He demonstrated that certain defendants (blacks, the poor, and other minorities) were far more likely to receive a death penalty than other defendants (whites and the wealthy) for similar offenses. Thus, the penalty was "cruel and unusual" because it was an extreme form of racial discrimination. Second, Amsterdam argued that a major rationale for the death penalty—that it served as a deterrent against the commission of future serious crimes—was faulty. Social scientists and criminologists had not demonstrated any linkage between the death penalty and deterrence. The death penalty, he continued, was "cruel" because it killed people for no good reason. Finally, he asserted that "evolving standards of decency" made the penalty increasingly unacceptable to society as a whole. Eleven states banned it, and public opinion polls in the 1960s indicated rising opposition to the penalty.

Beyond these constitutional arguments, the Justices were confronted with an excruciating moral dilemma. A tactic of the abolitionists in their campaign to banish capital punishment was to appeal every death sentence, ask for stays of execution again and again, and raise whatever procedural objections might be useful to delay the implementation of the sentences. The Legal Defense Fund, an arm of the National Association for the Advancement of Colored People, had adopted this strategy because of its view that the death penalty was, in practice, the most extreme form of racial discrimination extant. State courts and executives went along with this strategy of delay in the belief that the Supreme Court would soon have to confront the death penalty and resolve, once and for all, the question of its constitutionality.

These tactics were so successful that by 1972 no execution had occurred since 1965. Over six hundred persons were awaiting execution as *Furman* was heard. Several Justices expressed much distress over the possibility that a decision in favor of the death penalty would unleash a wave of pent-up execution orders. Fears of a legalized bloodbath loomed ominously.[2]

The *Furman* decision resulted in nine separate opinions, over 50,000 words, and 243 pages—one of the longest in the Court's history and a reflection of its collective anguish. Four Justices (Burger, Harry Blackmun, Lewis Powell, and Rehnquist) concluded that the Eighth Amendment did not forbid the death penalty; at most, it merely required that the punishment not be barbarously or inhumanely inflicted. The five Justices who agreed to overturn these death sentences, however, offered a curious and diverse mixture of reasons. Brennan and Marshall were the only Justices to declare that the death penalty was "cruel and unusual" per se—that a contemporary reading of the Eighth Amendment forbade capital punishment under *any* circumstances. The remaining three Justices agreed only that the death penalty was unconstitutional "in these cases." Douglas was offended by the evidence of racial discrimination in death sentences. Stewart argued that the randomness of the sentences made them "cruel and unusual." White took the curious line that because the death penalty was so infrequently imposed, it had lost its deterrent value and was therefore ineffective. White, however, expressed the sentiments of all three swing Justices when he pointed out, "I do not at all intimate that the death penalty is unconstitutional per se or that there is no system of capital punishment that would comport with the Eighth Amendment."

White's remarks implied that if death penalty statutes and procedures were made fairer, less discriminatory, or less capricious, they might pass constitutional muster. In the four years between *Furman* and *Gregg*, thirty-five state legislatures rewrote their death penalty statutes with those concerns in mind.[3] It was now clear, as it had not been in *Furman*, that "contemporary standards of decency," as manifested by popularly elected legislatures, were not offended by capital punishment.

These new death penalty statutes responded to the *Furman* decision in two categorically different ways. Fifteen states addressed the concerns of Stewart and Douglas about capriciousness and randomness by establishing specific standards and criteria for juries to use when considering the death penalty. Twenty states, in response to White's criticisms about the penalty's infrequent application, passed laws making capital punishment *mandatory* for certain categories of crime.[4] The legislatures had gotten the message.

Gregg, and its companion cases, compelled the Court to assess these new statutes in the light of both the Eighth Amendment and their individual opinions in *Furman*. Not surprisingly, the three swing votes in *Furman* (Stewart, White, and John Paul Stevens, who had replaced Douglas) now voted to support those death penalty statutes that established rigorous criteria intended to avert discrimination and arbitrariness. They voted with the two abolitionist dissenters, Marshall and Brennan, to overturn the "automatic death penalty" statutes, but the overall result was unambiguous. The death penalty was not unconstitutional.

The debate has not ended, although the moratorium on executions has. Cases continue to arise involving whether the death penalty may be imposed for certain offenses (rape or kidnapping) where murder is not committed or according to certain procedures (bifurcated or nonbifurcated trials) or with certain specific safeguards. This debate is continued in the essays that follow. The late Abe Fortas, noted lawyer (he "won" the famous *Gideon* case) and Associate Justice of the Supreme Court, sets forth many of the key arguments of the abolitionist position. Conservative social philosopher Ernest van den Haag offers a pointed rejoinder in defense of capital punishment.

Yes: The Case against Capital Punishment

Abe Fortas

I BELIEVE that most Americans, even those who feel it is necessary, are repelled by capital punishment; the attitude is deeply rooted in our moral reverence for life, the Judeo-Christian belief that man is created in the image of God. Many Americans were pleased when on June 29, 1972, the Supreme Court of the United States set aside death sentences for the first time in its history. On that day the Court handed down its decision in *Furman v. Georgia,* holding that the capital-punishment statutes of three states were unconstitutional because they gave the jury complete discretion to decide whether to impose the death penalty or a lesser punishment in capital cases. For this reason, a bare majority of five justices agreed that the statutes violated the "cruel and unusual punishment" clause of the Eighth Amendment.

The result of this decision was paradoxical. Thirty-six states proceeded to adopt new death-penalty statutes designed to need the Supreme Court's objection, and beginning in 1974, the number of persons sentenced to death soared. In 1975 alone, 285 defendants were condemned—more than double the number sentenced to death in any previously reported year. Of those condemned in 1975, 93 percent had been convicted of murder; the balance had been convicted of rape or kidnapping.

The constitutionality of these death sentences and of the new statutes, however, was quickly challenged, and on July 2, 1976, the Supreme Court announced its rulings in five test cases. It rejected "mandatory" statutes that automatically imposed death sentences for defined capital offenses, but it approved statutes that set out "standards" to guide the jury in deciding whether to impose the death penalty. These laws, the court ruled, struck a reasonable balance between giving the jury some guidance and allowing it to

Abe Fortas, from "The Case against Capital Punishment," *New York Times Magazine* (January 23, 1977), pp. 84, 92–93. Copyright 1977 by The New York Times Company. Reprinted by permission.

take into account the background and character of the defendant and the circumstances of the crime.

The decisions may settle the basic constitutional issue until there is a change in the composition of the Court, but many questions remain. Some of these are questions of considerable constitutional importance, such as those relating to appellate review. Others have to do with the sensational issues that accompany capital punishment in our society. Gary Gilmore generated an enormous national debate by insisting on an inalienable right to force the people of Utah to kill him. So did a district judge who ruled that television may present to the American people the spectacle of a man being electrocuted by the state of Texas.

The recent turns of the legislative and judicial process have done nothing to dispose of the matter of conscience and judgment for the individual citizen. The debate over it will not go away; indeed, it has gone on for centuries.

Through the years, the number of offenses for which the state can kill the offender has declined. Once, hundreds of capital crimes, including stealing more than a shilling from a person and such religious misdeeds as blasphemy and witchcraft, were punishable by death. But in the United States today, only two principal categories remain—major assaults upon persons, such as murder, kidnapping, rape, bombing and arson, and the major political crimes of espionage and treason. In addition, there are more than 20 special capital crimes in some of our jurisdictions, including train robbery and aircraft piracy. In fact, however, in recent years murder has accounted for about 90 percent of the death sentences and rape for most of the others, and the number of states prescribing the death penalty for rape is declining. . . .

Practically all scholars and experts agree that capital punishment cannot be justified as a significantly useful instrument of law enforcement or of penology. There is no evidence that it reduces the serious crimes to which it is addressed. Professor William Bowers, for example, concludes in his excellent study, "Executions in America", that statutory or judicial developments that change the risk of execution are not paralleled by variations in homicide rates. He points out that over the last 30 years, homicide rates have remained relatively constant while the number of executions has steadily declined. He concludes that the "death penalty, as we use it, exerts no influence on the extent or rate of capital offenses."

I doubt that fear of the possible penalty affects potential capital offenders. The vast majority of capital offenses are murders committed in the course of armed robbery that result from fear, tension or anger of the moment, and murders that are the result of passion or mental disorder. The only deterrence derived from the criminal process probably results from the fear of apprehension and arrest, and possibly from the fear of significant punishment. There is little, if any, difference between the possible deterrent effect of life imprisonment and that of the death penalty.

In fact, the statistical possibility of execution for a capital offense is extremely slight. We have not exceeded 100 executions a year since 1951, although the number of homicides in death-sentence jurisdictions alone has ranged from 7,500 to 10,000. . . . A potential murderer who rationally weighed the possibility of punishment by death (if there is such a person), would figure that he has considerably better than a 98 percent chance of avoiding execution in the average capital-punishment state. In the years from 1960 to 1967, his chances of escaping execution were better than 99.5 percent. The professional or calculating murderer is not apt to be deterred by such odds.

An examination of the reason for the infrequency of execution is illuminating:

(1) Juries are reluctant to condemn a human being to death. The evidence is that they are often prone to bring in a verdict of a lesser offense, or even to acquit, if the alternative is to impose the death penalty. The reluctance is, of course, diminished when powerful emotions come into play—as in the case of a black defendant charged with the rape of a white woman.

(2) Prosecutors do not ask for the death penalty in the case of many, perhaps a majority, of those who are arrested for participation in murder or other capital offenses. In part, this is due to the difficulty of persuading juries to impose death sentences; in part, it is due to plea bargaining. In capital cases involving more than one participant, the prosecutor seldom asks for the death penalty for more than one of them. Frequently, in order to obtain the powerful evidence necessary to win a death sentence, he will make a deal with all participants except one. The defendants who successfully "plea bargain" testify against the defendant chosen for the gallows and in return receive sentences of imprisonment.

This system may be defensible in noncapital cases because of practical exigencies, but it is exceedingly disturbing where the result is to save the witness's life at the hazard of the life of another person. The possibility is obvious that the defendant chosen for death will be selected on a basis that has nothing to do with comparative guilt, and the danger is inescapable that the beneficiary of the plea-bargain, in order to save his life, will lie or give distorted testimony. To borrow a phrase from Justice Byron R. White, "This is a grisly trade. . ." A civilized nation should not kill A on the testimony obtained from B in exchange for B's life.

(3) As a result of our doubts about capital punishment, and our basic aversion to it, we have provided many escape hatches. Every latitude is allowed the defendant and his counsel in the trial; most lawyers representing a capital offender quite properly feel that they must exhaust every possible defense, however technical or unlikely; appeals are generally a matter of right; slight legal errors, which would be disregarded in other types of cases, are grounds for reversal; governors have, and liberally exercise, the power to

commute death sentences. Only the rare, unlucky defendant is likely to be executed when the process is all over. . . .

It is clear that American prosecutors, judges and juries are not likely to cause the execution of enough capital offenders to increase the claimed deterrent effect of capital-punishment laws or to reduce the "lottery" effect of freakish selection. People generally may favor capital punishment in the abstract, but pronouncing that a living person shall be killed is quite another matter. Experience shows that juries are reluctant to order that a person be killed. Where juries have been commanded by law to impose the death penalty, they have often chosen to acquit or, in modern times, to convict of a lesser offense rather than to return a verdict that would result in execution.

The law is a human instrument administered by a vast number of different people in different circumstances, and we are inured to its many inequalities. Tweedledee may be imprisoned for five years for a given offense, while Tweedledum, convicted of a similar crime, may be back on the streets in a few months. We accept the inevitability of such discriminations, although we don't approve of them, and we constantly seek to reduce their frequency and severity. But the taking of a life is different from any other punishment. It is final; it is ultimate; if it is erroneous, it is irreversible and beyond correction. It is an act in which the state is presuming to function, so to speak, as the Lord's surrogate.

We have gone a long way toward recognition of the unique character of capital punishment. We insist that it be imposed for relatively few crimes of the most serious nature and that it be imposed only after elaborate precautions to reduce the possibility of error. We also inflict it in a fashion that avoids the extreme cruelty of such methods as drawing and quartering, though it still involves the barbaric rituals attended upon electrocution, the gallows or the firing squad.

But fortunately, the death penalty is and will continue to be sought in only a handful of cases and rarely carried out. So long as the death penalty is highly exceptional punishment, it will serve no deterrent or penological function; it will fulfill no pragmatic purpose of the state and inevitably, its selective imposition will continue to be influenced by racial and class prejudice.

All of the standards that can be written, all of the word magic and the procedural safeguards that can be devised to compel juries to impose the death penalty on capital offenders without exception or discrimination will be of no avail. In a 1971 capital-punishment case, Justice John Harlan wrote on the subject of standards. "They do no more," he said, "than suggest some subjects for the jury to consider during its deliberations, and [the criteria] bear witness to the intractable nature of the problem of 'standards' which the history of capital punishment has from the beginning reflected."

Form and substance are important to the life of the law but when the law deals with a fundamental moral and constitutional issue—the disposition of human life—the use of such formulas is not an acceptable substitute for correct decision on the substance of the matter.

The discrimination that is inescapable in the selection of the few to be killed under our capital-punishment laws is unfortunately of the most invidious and unacceptable sort. Most of those who are chosen for extinction are black (53.5 percent in the years 1930 to 1975). The wheels of chance and prejudice begin to spin in the police station; they continue through the prosecutor's choice of defendants for whom he will ask the death penalty and those he will choose to spare; they continue through the trial and in the jury room, and finally they appear in the Governor's office. Solemn "presumptions of law" that the selection will be made rationally and uniformally violate human experience and the evidence of the facts. Efforts to bring about equality of sentence by writing "standards" or verbal formulas may comfort the heart of the legislator or jurist, but they can hardly satisfy his intelligence.

If deterrence is not a sufficient reason to justify capital-punishment laws and if their selective application raises such disturbing questions, what possible reason is there for their retention? One other substantive reason, advanced by eminent authorities, is that the execution of criminals is justifiable as "retribution." This is the argument that society should have the right to vent its anger or abhorrence against the offender, that it may justifiably impose a punishment people believe the criminal "deserves." Albert Camus, in a famous essay, says of capital punishment: "Let us call it by the name which, for lack of any other nobility, will at least give the nobility the truth, and let us recognize it for what it is essentially: a revenge."

We may realize that deep-seated emotions underlie our capital-punishment laws, but there is a difference between our understanding of the motivation for capital punishment and our acceptance of it as an instrument of our society. We may appreciate that the *lex talionis,* the law of revenge, has its roots in the deep recesses of the human spirit, but that awareness is not a permissible reason for retaining capital punishment.

It is also argued that capital punishment is an ancient sanction that has been adopted by most of our legislatures after prolonged consideration and reconsideration, and that we should not override this history.

But the argument is not persuasive. If we were to restrict the implementation of our Bill of Rights, by either constitutional decisions or legislative judgments, to those practices that its provisions contemplated in 1791, we would indeed be a retarded society. In 1816, Thomas Jefferson wrote a letter in which he spoke of the need for constitutions as well as other laws and institutions to move forward "hand in hand with the progress of human mind." He said, "We might as well require a man to wear still the coat which fitted him when a boy, as civilized society to remain under the regimen of their barbarous ancestors."

As early as 1910, the Supreme Court, in the case of *Weems v. United States,* applied this principle to a case in which the defendant had been sentenced to 15 years in prison for the crime of falsifying a public document as part of an embezzlement scheme. The Court held that the sentence was excessive and constituted "cruel and unusual punishment" in violation of the Eighth Amendment. In a remarkable opinion, Justice Joseph McKenna eloquently rejected the idea that prohibitions of the Bill of Rights, including the Eighth Amendment, must be limited to the practices to which they were addressed in 1791, when the great Amendments were ratified. He said, "Time works changes, brings into existence new conditions and purposes. Therefore a principle, to be vital, must be capable of wider application than the mischief which gave it birth. This is peculiarly true of constitutions. They are not ephemeral enactments, designed to meet passing occasions." As to the "cruel and unusual punishment" clause of the Constitution, he said that it "is not fastened to the obsolete, but may acquire meaning as public opinion becomes enlightened by a humane justice. . . ."

We will not eliminate the objections to capital punishment by legal legerdemain, by "standards," by procedures or by word formulas. The issue is fundamental. It is wrong for the state to kill offenders; it is a wrong far exceeding the numbers involved. In exchange for the pointless exercise of killing a few people each year, we expose our society to brutalization; we lower the essential value that is the basis of our civilization: a pervasive, unqualified respect for life. And we subject ourselves and our legal institutions to the gross spectacle of a pageant in which death provides degrading, distorting excitement. Justice Felix Frankfurter once pointed out: "I am strongly against capital punishment. . . . When life is at hazard in a trial, it sensationalizes the whole thing almost unwittingly; the effect on juries, the bar, the public, the judiciary, I regard as very bad. I think scientifically the claim of deterrence is not worth much. Whatever proof there may be in my judgment does not outweigh the social loss due to the inherent sensationalism of a trial for life."

Beyond all of these factors is the fundamental consideration: In the name of all that we believe in and hope for, why must we reserve to ourselves the right to kill 100 or 200 people? Why, when we can point to no tangible benefit; why, when in all honesty we must admit that we are not certain that we are accomplishing anything except serving the cause of "revenge" or retribution? Why, when we have bravely and nobly progressed so far in the recent past to create a decent, humane society, must we perpetuate the senseless barbarism of official murder?

In 1971, speaking of the death penalty, Justice William O. Douglas wrote: "We need not read procedural due process as designed to satisfy man's deep-seated sadistic instincts. We need not in deference to those sadistic instincts say we are bound by history from defining procedural due process so as to deny men fair trials."

I hope and believe we will conclude that the time has come for us to join the company of those nations that have repudiated killing as an instrument of criminal law enforcement.

No: In Defense
of the Death Penalty:
A Legal-Practical-Moral Analysis

Ernest van den Haag

T HE Fifth Amendment states that no one shall be "deprived of life, liberty, or property without due process of law," thus implying that in compliance with "due process of law" we may deprive persons of life. The Eighth Amendment prohibits "cruel and unusual punishment." It is unlikely that the Eighth Amendment was meant to supersede the Fifth Amendment, since the amendments were simultaneously enacted in 1791. In any event, the Fourteenth Amendment, enacted in 1868, reasserted and explicitly extended to the states the implied authority to "deprive of life, liberty or property" by "due process of law." Thus, to regard the death penalty as unconstitutional one must believe that the standards that determine what is "cruel and unusual" have so evolved since 1868 as to prohibit now what was authorized then. What might these standards be? And what shape must their evolution take to be constitutionally decisive?

(1) *Consensus.* A moral consensus, intellectual or popular, could have evolved to find execution "cruel and unusual," but it did not. Intellectual opinion is divided. Polls suggest that today most people would vote for the death penalty for skyjacking under certain conditions. The representative assemblies of two-thirds of the states have reenacted capital punishment when previous laws were found constitutionally defective.

If, however, there were a consensus against the death penalty, the Constitution expects the political process to reflect it rather than judicial decisions. Courts are meant to interpret the laws made by the political process and to set constitutional limits to it—not to replace it by responding to a pre-

Ernest van den Haag, from "In Defense of the Death Penalty: A Legal-Practical-Moral Analysis," 14 *Criminal Law Bulletin* (1978), pp. 51–61. Reprinted by permission from the Criminal Law Bulletin, January–February 1978, Copyright 1978, Warren, Gorham & Lamont, Inc., 210 South Street, Boston, Massachusetts. All rights reserved.

sumed moral consensus. Surely the "cruel and unusual" phrase was not meant to authorize the courts to become legislatures. Thus, neither a consensus of moral opinion, nor a "moral discovery" by judges is to be disguised as a constitutional interpretation. Even when revealed by a burning bush, new moral norms were not meant to become constitutional norms by means of court decisions. To be sure, the courts in the past have occasionally done away with obsolete kinds of punishment—but never in the face of legislative and popular oppositions and reenactment. Abolitionists now press the courts to create rather than to confirm obsolescence. That courts are urged to do what so clearly is for voters and lawmakers to decide suggests that the absence of consensus for abolition is recognized by the opponents of capital punishment.

What then can the phrase "cruel and unusual punishment" mean today?

(2) *"Cruel"* may be understood to mean excessive, punitive without, or beyond, a rational-utilitarian purpose. Since capital punishment excludes rehabilitation and is not needed for incapacitation, the remaining rational-utilitarian purpose would be deterrence, the reduction of the rate at which the crime punished is committed by others. I shall consider this reduction further on. Here, I wish to note that if the criterion for the constitutionality of any punishment were an actual demonstration of its rational-utilitarian effectiveness, all legal punishments would be in as much constitutional jeopardy as the death penalty. Are fines for corporations deterrent? Rehabilitative? Incapacitative? Is a jail term for possession of marijuana? Has it ever been established beyond doubt that ten years in prison are doubly as deterrent as five, or at least sufficiently more deterrent?

The constitution certainly does not require a *demonstration* of rational-utilitarian effects for any punishment. Such a demonstration so far has not been available. To demand it for one penalty—however grave—and not for others, when it is known that no such demonstration is available, seems constitutionally unjustified. Penalties always have been regarded as constitutional if they can be plausibly intended (rather than demonstrated) to be effective (useful), and if they are not grossly excessive (i.e., unjust).

Justice, a rational but nonutilitarian purpose of punishment, requires that a sanction be proportioned to the gravity of the crime. Thus, constitutional justice authorizes, even calls for, penalties commensurate with the gravity of the crime. One cannot demand that this constitutionally required escalation stop short of the death penalty unless one furnishes positive proof of its injustice (i.e., disproportionality to the gravity of the crime punished and to other punishments), as well as ineffectiveness (i.e., uselessness in reducing the crime rate). If this be thought of as cruelty, then no proof exists of either aspect.

(3) *"Unusual"* is generally interpreted to mean either randomly capricious and therefore unconstitutional, or capricious in a biased, discrimina-

tory way so as to particularly burden specifiable groups. Random arbitrariness might violate the Eighth Amendment, while biased arbitrariness would violate the Fourteenth Amendment equal protection clause.

For the sake of argument, let me grant that either or both forms of capriciousness prevail, and that they are less tolerable with respect to the death penalty than with respect to milder penalties—which certainly are not meted out less capriciously. However prevalent, neither form of capriciousness would argue for abolishing the death penalty. Capriciousness is not inherent in that penalty, or in any penalty, but occurs in its distribution. Therefore, the remedy lies in changing the laws and procedures that distribute the penalty.

(4) *Unavoidable capriciousness.* If capricious distribution places some convicts, or groups of convicts, at an unwarranted disadvantage, can it be remedied sufficiently to satisfy the Eighth and Fourteenth Amendments? Some capriciousness is unavoidable. Decisions of the criminal justice system often rest on such accidental factors as the presence or absence of witnesses to an act, or the cleverness or clumsiness of police officers. All court decisions must rest on the available and admissible evidence for, rather than the actuality of, guilt. Availability of evidence is necessarily accidental to the actuality of whatever it is that the evidence is offered to demonstrate.

If possible, without loss of other desiderata, accident and capriciousness should be minimized. But discretionary judgments obviously cannot be avoided altogether. The Framers of the Constitution certainly were aware of the unavoidable elements of discretion which affect all human decisions, including those of police officers, of prosecutors, and of the courts. Because it always was unavoidable, discretion no more speaks against the constitutionality of the criminal justice system or of any of its penalties now than it did when the Constitution was written—unless something has evolved since, to make unavoidable discretion, tolerable before, intolerable now—at least for the death penalty. I know of no such evolution; and if it has occurred I would think it up to the legislative branch of government to register it.

The Constitution, although it enjoins us to minimize capriciousness, does not enjoin a standard of unattainable perfection or exclude penalties because that standard has not been attained. Although we should not enlarge discretion *praeter necessitatem,* some discretion is unavoidable and even desirable, and certainly is no reason for giving up any form of punishment.

(5) *Avoidable capriciousness.* Capriciousness should be prevented by abolishing penalties capriciously distributed only when it is so unavoidable and excessive that penalties are randomly distributed between the guilty and the innocent. When that is not the case, the abuses of discretion which lead to discrimination against particular groups of defendants or convicts certainly require correction, but not abolition of the penalty abused.

Regardless of constitutional interpretation, the morality and legitimacy of the abolitionist argument regarding capriciousness, discretion, or discrimination, would be more persuasive if it were alleged that those selectively executed are not guilty. But the argument merely maintains that some guilty, but favored, persons or groups escape the death penalty. This is hardly sufficient for letting others escape it. On the contrary, that some guilty persons or groups elude it argues for *extending* the death penalty to them.

Justice requires punishing the guilty—as many of the guilty as possible—even if only some can be punished, and sparing the innocent—as many of the innocent as possible, even if not all are spared. Morally, justice must always be preferred to equality. It would surely be wrong to treat everybody with equal injustice in preference to meting out justice to some. Justice cannot ever permit sparing some guilty persons, or punishing some innocent ones, for the sake of equality—because others have been unjustly spared or punished. In practice, penalties never could be applied if we insisted that they cannot be inflicted on any guilty persons unless we are able to make sure that they are equally applied to all other guilty persons. Anyone familiar with law enforcement knows that punishments can be inflicted only on an unavoidably capricious selection of the guilty.

Although it does not warrant serious discussion, the argument from capriciousness looms large in briefs and decisions. For the last seventy years, courts have tried—lamentably and unproductively—to prevent errors of procedure, or of evidence collection, or of decision-making, by the paradoxical method of letting defendants go free as a punishment, or warning, to errant law enforcers. Yet the strategy admittedly never has prevented the errors it was designed to prevent—although it has released countless guilty persons. There is no more merit in the attempt to persuade the courts to let all capital crime defendants go free of capital punishment because some have wrongly escaped it, than in attempting to persuade the courts to let all burglars go, because some have wrongly escaped detection or imprisonment.

Is the death penalty morally just and/or useful? This is the essential moral, as distinguished from the constitutional, question. Discrimination is irrelevant to this moral question. If the death penalty were distributed equally and uncapriciously and with superhuman perfection to all the guilty, but were morally unjust, it would be unjust in each case. Contrariwise, if the death penalty is morally just, however discriminatorily applied to only some of the guilty, it remains just in each case in which it is applied.

The utilitarian (political) effects of unequal justice may well be detrimental to the social fabric because they outrage our passion for equality before the law. Unequal justice also is morally repellent. Nonetheless unequal justice is still justice. The guilty do not become innocent or less deserving of punishment because others escaped it. Nor does any innocent deserve punishment because others suffer it. Justice remains just, however unequal, while injustice remains unjust, however equal. While both are desired, justice and equality are not identical. Equality before the law should be extended and enforced—but not at the expense of justice. . . .

The execution of innocents believed guilty is a miscarriage of justice that must be opposed whenever detected. But such miscarriages of justice do not warrant abolition of the death penalty. Unless the moral drawbacks of an activity or practice, which include the possible death of innocent bystanders, outweigh the moral advantages, which include the innocent lives that might be saved by it, the activity is warranted. Most human activities—medicine, manufacturing, automobile and air traffic, sports, not to speak of wars and revolutions—cause the death of innocent bystanders. Nevertheless, if the advantages sufficiently outweigh the disadvantages, human activities, including those of the penal system with all its punishments, are morally justified.

Is there evidence supporting the usefulness of the death penalty in securing the life of citizens? Researchers in the past found no statistical evidence for the effects sought, marginal deterrent effects, or deterrent effects over and above those of alternative sanctions. However, in the last few years new and more sophisticated studies have led Professor Isaac Ehrlich to conclude that over the period 1933–1969, "an additional execution per year . . . may have resulted (on the average) in 7 to 8 fewer murders." Other investigators have confirmed Ehrlich's tentative results. Not surprisingly, refutations have been attempted, and Professor Ehrlich has offered his rebuttals. The matter will remain controversial for some time. However, two tentative conclusions can be drawn with some confidence. First, Ehrlich has shown that previous investigations, that did not find deterrent effects of the death penalty, suffered from fatal defects. Second, there is now some likelihood—much more than hitherto—of statistically demonstrable marginal deterrent effects.

Thus, with respect to deterrence, we must now choose:

(1) To trade the certain shortening of the life of a convicted murderer against the survival of between seven and eight innocent victims whose future murder by others becomes more probable, unless the convicted murderer is executed;

(2) To trade the certain survival of the convicted murderer against the loss of the lives of between seven and eight innocent victims, who are more likely to be murdered by others if the convicted murderer is allowed to survive.

Prudence as well as morality command us to choose the first alternative.

If executions had a zero marginal effect, they could not be justified in deterrent terms. But even the pre-Ehrlich investigations did not demonstrate this. They merely found that an above-zero effect could not be demonstrated statistically. While we do not know at present the degree of confidence with which we can assign an above marginal deterrent effect to executions, we can be more confident than in the past. I should now regard it as irresponsible not to shorten the lives of convicted murderers simply because we cannot be altogether sure that their execution will lengthen the lives of innocent victims: It seems immoral to let convicted murderers survive at the probable—or even at the merely possible—expense of the lives of innocent victims who might have been spared had the murderers been executed. . . .

As an additional common sense observation, I should add that without the death penalty, we necessarily confer immunity on just those persons most likely to be in need of deterrent threats. Thus, prisoners serving life sentences can kill fellow prisoners or guards with impunity. Prison wardens are unlikely to prevent violence in prisons as long as they give humane treatment to inmates and have no threats of additional punishment available for the murderers among them who are already serving life sentences. I cannot see the moral or utilitarian reasons for giving permanent immunity to homicidal life prisoners, thereby endangering the other prisoners and the guards, and in effect preferring the life prisoners to their victims.

Outside the prison context, an offender who expects a life sentence for his offense may murder his victim, or witnesses, or the arresting officer, to improve his chances of escaping. He could not be threatened with an additional penalty for his additional crime—an open invitation. Only the death penalty could deter in such cases. If there is but a possibility—and I believe there is a probability—that it will, we should retain it.

However, deterrence requires that the threat of the ultimate penalty be reserved for the ultimate crime. It may be prevented by that threat. Hence, the extreme punishment should never be prescribed when the offender, because already threatened by it, might add to his crimes with impunity. Thus, rape, or kidnapping, should not incur the death penalty, while killing the victim of either crime should. This may not stop an Eichmann after his first murder, but it will stop most people before. The range of punishments is not infinite; it is necessarily more restricted than the range of crimes. Since death is the ultimate penalty, it must be reserved for the ultimate crime.

10
Regents of the University of California v. Bakke: Does Affirmative Action Mean Reverse Discrimination?

Glenn A. Phelps

A LLAN Bakke was not, at first glance, the sort of person whom one would suspect as likely to make a federal case out of anything. To most he seemed quiet, even shy. To say that Bakke was just an average guy would be a misstatement, however; he was in many ways exceptional. But nothing in his background indicated that he would instigate one of the most talked-about civil rights cases of the 1970s.

Those who knew Allan Bakke well were aware that he had a goal that bordered on obsession: he wanted to be a doctor. This realization had come to Bakke later in life than most. He had graduated from the University of Minnesota in 1962 with a degree in engineering. To fulfill his ROTC obligation he then served four years as an officer in the U.S. Marine Corps with a tour of duty in Vietnam. After his military service, he resumed his engineering career at the National Aeronautics and Space Administration (NASA), in the meantime obtaining a master's degree in engineering from Stanford University.

Vietnam changed many people in many ways. For Allan Bakke it was where he first realized he wanted to be a doctor. His association with medics and doctors there convinced him that he could serve his community more appropriately as a physician than as an engineer. That desire became an almost single-minded obsession on his return. He often worked early morning hours and evenings at NASA so that he would have time to commute to school, where he took the biology and chemistry courses needed as prerequisites for medical school. He also began working as a volunteer at the local hospital as an emergency room assistant. Those who know him there were struck by his dedication.

Among the medical schools to which he applied was the University of California at Davis (UCDMS). Ironically, at this point Bakke's greatest concern was about his age. He was thirty-two years old when he first applied to UCDMS, an age that many schools classified as too old for consideration due to the number of years that medical training requires. (Subsequent civil rights legislation now prohibits age discrimination.) Otherwise his credentials were impressive: a 3.5 grade point average combined with Medical College Admissions Test scores that were near the ninety-fifth percentile on three of the four tests. The admissions standards at Cal-Davis, though, were highly competitive for candidates seeking regular admissions. In 1973 2,173 applicants were vying for only 84 seats (an acceptance rate of one in twenty-six). Bakke's record, however, was sufficiently impressive to advance him to the interview stage, after which the five evaluators gave him a cumulative score of 468 (out of a possible 500). The benchmark score for advancing further in the admissions process was 470, so he was denied admission. In another curious turn to the story, had Bakke's application been received several months earlier, the record suggests that his score would have been sufficiently high for admission under the early consideration process, and *Regents v. Bakke* (438 U.S. 265, 1978) would have never occurred.

Bakke applied to UCDMS again in 1974, this time early enough to be considered in the rolling admissions process that he had missed the year before. Although there were 3,109 applicants (almost 50 percent more than in 1973), he again reached the interview process. This time six evaluators assigned him a score of 549 out of 600, marginally lower than in 1973, and he was rejected for a second time.

Bakke had discovered, however, that Cal-Davis had two admissions review processes: one for regular applicants, like himself, and one for special applicants. The special admissions process was intended to review carefully applicants who might in some way be considered "disadvantaged." On the surface, there was nothing to prevent a white male from being reviewed by this special process, perhaps because of poverty, physical handicaps, age, or some other factor that would make him *personally* "disadvantaged." In practice, though, the only persons offered admission to UCDMS by the special review process were racial minorities. Of the sixty-three special admittees between 1971 and 1974, thirty were Hispanic, twenty-one were black, and twelve were Asian. The grade averages and MCAT scores for these special admittees were considerably lower than Bakke's.

Allan Bakke now found himself the odd man out in a conflict between two principles, each with an authentic civil liberties pedigree and each using the Equal Protection Clause of the Fourteenth Amendment for its justification. The antidiscrimination principle sees the Equal Protection Clause as asserting that race must not be a consideration when making public policy. U.S. history has been so fraught with infamies resulting from discrimination based on race that that road ought to be singularly avoided. Accordingly persons ought to be judged by their individual talents, character, and abilities rather than by irrelevancies like race.[1]

The second principle, "affirmative action," also anchors itself in the

Fourteenth Amendment. In assessing the history of that Amendment, supporters of "affirmative action" note that the purpose of the Equal Protection Clause was to guarantee that the civil rights of blacks as a group were protected and promoted. To be satisfied with an end only to *de jure* discrimination would leave historically disadvantaged blacks to compete with historically advantaged whites, a competition many observers analogized to a foot race in which some runners are shackled at the beginning and then released to compete on an "equal" basis with those far down the track.[2] Thus, government would be justified in seeking to remedy for past discriminations by encouraging "affirmative action" through various means including quotas, targets, and set-asides.

Cal-Davis chose to adhere to the "affirmative action" principle in its admissions policy by setting aside sixteen of the one hundred places in each medical school class for "disadvantaged" applicants. The university was concerned especially about the underrepresentation of blacks and other minorities in the medical professions. Who, they wondered, would serve the needs of those, often poor, minority communities? Allan Bakke, on the other hand, saw himself as a victim of "reverse discrimination." He believed he would have received one of the sixteen set-aside places had they been open to all candidates regardless of race. (In truth, his assertion was probably true only for 1973. His 1974 benchmark score was probably not within the highest one hundred applicants.)

The Court's resolution of the antidiscrimination versus "affirmative action" conflict raised by *Bakke* was eagerly anticipated because of the disappointing results of an earlier "reverse discrimination" case, *DeFunis v. Odegaard* (416 U.S. 312, 1974). Marco DeFunis was a white Jewish male who had applied for admission to the University of Washington Law School (UWLS). He, too, complained that he was a victim of "reverse discrimination": that thirty applicants from designated minorities were admitted despite having PFYA (predicted first-year average) scores significantly lower than his. Despite enormous public interest, however, the Supreme Court declined the opportunity to make a definitive ruling. The original trial court had ordered UWLS to admit DeFunis in 1971 as a temporary measure until the issue could be resolved; he was now about to graduate. Thus, the Court determined that the issue, at least in DeFunis's case, was moot.

No such opportunity for nondecision existed in *Bakke,* though. The result was one of the most curious decisions in the Supreme Court's history. Instead of a clear majority for one party or other, the Court offered a bizarre one-person plurality. Justice Powell wrote the opinion for the Court, but to do so he was compelled to negotiate an unusual 4-1-4 coalition between two diametrically opposed blocs.

One group of four justices (Brennan, White, Marshall, and Blackmun) accepted the "affirmative action" principle as decisive. While recognizing that discriminations based on race were "suspect" and merited "strict scrutiny," they noted that the Equal Protection Clause did not demand that racial classifications could *never* be constitutional. Rather, it was imperative that such classifications be both benign *and* essential for some legitimate state purpose. The "affirmative action four" were impressed with Cal-Davis's claims regarding the shortage of black and minority doctors and agreed that rectifying this situation, a result of past discrimination, was a legitimate state purpose. In addition, they asserted that the special admissions program was benign rather than invidious:

> Unlike discrimination against racial minorities, the use of racial preferences for remedial purposes does not inflict a pervasive injury upon individual whites in the sense that wherever they go or whatever they do there is a significant likelihood that they will be treated as second-class citizens because of their color.

Justice Marshall stated his support for "affirmative action" even more passionately:

> It must be remembered that, during most of the past 200 years, the Constitution as interpreted by this Court did not prohibit the most ingenious and pervasive forms of discrimination against the Negro. Now, when a State acts to remedy the effects of that legacy of discrimination, I cannot believe that this same Constitution stands as a barrier.

The "anti-discrimination four" (Justices Burger, Stewart, Stevens, and Rehnquist), on the other hand, argued that race could not be used to discriminate against *anyone* in the allocation of public benefits. Moreover, they noted that the specific language of the Civil Rights Act of 1964 went beyond the Equal Protection Clause. Title VI of this act states that "race cannot be the basis of excluding anyone from participation in a federally funded program." To this bloc, Bakke was clearly excluded from consideration solely because of his race.

Powell carved out an interesting compromise position. His opinion was critical of the quota aspect of the UCDMS plan. Setting aside sixteen places for minorities only struck Powell as the kind of overt racial discrimination prohibited by both the Fourteenth Amendment and Title VI. Moreover, Cal-Davis had no institutional history of racial discrimination (the medical school opened in 1968, long after the official demise of race-conscious school systems), so its claims of remedying the effects of past discrimination were unconvincing. Thus, the Court commanded that Bakke be admitted.

But Powell did not go so far as to say that race could *never* be a consideration in the admissions process. Universities have long considered many factors other than grades and test scores in attracting a diverse student body.

Scholarships can be offered to candidates with superior athletic ability, or to musicians, or to the needy, among others. Colleges may wish also to examine factors such as geographic distribution or socioeconomic class or veteran status. In this light, Powell argued that universities may consider race as *a* factor in the admisssions process but only if it is considered as one among many such special factors. Powell thus concluded with an invitation to other interested parties to redesign their admissions process: quotas, no; affirmative action, yes.

The ambiguity of Powell's decision (accepting the antidiscrimination principle in part and the "affirmative action" principle in part) appeared Solomon-like, but it did not resolve the conflict. Both opponents and supporters of "affirmative action" hailed it as a victory. Shortly thereafter the Court decided that "affirmative action" in the private sector was constitutional (*United Steelworkers v. Weber,* 443 U.S. 193, 1979), as was a federal law requiring that 10 percent of all government contracts be allocated to minority businesses (*Fullilove v. Klutznick,* 448 U.S. 448, 1980).

The controversy continues unabated. In the essays that follow, John C. Livingston, professor of government at California State University-Sacramento, offers a spirited moral and practical defense of the "affirmative action" principle. Henry J. Abraham, professor of government and foreign affairs at the University of Virginia, supports the antidiscrimination principle with some interesting personal comments about life in the United States as a Jew.

Yes: Some Post-*Bakke* Reflections on "Reverse Discrimination"

Henry J. Abraham

TIPULATING the audience of these ruminations to be educated, intelligent human beings, who read, see and/or hear the news that informs our *vie quotidienne,* I am comfortable in assuming a basic familiarity with the issues involved. I am also aware that—and I daresay, without exception—any listener or reader will have strong feelings on the matter. So do I. We would not be human if we did not; while they operate on a host of levels and are triggered at vastly diverse moments, we all have consciences. Stipulating these facets, I should first endeavor to make clear what "reverse discrimination" is *not:* (1) It is *not* action, be it in the governmental or private sector, designed to remedy the absence of proper and needed educational preparation or training by special, even if costly, primary and/or secondary school level preparatory programs or occupational skill development, such as "Head Start," "Upward Bound," etc., always provided that access to these programs is not bottomed on race but on education, and/or economic need, be it cerebral or manual. (2) It is *not* the utilization of special classes or supplemental tutoring or training, regardless of the costs involved (assuming, of course, that these have been properly authorized and appropriated) on any level of the educational or training process, from the very pre-nursery school bottom to the very top of the professional training ladder. (3) It is of course *not* the scrupulous exhortation and enforcement of absolute standards of non-discrimination on the basis of race, sex, religion, nationality, and also now of age (at least up to 70, with certain exceptions, some of which will be discontinued by 1982). (4) It is *not* the above-the-table special recruiting and utilization efforts which, *pace* poo-pooing by leaders of some of the recipient groups involved, are not only pressed vigorously, but have been and are being pushed and pressed on a scale that would make a Bear Bryant and Knute

Henry J. Abraham, from "Some Post-*Bakke, Weber,* and *Fullilove* Reflections on Reverse Discrimination," 14 *University of Richmond Law Review* (1980), pp. 373–88.

Rockne smile a knowing well-done smile. (5) It is *not* even an admission or personnel officer's judgment that, along with sundry other criteria, he or she may take into account an individual applicant's racial, religious, gender, or other characteristics as a "plus"—to use Mr. Justice Powell's crucial *Bakke* term—but only if that applicant can demonstrate the presence of demonstrable explicit or implicit merit in terms of ability and/or genuine promise. For I shall again and again insist that *the* overriding criterion, *the* central consideration, must in the final analysis be present or arguably potential merit. It must thus be merit and ability, not necessarily based exclusively upon past performance, but upon a mature, experienced judgment that merit and ability are in effect in the total picture either by their presence or by their fairly confident predictability. These five aforementioned "nots", which are all aspects of the concept of "affirmative action"—are naturally not an exhaustive enumeration. Yet they are illustrative of common practices that, in my view, do *not* constitute "reverse discrimination"—always provided that they remain appropriately canalized within proper legal and constitutional bounds—for they give life to the basic American right of equality of *opportunity*. One of the major problems, alas, is that militant pro-"reverse discrimination" advocates insist on substituting a requirement of equality of *result* for the requirement of equality of *opportunity*—a requirement based on the dangerous notion of statistical group parity, in which the focal point becomes the *group* rather than the individual.

This brings me to the necessary look at the quintet of what "reverse discrimination" is: (1) It *is*, above all, what in the final analysis, the *Bakke*, *Weber* and *Fullilove* cases fundamentally were all about, namely the setting aside of quotas—be they rigid or quasi-rigid—i.e., the adoption of a *numerus clausus*, on behalf of the admission of recruitment or training of employment or promotion of groups identified and classified by racial, sexual, religious, age or nationality characteristics. For these are characteristics that are, or should be, proscribed on both legal *and* constitutional grounds, because they are *non-sequiturs* on the fronts of individual merit and ability and are, or certainly should be, regarded as being an insult to the dignity and intelligence of the quota recipients. "Our Constitution is color-blind," thundered Mr. Justice John Marshall Harlan in lonely dissent in the famous, or infamous, case of *Plessy v. Ferguson* in 1896, "and neither knows nor tolerates classes among citizens." His dissent, which became the guiding star of the Court's unanimous holding in the monumental and seminal 1954 ruling in *Brown v. Board of Education of Topeka, Kansas*, now prompts us to ask the question whether, as the proponents of "reverse discrimination" urge, the "Constitution must be *color-conscious* in order to be color blind?" But to continue what "reverse discrimination" is, it *is* (2) the slanting of what should be neutral, pertinent, and appropriate threshold and other qualification examinations and/or requirements; double-standards in grading and rating;

double-standards in attendance and disciplinary requirements. It *is* (3) the dishonest semanticism of what are called *goals* or *guidelines,* that the latter day bureaucracy has simply pronounced legal and/or constitutional on the alleged ground that they differ from rigid *quotas,* which admittedly would be presumably illegal and/or unconstitutional. Supported by Mr. Justice Powell's dismissal of them in the *Bakke* decision as a "semantic distinction" which is "beside the point," I submit that this distinction is as unworkable as it is dishonest—in the absence of, to use a favorite Department of Health, Education and Welfare, (and later Health, Education and Human Services), Department of Labor, and O.E.E.O. term, "good faith" vis-a-vis the far-reaching efforts of affected educational institutions and employers to function under the concept of "goals" or "guidelines."

But while going to enormous lengths to deny any equation of "goals" or "guidelines" with "quotas," the largely Messianic enforcement personnel of the three aforementioned powerful and well-funded agencies of the federal government—personnel that, certainly in the realm of the administration of higher education, often lacks the one-would-think-essential experience and background—in effect *require* quotas while talking "goals" or "guidelines." Indeed, within hours, if not minutes of the *Bakke* decision, for example, Eleanor Holmes Norton, then the aggressive head of the O.E.E.O., announced that the Supreme Court holding would make no difference, whatever, in the agency's established policies! Thus, there is extant an eager *presumption* of a lack of a good faith effort against the background-imposition of rigid compliance quotas, based upon frequently irrelevant group statistics, statistics that are demonstrably declared *ultra vires* by the Title VII, Sec. 703(j) of the Civil Rights Act of 1964. (4) Reverse discrimination *is* such a statutory provision . . . as that mandated under the Public Works Employment Act of 1977. Under that Act, Congress enacted a rigid requirement, adopted on the floor without committee hearings as a result of shrewd strategy by the Congressional Black Caucus, that 10 percent of all public works contracts designed to stimulate employment go to "minority business enterprises" regardless of the competitiveness of their bid. Known as "M.B.E.'s", they are identified statutorily as private businesses that are at least half-owned by members of a minority group or publicly held businesses in which minority group members control a majority of the stock. For purposes of the Act, "minorities" are defined as "Blacks, Orientals, Indians, Eskimos, Aleuts," and what is termed "the Spanish-speaking." At issue, in what quickly came to be known as the "1977 Ten Per Cent Set-Aside Quota Law," were thousands of construction jobs and billions of dollars worth of Government contracts. But when the U.S. Supreme Court initially had the case before it a few days after it handed down its *Bakke* desision, it ducked the problem on the ground that the award involved had already been consummated and the money expended, the issue thus being moot. However, the Court did then reexamine the matter in 1980 in the seminal case of *Fullilove v. Klutznick.* And reverse discrimination *is* (5) the widely advanced notion, a favorite of officials at the very highest level of all branches of Administration that, somehow, two wrongs make a right; that the children must pay for the sins of their fathers by self-destructive actions; that of the practice, in the words of Chief Justice Burger's dissenting opinion in the pro-reverse discrimination *Franks* decision in 1976, of "robbing Peter to pay Paul."

It is, of course, the latter issue—one I suggested as my fifth illustration of what "reverse discrimination" *is*—that lies at the heart of the matter. To put it simply, but not oversimplifiedly, it is the desire, the perceived duty, the moral imperative, of compensating for the grievous and shameful history of racial and collateral discrimination in America's past. That discrimination is a fact of history which no fair person can deny and the reappearance of which no decent or fair person would sanction, let alone welcome. America's record since the end of World War II, and especially since the *Brown* decision, is a living testament to the far-reaching, indeed exhilarating, ameliorations that have taken place, and are continuing to take place, on the civil rights front. This is a fact of life amply documented and progressively demonstrated, and I need not do so here. . . . I presume it all depends "whose ox is being gored"— to use Al Smith's felicitous phrase—and at which moment in history. Anyone who denies the very real progress *cum* atonement that has taken place, and is continuing to take place, in both the public and the private sector is either a fool, dishonest, or does so for political purposes—and the largest numbers, understandably, fall into the latter category. American society today is abso- lutely committed to the fullest measure of egalitarianism under our Constitu- tion, mandated in our basic document by the "due process" clause of Amend- ments Five and Fourteen and the latter's "equal protection of the laws" clause as well as in a plethora of legislation. But that Constitution, in the very same Amendments, safeguards *liberty* as well as equality—a somber reminder that rights and privileges are not one-dimensional.

It is on the frontiers of that line between equality and liberty that so much of the "reverse discrimination" controversy, both in its public and private manifestations, has become embattled. It is here that the insistent, often strident, calls for compensatory, preferential, "reverse discrimination" action are issued—and, more often than not, they issue from a frighteningly pro- found guilt complex, a guilt complex that has become so pervasive as to brush aside as irrelevant on the altar of atonement even constitutional, let alone legal, barriers—witness, for example, the opinions by Justices Brennan and Blackmun in both the *Bakke* and *Weber* rulings. To cite just one or two cases in point: One argument that veritably laces the pro-"reverse discrimina- tion" arguments of the briefs in *Bakke, Weber,* and *Fullilove,* especially those by the American Civil Liberties Union, the Association of American University Professors, Harvard University, Stanford University, the University of Pennsylvania, Columbia University, and the NAACP, among others, is that the injustices of the past justify, indeed demand, a "*temporary* use of affirmative action including class-based hiring preferences and admission goals" in favor of racial minorities. In other words, the record of the past creates the catalyst *cum* mandate for the imposition of *quotas* like the 16 places out of 100 admittedly set aside by the Medical School of the University of California at Davis for the "special" admission of members of certain minority groups. What the school did is entirely straightforward and clear: it *did* deny admission to a fully qualified white applicant, Allan Bakke, on racial grounds—which as Mr. Justice Stevens' stern opinion for himself and his colleagues Burger, Stewart, and Rehnquist, makes clear, is *ipso facto* forbidden by the plain language of Title VI of the Civil Rights Act of 1964. The University had justified its action on the grounds of redress for past racial discrimination (although it had *never* practiced discrimination—and had, and has, never been accused of such until it denied Allan Bakke's admission); on the need for compensatory action; and a commitment to "genuine equal opportunity. . . ."

A related, although somewhat different justification advanced on the altar of redressing past wrongs by temporarily—or perhaps not-so-temporarily?—winking at legal and constitutional barriers, on I prefer to call the "I am not really pregnant, just a little bit," approach to the problem, is illustrated by Ronald Dworkin, Professor of Jurisprudence at Oxford University, in his following 1977 defense of the use of racial criteria in connection with the well-known 1974 Washington Law School "reverse discrimination" case of *De Funis v. Odegaard.*

> Racial criteria are not necessarily the right standards for deciding which applicants should be accepted by law schools for example. But neither are intellectual criteria, nor indeed, any other set of criteria. [*Sic!*] The fairness—and constitutionality—of any admissions program must be tested in the same way. It is justified if it serves a proper policy that respects the right of all members of the community to be treated as equals, but not otherwise. . . We must take care not to use the Equal Protection of the Laws Clause of the Fourteenth Amendment to cheat ourselves of equality.

Which, of course, is exactly what he in effect counsels—in addition to the inequality of "reverse discrimination." In other words, the desired end justifies the means—no matter what the Constitution may command! We have here another patent illustration of the guilt complex syndrome which, not content with equal justice under law and equality of opportunity, insists upon, in Raoul Berger's characterization, the attainment of "justice at any cost." Yet it represents the gravamen of the concurring opinion in *Bakke* by Justices Brennan, Marshall, and Blackmun; the controlling holding in the *Weber* case via the pen of Mr. Justice Marshall in *Fullilove,* which was joined by his colleagues Brennan and Blackmun.

Along with the good many others who consider themselves *bona fide* civil libertarians and are certifiable champions of civil rights, who decades ago fought the good fight for equal justice and non-discrimination—when fighting it was far more fraught with professional and personal risks than it is now—I confess, however, that I do not have a guilt complex on that issue. Myself a sometime victim of discrimination, of prejudice, and of the *numerus clausus*, i.e., of quotas, I know that two wrongs not one right make; that any so-called "temporary suspension" of constitutional rights, is a cancer upon constitutionalism; that there is no such thing as being a little bit pregnant. Because of our religious persuasion my parental family and I were exiled from, and a number of members of our family were exterminated by, a land where our ancestors had lived for 500 years. As relatively recently as 1952, I was told quite frankly by an administrator at a major Northern University—one of the first proudly to carry the *anti*-Allan Bakke banner twenty-five years later—that I could not be promoted because "we have already promoted one Jew this year." To which he added, and he was wholly sincere, "no personal offense meant." Happily those times are gone—and I, for one, will not support their return on the altar of siren-like calls for atonement for past wrongs, etched in socio-constitutional rationalizations and manifestations of preferential treatment, compensatory standards, and quotas that are based on criteria and considerations other than those of fundamental merit, of ability, of equality of opportunity, and of equality before the law. . . .

A concluding word on the desirability of "reverse discrimination" *per se.* I hope I have demonstrated what I regard as its tenets; what it *is,* and what it is *not.* Whether or not one agrees with that position, and regardless of how one perceives or reads the inherent statutory and constitutional issues, what of the merits of the proposition of adopting racial, or sexual, or religious, or nationality quotas, or by whatever other noun they may be perfumed? Resounding to that *quaere,* I shall call as my star witness upon someone whose credentials on the libertarian front are indisputably impeccable: Justice William O. Douglas. In his 1974 dissenting opinion in *De Funis v. Odegaard,* after finding that Marco De Funis had been rejected by the University of Washington School of Law "solely on account of his race," Douglas lectured at length on the classification, styling it at the outset as introducing "a capricious and irrelevant factor working an invidious discrimination," and insisting that the Constitution and the laws of our land demand that each application for admission must be considered in "a racially neutral way," a phrase he italicized and one, incidentally, quoted with approval by Mr. Justice Powell in *Bakke,* "Minorities in our midst who are to serve actively in our public affairs," he went on, "should be chosen on talent and character alone, not on cultural orientation or leanings. . . ."

Justice Douglas—who in his last book, wrote that, "Racial quotas, no matter how well-intentioned—are a wholly un-American practice, quite inconsistent with equal protection"—had concluded his *De Funis* dissent on a note that, for me, hits the essence of the entire issue: "The Equal Protection Clause," he insisted

> commands the elimination of racial barriers, not their creation in order to satisfy our theory as to how society ought to be organized. The purpose of the University of Washington cannot be to produce Black lawyers for Blacks, Polish lawyers for Poles, Jewish lawyers for Jews, Irish lawyers for the Irish. It should be to produce good lawyers for Americans. . . .

That, I submit in all humility, is the *sine qua non* of the matter. It is my fervent hope, though very far from a confident expectation—especially in view of the unsatisfactory, multifaceted, evasion-inviting response given by the Court in *Bakke* and the high tribunal's patent violation of the language and intent of Title VII in *Weber*—that we will still, at this late hour, resolve to heed the now deceased Justice's admonition and substitute for "lawyers" whatever educational, occupational, or professional noun may be appropriate in given circumstances in the justly egalitarian striving of all Americans, regardless of race, sex, creed, nationality, or religion, for a dignified, happy, prosperous, and free life, blessed by a resolute commitment to and acquiescence in equal justice under law—which is as the cement of society.

No: Reverse Discrimination?

John C. Livingston

T HE charge of reverse discrimination is rooted in the high moral ground claimed by opponents of affirmative action. They appeal to the principle of color-blindness—the principle that individuals should be judged exclusively on their individual merits without regard to race or color. The principle of color-blindness challenges all historical forms of legalized and institutionalized preference for whites and proposed forms of preference for others. It proposes that racism can only be overcome by ruling out all forms of racial preference. Viewed in this light, a racial quota—or any form of racial preference—appears to be reverse discrimination.

Too often the supporters of affirmative-action programs have accepted the phrase "reverse discrimination" as describing the effects of racial preference, and then have sought to justify, or evade, it. But to do so is to accept an unfair and unnecessary burden. What needs to be challenged is the proposition that racial quotas or other forms of racial preference for colored minorities involve reverse discrimination. They do not. And in the claim that they do lies a basic flaw in the case against affirmative action.

However implausible it may appear at first glance, the point can be made without hedging: *a quota system that gives preference to minorities does not discriminate against whites.* Even a compensatory quota of 100 percent, I will later argue, would not discriminate against whites as a group.

The charge of reverse discrimination rests on the implicit premise that whites are denied access to advantages to which they are entitled, and which they would have achieved had not preference been given to minorities. This assumption appears to make obvious sense—until one stops to think about it. Consider, for example, the Bakke situation. Let's assume, for the sake of argument, that Bakke was qualified by past performance and motivation and that he stood next in line for selection so that his place could be said to have been taken by someone admitted under the minorities quota whose qualifications were inferior to his. On those assumptions, was Bakke discriminated against on the basis of his race? Was he treated unfairly? Was he a victim of reverse discrimination, of the same sort of denial of equal protection under which minorities have suffered in the past?

My argument is that the answer to all these questions is no. Quotas are not reverse discrimination, for the simple reason that they do not imply or result in discrimination. To discriminate, in the relevant meaning of the word, is not simply to treat differently, but to treat unjustly or unfairly on the basis of prejudice. Our common sense and our common experiences teach us this difference. As every parent knows, one of the most striking and frustrating characteristics of children is their inability to distinguish between different treatment and discriminatory treatment—a deficiency of judgment that leads younger siblings to perceive their lesser privileges as clear instances of parental discrimination. As every parent learns, an important part of the parental role is to enable children to become adults by equipping them to judge between different and unjust treatment. By just this sort of judgment, after all, the issue of justice is tested.

It should be clear, then, that the question of whether white males are victims of discrimination under affirmative-action programs is not answered by merely noting that they are treated differently from ethnic minorities. The question is whether they are deprived, on the basis of prejudice, of what they are fairly entitled to have. . . .

If white males excluded by a quota are not victims of prejudice, it still may be claimed that they are deprived of places to which they are fairly entitled. What then is the basis of this claim to entitlement? It is not enough to say that the qualifications of a rejected white are superior to those of a minority person who was admitted. The argument must be the more general one that the only way to be fair to individuals is to act, in allocating rewards, as if racial (and other) differences are irrelevant, so that individual achievement is the only criterion.

But, if to the winners go the laurels because they have run a faster race, the race itself must be fairly run. If winners are to be selected and rewarded on the basis of individual achievement, without regard to race, color, or sex, then fairness requires that those characteristics cannot have been determinants of the losers' chances. Justice involves giving people, not what their achievements warrant, but rewards commensurate with their achievements *in a fair race.* . . .

Where would Bakke have stood at the finish if the conditions of justice (as Bakke's supporters defined them) had been met, if the race had been run fairly, if opportunities had been genuinely equal, and if racial prejudice had not been a factor in the chances of some of Bakke's competitors? The answer must be that he would not have ranked higher than the quota applicants. For, unless we are prepared to accept the racist premise of genetic inequality, we must conclude that the performances of minority competitors reflected the social and cultural consequences of racism. And we must conclude that, in the absence of the arbitrary handicaps imposed by racism, colored minorities would have performed as competently on the average as whites. Fair competition would have produced equality of group results, and the quota positions would have been filled by minorities through the normal processes of meritocratic competition.

The crucial fact is that Bakke could not have earned the qualifications for admission in a fair race (unless, of course, it was unfair to deny him admission on account of his age, which is another matter, and one between him and his younger white competitors). He was, therefore, not entitled as a matter of justice to the position and he had not originally been denied it for being white. . . .

An implicit, but subtle, racism in some reactions against affirmative action is suggested by another consideration. When the question is raised about reverse discrimination on the basis of race, we are inclined to discuss the issue as if racial preference were the only departure from a strict regime of competitive, individual merit. This assumption, of course, is far from the truth. In prestigious universities and colleges, in professional schools, and in business and industry, a wide range of arbitrary criteria is invoked to offer advantage on other grounds than merit. Preference often goes to the boss's son, the foreman's friend, the alumni's offspring, the children of influential politicians and potential donors, the bed partners, the politically conventional, the con-artists, and the positive thinkers—anyone with experience in the competition for place and power in American society could add to the list. None of these practices, of course, is justifiable on the premises of meritocracy. We grumble to our wives, husbands, and close friends about their unfairness. But we find them tolerable. They do not give rise to a backlash or the sort of resentment that threatens social stability. But quotas do. Why? Clearly, it cannot be because quotas are more important in their overall effect. Probably, the arbitrary preference accorded to persons on the basis of who their parents are exceeds in magnitude the consequences of a full-fledged quota system.

Is it, then, because these other arbitrary criteria are somehow less arbitrary, more morally defensible, than preference on the basis of race? To ask the question is to answer it. It is morally irresponsible even to put racial preference for oppressed groups on the same moral plain as customary forms of preference—as the key opinion of Justice Powell reveals in the *Bakke* decision. In his effort to justify the use of race as a factor in admissions decisions, Powell found that the justifying public purpose lies in the university's goal to a diversified student body. As Justice Blackmun noted, the effect of this reasoning gives preference that serves the cause of remedying racial injustice the same constitutional standing as preferences accorded "to those possessed of athletic skills, to the children of alumni, to the affluent who may bestow their largess on the institutions and to those having connections with celebrities, the famous, and the powerful." Our moral sense protests against this result. And our common sense tells us that our unconscious racism provides an unpleasant but plausible explanation of why we are so much more disturbed about racial preference than about preference derived from parentage or other arbitrary considerations.

Most affirmative-action programs aim to assign a proportion of available positions to minorities on the basis of their proportions of the relevant population. They may be described as "fairness quotas," since they indicate what the results would be if the competition were fair—if, more specifically, white racism had not crippled the chances of nonwhite competitors. The upper limit of a fairness quota for minorities in the *Bakke* situation, for example, would have been 25 percent.

A second type of quota may be described as "compensatory." By setting the figure higher than the proportion of minorities to the total relevant population, a compensatory quota aims at reaching a proportional result in the profession or occupation more rapidly. A compensatory hiring or admissions quota—even one of 100 percent—would not lead to reverse discrimination against whites as a group. Its goal is to achieve a proportional share for minorities in the particular profession—the share required by justice in a system of equal opportunity. A compensatory quota, however, would discriminate against white *individuals*—or, more accurately, against the class of young whites just entering the job or career market. The misperception that this discrimination occurs under fairness quotas has led to much of the white backlash and increased racial tension in recent years.

But even under compensatory quotas, the injustice done to young white males does not result from the preference given to minorities. It results rather from the accumulated historical preference enjoyed by older white males. The grievance of young white males under a compensatory quota is against their fathers, uncles, and cohorts—not their colored contemporaries. For, among those older white males, some occupy their positions unfairly and undeservedly. Some of these older white males would not be where they are if their potential ethnic competitors had been able to compete fairly. True, we cannot identify these individuals in any satisfactory or just way, but that is irrelevant to the question of racial justice. Group larceny does not make its victims less victimized or deprive them of the right of redress. To say this is not to imply, of course, that older white males have gotten their unearned advantages through personal acts of discrimination or displays of prejudice. They may well have belonged to the NAACP and the ACLU. In a sense, they couldn't avoid being favored for the color of their skins.

The trouble with compensatory quotas, then, is not that they are unjust in imposing injuries on whites—remedying racial injustice can never be costless to its beneficiaries—but that they impose the entire cost on the generation of white males just entering the career market. To put the matter bluntly, under a system of fairness quotas, older, successful white males are able to hang onto their undeserved advantages at the same time that it goes unnoticed that they are the beneficiaries of group larceny. Our sons do not blame us for frustrated careers; they blame our victims. They don't say, "I want to be a professor and you're sitting in my chair." They don't even say, "There aren't enough chairs—create some more." They say, instead, "Those blacks and Chicanos are getting places that rightfully belong to me." And they use the slogans we've taught them, albeit innocently, to put a moral gloss on their careerism: Individual merit is the only legitimate test. Sure, blacks and others have been victimized in the past, but two wrongs don't make a right. . . .

Compensatory quotas, of course, are not the source of the recent and continuing fervor over affirmative action. After a brief trial in a very few places in the late 1960s, compensatory quotas were rapidly abandoned in the face of a white, largely intellectual, backlash. The debate now rages over fairness quotas. And on that level, no question of discrimination is involved.

Quotas are not reverse discrimination in either an individual or a group sense, and the insistence on describing them that way serves only to protect white interests while soothing white consciences. In letters to the editor and in casual conversation, one is struck by the vehemence, the moral outrage, and the righteous indignation that accompanies the charge of reverse discrimination. A nation with such reserves of easily triggered moral indignation and such a keen eye for discrimination might be expected to be a little further down the road to racial justice by now! This capacity to get in a moral lather over reverse discrimination against whites (which does not exist), while whites continue to enjoy the advantage of a racist heritage (which still exists) says something about the adequacy of our perceptions and the seriousness of our moral claims.

But if quotas do not produce reverse discrimination, another and more valid charge may be made against them and against all other forms of racial preference. They seek to produce the conditions that would exist if there were no discrimination against minorities, without eliminating discrimination against minorities. They would thus approximate the results of equal opportunity without achieving the conditions of equal opportunities. This is a valid charge, but not a morally weighty one, if we can't have both—at least in the immediate future—we're better off with one than we would be without either. We have been tragically unsuccessful in eliminating racism, especially in its subtler forms. Very likely its roots go so deep in our culture, our institutions, and our psychological makeup that it will take generations.

So our choices for the near future involve continuing to live with racism and its social and economic consequences, or altering the social and economic consequences of racism without waiting for its roots to wither.

So our choices for the near future involve continuing to live with racism and its social and economic consequences, or altering the social and economic consequences of racism without waiting for its roots to wither.

Is there not a serious moral flaw in a concept of meritocratic justice, advanced by whites, that argue the whites are morally justified in continuing to play with a loaded deck? Why, in any event, should aggrieved minorities be expected to wait patiently on the processes of cleansing white souls for changes in the objective economic conditions of their lives? Moreover, a powerful case can be made that changes in the social and economic status of minorities will be, in the long run, a powerful factor in speeding changes in white attitudes. In the American gospel of equal opportunity, it is a short step from being poor and black to being judged poor because black. Whites are generally willing to accept equality before the law as a close enough approximation of social justice built into the law, a fair chance as a substitute for real equality of opportunity, and the results of unequal opportunities as a satisfactory measure of the relative merit of the competitors. Under these conditions, inequality of group results will continue to feed white prejudice and, however unconsciously, delusions of white superiority.

Equality of group results, even though achieved through programs of racial preference, may in the long run benefit from the great American tendency to use the slogan of equal opportunity to legitimize whatever the winners have come by. In the old American adage, "nothing succeeds like success." It's worked that way in the past for successful whites. Why not for blacks in the future?

Even if it is granted that fairness quotas produce a sort of justice, it still may be objected that they do it too crudely. It may be objected that not all blacks are equally disadvantaged, that there are other sources of disadvantage that are not touched by racial quotas, the chief of which is being poor. There is truth in the objection, but such moral fastidiousness is unbecoming in a people who have been able to stomach without apparent distress the rough textures of success in American life. In any event, doing justice is always, for fallible man, a rough business. The old principle that the good should not be allowed to become the enemy of the better is still a solid ground for moral conduct.

11

Frontiero v. Richardson:
Is an Equal Rights Amendment Necessary
to Provide Equal Protection for Women?

Glenn A. Phelps

T HE proposed Equal Rights Amendment (ERA) to the Constitution is brief and straightforward: "Equality of Rights under the Law shall not be denied or abridged by the United States or by any State on account of sex." One might not expect twenty-four words to be capable of eliciting such impassioned controversy. Yet the ERA, during a ten-year struggle for ratification that eventually failed, evoked a political debate that was to divide many friends, households, churches, and even civil libertarians into warring camps. Although the ERA ratification process died, the issues that it raised linger on.

Like most other contemporary civil liberties problems, the controversy about women's rights under the Constitution is at least partly a vestige of the eighteenth-century values of the Framers. Even such a committed civil libertarian of that period as Thomas Jefferson could write that the purest of democracies would have to exclude women, "who, to prevent depravation of morals and ambiguity of issue, could not mix promiscuously in the public meetings of men."[1] For the founding generation, it was not mankind that was created equal but *men.*

The Civil War Amendments would establish a constitutional foundation for the eventual extension of full civil and political rights to another group specifically excluded by the founders: blacks. Many women's rights activists of the postwar period saw the debate over adoption of these amendments as an opportunity to clarify the status of women. But the final wording of the Fourteenth and Fifteenth Amendments proved to be a disappointment to their cause. Section 2 of the Fourteenth Amendment used the term *male* for the first time in the Constitution—by implication placing a "males-only" membership requirement in the community of equal rights. When the Fifteenth Amendment was proposed so as to prevent the abridgement of the vote "on account of race, color, or previous condition of servitude," feminists sought to add the words "or sex" but again without success.

Thus it was no surprise (indeed, it probably reflected the prevailing attitude of the times) that the Supreme Court, three years later, could find no substance to the claim that women had the same "privileges and immunities" as guaranteed to men by the Fourteenth Amendment. Myra Bradwell had applied for admission to the Illinois bar and had passed the examination, but the Illinois Supreme Court denied her admission to the bar because she was a woman.[2] In agreeing with the state court's decision, three Justices of the U.S. Supreme Court, led by Joseph P. Bradley, commented on the appropriateness of women seeking equal rights by the Fourteenth Amendment:

> The civil law, as well as nature herself, has always recognized a wide differ-
> ence in the respective spheres and destinies of man and woman. Man is, or
> should be, woman's protector and defender. The natural and proper timidity
> and delicacy which belongs to the female sex evidently unfits it for many of
> the occupations of civil life. . . . The harmony, not to say identity, of inter-
> ests and views which belongs, or should belong, to the family institution is
> repugnant to the idea of a woman adopting a distinct and independent career
> from that of her husband. . . . The paramount destiny and mission of woman
> are to fulfill the noble and benign offices of wife and mother. This is the law
> of the Creator. And the rules of civil society must be adapted to the general
> constitution of things. (*Bradwell v. Illinois,* 1873, 83 U.S. 130)

For most of the next hundred years the Equal Protection Clause was deemed not to apply to females in the same way that it applied to males. Every state statute book was filled with examples of legislation that treated women differently. Most of these were justified by the need to grant "special protections" for wives and mothers in their familial roles or to protect women from being taken advantage of in the workplace. In that many women were denied access to careers as a result of these male-inspired "special protections," this protective legislation was perceived by some women as more oppressive than liberating.

Efforts to seek a constitutional solution to the indifference of the Four-teenth Amendment did not end with *Bradwell,* though. Beginning in 1923, a constitutional amendment guaranteeing equal rights for men and women before the law was introduced annually in Congress, though it rarely pro-gressed even to committee consideration. But in 1972 Congress at last approved an equal rights amendment and submitted it to the states for rati-fication.

Although the ERA was supported by most feminists and civil libertarians and opposed by those (male and female) who felt threatened by the idea of equal rights, an interesting debate occurred within the ranks of constitutional scholars, most of whom shared a commitment to women's rights. As Peter Coogan has noted, the concerns of these scholars were several.[3] One objec-tion was based on the view that the Constitution ought not be amended when the same social policies could be achieved by statutory means or judicial interpretation of existing constitutional provisions. Rather than adding another amendment to the Constitution, advocates of equal rights for women should, according to this view, seek statutory action of the kind that promoted the black civil rights movement of the 1960s (such as the Civil Rights Acts of 1960 and 1964). They should also pursue litigation that would lead the Supreme Court to interpret the Equal Protection Clause as applying to women in the same way as it applies to blacks—that laws discriminating against women were a "suspect classification."

Frontiero v. Richardson (411 U.S. 671, 1973), decided just a few months after Congress had submitted the ERA for ratification, suggests why ERA supporters are skeptical of the approach suggested by the constitutional "purists." Congress, in an attempt to encourage career enlistments in the military, had established several programs that provided additional benefits to married military personnel. One program offered supplemental payments (quarters allowance) to offset the additional costs of supplying housing for the soldier's dependents. A second program provided comprehensive medical and dental care for all dependents.

Sharron Frontiero was a married lieutenant in the U.S. Air Force. She applied for the quarters allowance and medical benefits, fully expecting to receive the additional benefits for her spouse. She soon discovered otherwise. Female soldiers could claim these benefits *only* if they could demonstrate that they provided more than one-half of the living expenses of their husbands. Joseph Frontiero was a veteran attending a nearby college as a full-time student. It was determined that his share of the couple's living expenses was $354 per month. His Veterans' Administration (VA) benefits paid him $205 per month. Because this amount was more than half of Joseph's living expenses, the Air Force refused to allow Sharron Frontiero to claim him as a dependent and denied her any additional benefits. What especially angered the Frontieros was that no such means test was applied to male military personnel. The benefits for dependents were granted to all male soldiers regardless of the income levels of their wives. The proffered reason was clear: a man was presumed to be the head of the household and provider for his family. A woman's claim as the principal earner was, on the other hand, to be examined carefully because such a role was "atypical." Thus, by these rules a male soldier whose wife earned $30,000 per year as, say, a college professor would be paid full benefits. Indeed, the Air Force would not even examine the question of who earned what. But a female soldier whose husband received $2,400 per year as a college *student* would be denied those same benefits because *her* claim would be evaluated on a case-by-case basis according to the means test.

The question before the Supreme Court was not whether the military pay act was discriminatory. All laws, after all, ultimately benefit some groups and disadvantage others. Traditional application of the Equal Protection Clause merely requires that a law be "reasonable" and that it not "arbitrarily" discriminate against some class of people. In this case, the Air Force argued that the rules were reasonable because they were administratively convenient. Males comprise 99 percent of all Air Force personnel, so a procedure that required examination of all claims would be enormously costly. On the other hand, there are not only fewer women soldiers, they are *statistically* less likely to be the breadwinners of their households. Such rationalizations had been accepted by the Supreme Court for many years as a justification for sex discrimination.[4]

If a law discriminates against a "suspect class," however, a different kind of analysis is required: that of "strict scrutiny." Such a law would have to be more than merely reasonable; it would have to be "essential" to a "fundamental state interest," a standard extremely difficult for any statute to meet. The Court has asserted that classifications based on race, alienage, or national origin are inherently suspect. Activists for women's rights hoped that the *Frontiero* case would add gender to the list of suspect classifications and thus expose sex discriminations to the same severe standard of "strict scrutiny."

Eight Justices (Rehnquist dissenting) agreed that the Frontieros had been denied equal protection of the laws, but there was disagreement among them as to why. Justice Brennan and three other Justices argued that gender ought to be treated as a suspect classification. Women were a "discrete and insular minority" (at least politically) that had suffered from a history of "invidious discrimination." This was language previously used to extend strict scrutiny to discrimination based upon race.

The remaining four Justices, but principally Justice Powell, agreed that the classification scheme in question did not pass constitutional muster, but they were unwilling to embrace Brennan's plea for a new suspect classification. Their reasons are especially intriguing in the light of the claim by the constitutional "purists" that the ERA was unnecessary and that the Fourteenth Amendment was capable of rectifying the problem of sex discrimination. Powell agreed that the discrimination against Frontiero was unconstitutional but only because "administrative convenience" was an insubstantial justification for the government's action. Powell then went on to note:

> There is another . . . reason for deferring a general categorizing of sex classifications as invoking the strictest test of judicial scrutiny. The Equal Rights Amendment, which if adopted will resolve the substance of this precise question, has been approved by the Congress and submitted for ratification. . . . By acting prematurely and unnecessarily . . . the Court has assumed a decisional responsibility at the very time when state legislatures . . . are debating the proposed Amendment. It seems to me that this reaching out to pre-empt by judicial action a major political decision which is currently in process of resolution does not reflect appropriate respect for duly prescribed legislative process.

Ironically then, at the same time that numerous scholars were claiming that judicial interpretation of the Fourteenth Amendment made the ERA redundant and unnecessary, the Court was suggesting that the ERA was the appropriate instrument for resolving the issue of sex discrimination—a catch-22 indeed.

Since *Frontiero* the Court has applied a standard of review lying somewhere between "reasonableness" and "strict scrutiny," but the lack of clear criteria has led to a confusing array of decisions. For example, rules requiring pregnant public school teachers to quit at least five months before the expected birth were declared unconstitutional[5] but similar rules requiring pregnant airline stewardesses to take maternity leave were deemed reasonable.[6] A male-only draft is not unconstitutional,[7] but a law prohibiting beer sales to men under the age of twenty-one and to women under eighteen is unconstitutional.[8]

The ERA might not have resolved these matters any differently, but its failure in 1982 means that the debate over the scope of sex discrimination and its remedy will continue unabated. Typical of this debate are the following essays by two of the most noted constitutional scholars in the United States. Thomas I. Emerson is Professor of Law at Yale Law School. Paul Freund holds a similar position at Harvard Law School.

Yes: In Support of the Equal Rights Amendment

Thomas I. Emerson

THE basic premise of the Equal Rights Amendment is that sex should not be a factor in determining the legal rights of women, or of men. Most of us, I think, agree with this fundamental proposition. For example, virtually everybody would consider it unjust and irrational to provide by law that a person could not go to law school or be admitted to the practice of law because of his or her sex. The reason is that admission to the bar ought to depend upon legal training, competence in the law, moral character, and similar factors. Some women meet these qualifications and some do not; some men meet these qualifications and some do not. But the issue should be decided on an individual, not a group, basis. The fact of maleness or femaleness should be irrelevant. This remains true whether or not there are more men than women who qualify. It likewise remains true if there be no women who presently qualify, because women potentially qualify and might do so under different conditions of education and upbringing. The law, in short, owes an obligation to treat females as persons, not statistical abstracts.

What is true of admission to the bar is true of all legal rights. If we examine the various areas of the law one by one we will, I believe, reach the same conclusion in every case. Sex is an impermissible category by which to determine the right to a minimum wage, the custody of children, the obligation to refrain from taking the life of another, and so on. The law should be concerned with the right to a living wage for all, the welfare of the particular child, the protection of citizens from murder—that is, with the real issues—not with stereotypes about one or the other half of the human race.

The fundamental principle underlying the Equal Rights Amendment,

Thomas I. Emerson, from "In Support of the Equal Rights Amendment," 6 *Harvard Civil Rights–Civil Liberties Law Review* (1971), pp. 225–33. Copyright 1971 by the Harvard Civil Rights–Civil Liberties Law Review.

then, is that the law must deal with the individual attributes of the particular person, rather than make broad classifications based upon the irrelevant factor of sex. The aim of the Equal Rights Amendment is simply to establish these philosophic truths as principles of law.

It should be noted at this point that there is one type of situation where the law may properly focus on a sexual characteristic. When the legal system deals directly with a physical characteristic that is unique to one sex, in a certain sense, the individual obtains a benefit or is subject to a restriction because he or she belongs to one or the other sex. Thus a law providing for payment of the medical costs of childbearing would cover only women, and a law relating to sperm banks would apply only to men. Such legislation cannot be said to deny equal rights to the other sex. There is no basis here for seeking or achieving equality.

Instances of this kind, involving legislation directly concerned with physical differences found either in all women or in all men, are relatively rare. They may be distinguished from cases where the physical characteristic is not unique to one sex, and from cases of real or assumed psychological or social differences. A legislative distinction between sexes based on some physical characteristic not unique to one seems clearly inappropriate. Consider a determination that only men may be licensed to drive commercial vehicles because they are presumed to be stronger. Insofar as superior strength is not a characteristic of all men, such a determination unreasonably and thus unjustifiably discriminates against large numbers of women. Psychological and social differences between the sexes are similarly unjustifiable bases for discrimination since there is no clear evidence that such traits are unique to one sex or the other. Unless the difference is one that is characteristic of *all* women and *no* men, or *all* men and *no* women, it is not the sex factor but the individual factor which should be determinative.

The theoretical basis for prohibiting differential treatment in the law based upon sex is thus quite clear. The practical reasons for doing so are equally compelling. History and experience have taught us that a legal system which undertakes to confer benefits or impose obligations on the basis of sex inevitably is repressive. It is perhaps too much to expect that the sex which wields the greater influence in formulating the law will not use its power to entrench its position at the expense of the other. At least this has been the outcome of sex differentiation in the American legal system. . . .

It is unnecessary to press these matters further. That our present legal system grossly discriminates against women cannot seriously be questioned. The major portion of that indictment is indeed admitted by most observers, and the critical need for substantial and immediate revisions in our legal structure is likewise conceded. The only remaining issue concerns the method which should be utilized to achieve reform.

There appear to be three basic methods by which discrimination against women can be eliminated from our legal system. The first, the legislative approach, must begin with the repeal or revision of each separate piece of existing legislation through action by the federal, state and local legislatures having jurisdiction, and change of each separate administrative rule or practice through similar action by every federal, state and local executive agency concerned with administration. It goes without saying that such a procedure would involve interminable delay. It is unlikely that proponents of women's rights will be able to eliminate all discriminatory statutes and practices when forced to fight over every separate issue on innumerable fronts. Even if such an effort were successful, it would have no prospective effect, and there would be no protection against future discriminatory legislation and practices. The legislative approach then lacks any guarantee of ultimate success. The struggle would be justified only if no other course of action were possible.

A second method is through court action under the Equal Protection Clause of the Fourteenth Amendment and the comparable provision of the Fifth. This procedure has the advantage of affording a more broad-scale attack upon the problem, with a single agency of government, the United States Supreme Court, playing the primary role. Moreover, some progress has already been made. It is of course recognized that women are "persons" within the embrace of the Fourteenth and Fifth Amendments, and are entitled to "equal protection of the laws" under those decisions upholding equality of rights for women under the existing constitutional provisions. I feel reasonably confident that in the long run the United States Supreme Court would reach a position very close to or identical with that of the proponents of the Equal Rights Amendment. Nevertheless, there are serious drawbacks to this approach.

In the first place there are some Supreme Court decisions and some lower court cases which move in the wrong direction. The task of overcoming or distinguishing these decisions could be a long and arduous one. There is, in short, a certain amount of legal deadwood which would have to be cleared away before the courts could make clear-cut and rapid progress. In the second place the Supreme Court has been subjected over a period of time to powerful attack for moving too fast and too far in frontier areas of the law. The Court may consequently be somewhat reluctant to take the lead in bringing about another major social reform, regardless of how constitutionally justified that reform may appear to be. Hence it would be important for the courts, in performing such a task, to have the moral support of the other institutions of government and the people as a whole.

Third, and most important, the problems involved in building a legislative framework assuring equality of rights to women are somewhat different from those which the courts have faced in other areas of equal protection law. In ordinary cases, when a claim is made that equal protection of the laws has been denied, the Supreme Court will apply the rule that differential treatment is valid providing there is a reasonable basis for the classification; and the Court will accept the legislative judgment that the classification is reasonable unless that judgment is beyond the pale of rationality. Yet such a legal doctrine is not appropriate where the differential treatment is based on sex. For reasons stated above, classification by sex, except where the law pertains to a unique physical characteristic of one sex, ought *always* to be regarded as unreasonable. It would be inappropriate, time consuming, and ultimately futile for the courts to investigate in each case whether a legislature was justified in deciding that a particular piece of legislation or administrative practice favored women, disfavored women, benefited society as a whole, and so on. That decision—namely, that all discrimination is outlawed—must be fundamental and not subject to relitigation.

In cases where differential treatment is based upon race, the courts have developed a special rule under the equal protection clause. In racial cases the constitutional doctrine is that classification by race is a "suspect" classification, and the legislature has the burden of showing that it is not an "invidious" or harmful classification or that it is justified by the most compelling reasons. Yet, taken as a whole, the problems of race discrimination are somewhat different from those of sex discrimination. For example, questions of benevolent quotas, compensatory treatment, culture bias in psychological testing, separatism, and other issues may need differing treatment. The increasingly complex doctrines being developed in the field of race discrimination are therefore not necessarily applicable to the field of sex discrimination.

The same can be said of other areas of equal protection law. Discriminatory treatment on account of poverty or illegitimacy, classifications in economic regulatory legislation, denial of the right of franchise through malapportionment of legislative districts—all these present issues peculiar to their own spheres. In short, the establishment of equal rights for women poses questions that are in important ways sui generis. An effective solution demands a separate constitutional doctrine that will be geared to the special character of the problem. Furthermore, as stated before, unless Congress and the states, through adoption of a constitutional amendment, express the firm conviction that this reform must be promptly and vigorously undertaken, progress is bound to be slow and faltering.

We come then to the conclusion that the third method—a contitutional amendment—is by far the most appropriate form of legal remedy. The final question is whether the Equal Rights Amendment now before us furnishes a satisfactory constitutional framework upon which to achieve the goal of equal rights for women. I believe that it does.

The proposed amendment states clearly and simply the fundamental objective: "Equality of rights under the law shall not be denied or abridged by the United States or by any State on account of sex." In this respect it follows the tradition of the great provisions of the Constitution guaranteeing freedom of religion, freedom of speech, due process of law, protection against cruel and inhuman punishment, and other rights.

The word "rights," it seems clear, includes not only rights in the narrow sense of the term, but all forms of rights, privileges, immunities, duties and responsibilities. Thus service on juries, whether it be looked upon as a "right" or a "duty," plainly falls within the scope of the amendment.

The term "equality," interpreted in light of the basic philosophy of the amendment, means that women must be treated by the law in the same way as other persons: their rights must be determined on the basis of the same factors that apply to men. The factor of femaleness or maleness is irrelevant. This principle is subject to the proposition, already noted, that laws may deal with physical characteristics that exclusively pertain to one sex or the other without infringing upon equality of rights. As previously stated, such instances would only rarely occur.

The phrase "shall not be denied or abridged" constitutes an unqualified prohibition. It means that differentiation on account of sex is totally precluded, regardless of whether a legislature or administrative agency may consider such a classification to be "reasonable," to be beneficial rather than "invidious," or to be justified by "compelling reasons." Furthermore, for much the same reasons as in the racial area, the clause would not sanction "separate but equal" treatment. Power to deny equality of rights on account of sex is wholly foreclosed.

The Equal Rights Amendment applies only to governmental conduct, federal or state. It does not affect conduct in the private, nongovernmental sector of society. The problems of "state action" raised here are similar to those the courts have dealt with under the Fourteenth and Fifteenth Amendments. The basic legal doctrines that govern are the same, though they may have somewhat different application in the area of sex discrimination.

Finally, it should be noted that the Equal Rights Amendment fits into the total framework of the Constitution and should be construed to mesh with the remainder of the constitutional structure. One particular aspect of this is worth brief attention. It concerns the constitutional right to privacy.

In *Griswold v. Connecticut* the Supreme Court recognized an independent constitutional right of privacy, derived from a combination of various more specific constitutional guarantees. The scope and implications of the right to privacy have not yet been fully developed by the courts. But I think it correct to say that the central idea behind the concept is the existence of an inner core of personal life which is protected against invasion by the laws and rules of the society, no matter how valid such laws and rules may be outside the protected sphere. If this is true, the constitutional right of privacy would prevail over other portions of the Constitution embodying the laws of society in its collective capacity. This principle would have an important impact, at some points, in the operation of the Equal Rights Amendment. Thus I think the constitutional right of privacy would justify police practices by which a search of a woman could be performed only by another woman and search of a man, by another man. Similarly the right of privacy would permit, perhaps require, the separation of the sexes in public rest rooms, segregation by sex in sleeping quarters of prisons or similar public institutions, and a certain segregation of living conditions in the armed forces. The concern over these issues expressed by opponents of the Equal Rights Amendment seems to me to have been magnified beyond all proportion, and to have failed to take into account the young, but fully recognized, constitutional right of privacy. . . .

My conclusion for this survey of the legal problems raised by the Equal Rights Amendment is that the method chosen is the proper one and the instrument proposed is constitutionally and legally sound.

$$\left[\begin{array}{l}\textit{Is an Equal Rights Amend-}\\ \textit{ment Necessary to Provide}\\ \textit{Equal Protection for}\\ \textit{Women?}\end{array}\right]$$

No: The Equal Rights Amendment Is Not the Way

Paul A. Freund

T HE issue has always been over choice of means, not over ends. The objective is to nullify those vestigial laws that work an injustice to women, that are exploitative or impose oppressive discriminations on account of sex. Although such laws have been progressively superseded or held to be violative of equal protection, some of these laws still disfigure our legal codes. Beyond this, the Women's Rights Movement seeks to achieve equal opportunity and equal treatment for women in business, professional, domestic, and political relationships, but unless equality is denied by a public agency or because of a law the Equal Rights Amendment by its terms has no application. If we want to see more women in law firms, in the medical profession, in the Cabinet—and I, for one, do—we must turn elsewhere than to the proposed amendment. The point is not the smug argument that we must change hearts and minds and attitudes (though that too is involved) rather than look to law; the point is that within the realm of law we have to compare the effects and effectiveness of a constitutional amendment on the one hand and the mandate of congressional legislation and judicial decisions on the other.

The proposed amendment attempts to impose a single standard of sameness on the position of the sexes in all the multifarious roles regulated by law—marital support, parental obligations, social security, industrial employment, activities in public schools, and military service—to mention the most prominent. It is necessary to try to analyze all these various applications of the single-standard formula in order to discern whether anomalies, uncertainties, and injustices would result. Unfortunately we have no definitive

Paul A. Freund, from "The Equal Rights Amendment Is Not the Way," 6 *Harvard Civil Rights–Civil Liberties Law Review* (1971), pp. 234–42. Copyright 1971 by the Harvard Civil Rights–Civil Liberties Law Review.

guide in such an exploration, for neither in the House nor in the Senate was there a committee report on the amendment, which might have focused attention on concrete issues rather than on a generalized slogan—"equal rights under law"—which is intended to supplant "equal protection of the laws." The alternative legal course is to achieve changes in the relative position of women through paramount federal standards or to overcome invidious classifications on the ground that they are presently unconstitutional. The choice resembles that in medicine between a single broad-spectrum drug with uncertain and unwanted side-effects and a selection of specific pills for specific ills. . . .

Congressional power under the commerce clause, as the civil-rights legislation shows, is adequate to deal with discrimination (whether private or governmental) based on sex, as on race. This authority has been utilized to some extent in relation to sex discrimination in employment practices but not to such discrimination in places of public accommodation. Discrimination in matters of family law could be reached under Congress' power to enforce the equal-protection guarantee, as set forth in *Katzenbach v. Morgan*. . . .

So far I have set out reasons why the amendment is not necessary or appropriate. Before leaving this point, let me add that even if the amendment were adopted, legislation on the state or federal level would be necessary to carry it out in its myriad applications. Four words will not in themselves remake the laws of age of consent, marital property rights, marital and parental legal duties, and protective factory legislation. The energies that have been spent for forty years in an effort to secure the submission of the amendment by Congress to the states would have to be followed, even if ultimately successful, by efforts to revise the laws in a satisfactory way. It is hard to believe that this preliminary struggle to obtain the support of two-thirds of Congress and three-fourths of the states is other than a diversion of energy from the essential task of revising the laws themselves.

In some fields a national mandate to the states is a useful, even necessary, prelude because there is a bloc of recalcitrant states or because individual states fear a loss of competitive advantage in raising their standards. The latter was the case, for example, with unemployment compensation, which lagged in the states until federal tax credit legislation took away the supposed advantage of holding out. So far as women's rights are concerned, a similar situation conceivably might exist with respect to a disadvantaged position in industry; but there is a twofold answer to this supposition. So far as merely private discrimination is concerned, the amendment has no application, and all discrimination, private or governmental, is subject to the paramount power of Congress under the commerce clause. In noncommercial fields, such as marital property or parental duties, there is no need to go to the states for a preliminary mandate to change their laws. If three-fourths of the states are prepared to ratify the amendment, it is hard to see why they must first thus admonish themselves to do justice before they are prepared in fact to do justice. Although forty years of frustration ought to have carried a lesson, no doubt it seems easier to place a resounding and all-encompassing phrase in the Constitution than to identify specific wrongs and draft model laws to correct them. Yet it is the latter that sooner or later will have to be done, whatever the fate of the amendment—and I suggest that it be sooner.

Still, it may be suggested, the amendment would serve importantly as a symbol—a symbol that the nation has made a commitment to justice for women under law. One gets the impression that much of the drive for the amendment owes its force to this psychological wellspring. The value of a symbol, however, lies precisely in the fact that it is not to be taken literally, that it is not meant to be analyzed closely for its exact implications. A concurrent resolution of Congress, expressing the general sentiment of that body, would be an appropriate vehicle for promulgating a symbol. When, however, we are presented with a proposed amendment to our fundamental law, binding on federal and state governments, on judges, legislatures, and executives, we are entitled to inquire more circumspectly into the operational meaning and effects of the symbol. Lawyers, in particular, have an obligation to ask these questions and to weigh the answers that are given. For if the amendment is not only a needless misdirection of effort in the quest for justice, but one which would produce anomalies, confusion, and injustices, no symbolic value could justify its adoption. We turn, then, to these issues of meaning and effect.

A mandate that equal rights under law shall not be denied or abridged by the United States or any state on account of sex can have either of two conceivable meanings. It can mean that any classification based on sex must be justified by some good (or very good, or compelling) reason, or it can mean that no such classification can pass muster. To this question there is no authoritative answer to be found in the congressional history of the proposed amendment, but the literature of its main sponsors insists on an absolute meaning. This interpretation has been reinforced by the recent experience with the amendment in the Senate. After the original version was amended to death, Senator Bayh and other proponents offered a revised version, using the language "equal protection of the laws shall not be denied or abridged . . . on account of sex." This formulation, adopting the language of the Fourteenth Amendment but explicitly stressing its application to classifications based on sex, would have been accepted by a number of opponents of the original version. (I would not feel impelled to oppose the revised version, though doubting its necessity). But it was the most active groups behind the amendment that refused to accept the substitute. They protested that courts or legislatures might find compelling reasons for certain classifications, and this result was unacceptable. I should have thought that if there are compelling reasons and if the amendment would allow them to prevail, that outcome would be cause for satisfaction, not intransigent complaint.

A doctrinaire equality, then, is apparently the theme of the amendment. And so women must be admitted to West Point on a parity with men; women must be conscripted for military service equally with men (though classification on an individual basis for assignment to duties would be valid, it is asserted); girls must be eligible for the same athletic teams as boys in the public schools and state universities; Boston Boys' Latin School and Girls' Latin School must merge (not simply be brought into parity); and life insurance commissioners may not continue to approve lower life insurance premiums for women (based on greater life expectancy)—all by command of the Federal Constitution.

Perhaps the country ought to consider conscripting women equally with men. My point is not that we must maintain the status quo; it is that a change so far-reaching and inflexible ought surely not be brought about as the half-hidden implication of a constitutional motto. Changes of far less import in the draft law have been the subject of full-scale hearings, committee reports, and debate in and out of Congress. Can we assume that every member of Congress who is prepared to vote for the amendment is equally prepared to explain and justify its effect on military service and to support that result before his constituents? A similar question has to be raised about each of the other foregoing illustrative consequences of the amendment. The irreverent thought obtrudes itself that either not every member of Congress has been adequately briefed on the amendment's implications or not every member takes seriously the possibility of its ratification. This irreverence is reinforced when it is remembered that such subjects as selective service or admission to West Point are wholly in the control of Congress, and there is no reason to wait for the mandate of three-fourths of the states if Congress really regards sex differentiation in those institutions as unacceptable and is bent on ending it. Indeed, the change could be brought about by simple majority vote, not the two-thirds required to submit a constitutional amendment.

Special scrutiny should be given to the field of domestic relations, with its complex relationships of marital duties and parental responsibilities. Every state makes a husband liable for the support of his wife, without regard to the ability of the wife to support herself. The obligation of the wife to support her husband is obviously not identical to this; if it were, each would be duty bound to support the other. Instead, the wife's duty varies from state to state. In some jurisdictions there is no obligation on the wife, even if the husband is unable to support himself. In others, the wife does have a duty of support in such a case. . . .

Is the favorable treatment now everywhere accorded to wives in respect of support a manifestation of male oppression or chauvinism or domination?

Can it be expected that all the states will make an about-face on the law of support within a year of the adoption of the amendment; and if they do not, what will be the reaction of wives to the Equal Rights Amendment when husbands procure judicial decisions in its name relieving them of the duty of support because an equal duty is not imposed on their wives?

It is sometimes said that a rigid requirement of equality is no less proper for the sexes than for the races, and no less workable. But the moral dimensions of the concept of equality are clearly not the same in the two cases. To hold separate Olympic competitions for whites and blacks would be deeply repugnant to our sensibilities. Do we—should we—feel the same repugnance, that same sense of degradation, at the separate competitions for men and women? A school system offering a triple option based on race—all-white, all-black, and mixed schools—would elevate freedom of choice over equal protection in an impermissible way. Are we prepared to pass that judgment as readily on a school system that offers a choice of boys', girls', and coeducational schools? A family that prefers to send its daughter to a girls' school or college and its son to a boys' school or college is not thereby committing an invidious discrimination; their judgment of relative educational advantages may be wise or unwise, but it is not so far beyond the bounds of legitimate discretion, experimentation, and good will as to call for a uniform constitutional mandate closing off that area of choice. One of the prime targets of the equal-rights movement has been the color-segregated public rest room. Whether segregation by sex would meet the same condemnation is at least a fair question to test the legal assimilation of racism and "sexism."

The answer proffered is that a counter-principle, a constitutional right of privacy, would be invoked at this point. But this is only to restate the problem, which is whether there are not considerations other than identical treatment that ought to be taken into account in the various contexts of relations between the sexes. If privacy is one such consideration, though unexpressed in the amendment, when will it prevail and when will it not? Is privacy in fact the only unexpressed countervailing interest? Freedom of association is a constitutional right enjoying recognition even longer and firmer than privacy. It has been invoked without avail, as has the interest in privacy, to blunt the force of equal protection in the field of racial separation. Is it to have greater recognition (as in the area of public education) where relations between the sexes are concerned? Moreover, interests more social, less individual, than privacy or association are actually involved. If a public school conducts separate physical education classes for boys and girls, or a prison maintains separate cells for men and women, would the validity of the separation depend on a claim of privacy? If the pupils or prisoners waived any interest in privacy and wished to amalgamate the classes or the cells, would the school or the prison be required to conform? Or could the law respect a wider community sentiment that separateness was fitter and not invidious?

Constitutional amendments, like other laws, cannot always anticipate all the questions that may arise under them. Remote and esoteric problems may have to be faced in due course. But when basic, commonplace, recurring questions are raised and left unanswered by text or legislative history, one can only infer a want of candor or of comprehension.

I would not wish to leave the subject on a purely negative note. My concern, as I have said, is with the method proposed, which is too simplistic for the living issues at stake. It remains, then, to suggest alternative approaches. A great deal can be done through the regular legislative process in Congress. . . .

Moreover, a few significant decisions of the Supreme Court in well-chosen cases under the Fourteenth Amendment would have a highly salutary effect. And decisions under Title VII of the Civil Rights Act will clarify the role of state laws regulating employment in light of the statutory concept of bona fide occupational qualifications.

Finally, Congress can exercise its enforcement power under the Fourteenth Amendment to identify and displace state laws that in its judgment work an unreasonable discrimination based on sex. In this connection let me point out a serious deficiency in the proposed amendment. Its enforcement clause gives legislative authority to Congress and the states "within their respective jurisdictions." This is a more restrictive authorization to Congress than is to be found in any other amendment, including the Fourteenth. If the new amendment is deemed to supersede the Fourteenth concerning equal rights with respect to sex, Congress will be left with less power than it now possesses to make the guarantee effective. This is the final anomaly. . . .

12
Roe v. Wade: Does a Right to Privacy Include the Right to Have an Abortion?

Glenn A. Phelps

ORMA McCorvey was a down-on-her-luck twenty-five-year-old woman who, one hot August evening in Texas, was brutally gang raped by three men. Little more is known of the incident. Whether because of fear, shame, distrust of the criminal justice system, or trauma, McCorvey did not report the rape to the police. In that regard her response was not untypical of many other raped and physically abused women. There the story might have ended—one more uncounted victim of sexual violence— but McCorvey soon learned that she was pregnant. Faced with carrying an unwanted child for nine months, inflicted on her without her consent, she decided to seek an abortion. She soon discovered that abortions were forbidden by law in Texas. Lacking money to go to a state where abortions were legal (such as California) or to pay the fee of one of the many doctors providing underground abortions, she was forced to carry the child to term and offer it for adoption.[1]

Norma McCorvey's name appears nowhere in the annals of U.S. constitutional law. Yet her frustration and anger led to the most talked about, most hotly debated case of the 1970s. Norma McCorvey is more familiar to constitutional scholars as Jane Roe, the anonymous personage who would lend her name to *Roe v. Wade* (410 U.S. 113, 1973).

Other women were also angry and frustrated at the dilemma of choosing between criminality and unwanted pregnancy. Lawyers for Jane Roe filed a class action suit on behalf of all the "Jane Roes" present and future. (A class action suit was a practical necessity. Individual pregnancies last nine months. This case would not be decided until 1973, more than three years after Norma McCorvey had given birth, an event that would have made this or any other normal case moot.)

Nothing in the specifics of the Constitution offered much encouragement to Roe. There was no clear statement that persons had a right to privacy, much less the more expansive concept of a right to an abortion. Yet the opponents of the Texas antiabortion statute were not without hope. The boundaries of U.S. civil liberties are not determined solely by the Constitution and its amendments. Indeed, Justice Frank Murphy had argued in a number of opinions that the Bill of Rights merely stated the *minimum* standards of liberty, freedom, and equality. In his view there was nothing to prevent Congress or the states from amplifying or broadening the scope of these constitutional rights or even creating new rights out of whole cloth.

Might it be possible for the Supreme Court, through its powers of interpretation, to share in this process of civil liberties expansion? Scholars disagree on this point. However, the Court has on occasion allocated this authority to itself. When it does, controversy inevitably follows. Such was the case with the Court's "discovery" of the right to privacy.

The idea that privacy is a fundamental right in a democratic society was not new in 1973. Indeed, Charles Warren and Louis Brandeis (later to be a Supreme Court Justice) had written a famous law review article in 1890 on privacy. They asserted that respect for privacy had a long history in English common law and that the value of privacy undergirded many of the explicit protections of the Bill of Rights.[2]

For nearly seventy years, however, privacy as a fundamental individual right was an intellectual concept with no basis in law. *Griswold v. Connecticut* (381 U.S. 479, 1965) changed all that. The policy issues in *Griswold* had been in conflict for decades. Connecticut was one of many states that had legislated against any form of artificial birth control. Connecticut justified these laws with reference to the ample police powers reserved to the state. Broadly defined, these police powers authorize states to pass any laws necessary to promote the health, safety, and public welfare of their citizens. The only limitations on these police powers are those found in the federal Constitution and, in particular, the Fourteenth Amendment.

Connecticut's statutes had been enacted in 1879, a time when the moral standards of the community were fervently antiabortion and antibirth control. The state presumed that its police powers extended into these areas of public morality; thus it responded to the political demands of the majority of its citizens. The statutes in question made "any person who uses any drug, medicinal article or instrument for the purpose of preventing conception" guilty of a crime. Giving advice about birth control was also illegal.

Estelle Griswold was a long-outspoken supporter of birth control and served as Director of Connecticut's Planned Parenthood League. She believed that the state's antibirth control laws were both bad policy (she was convinced that uncontrolled population growth created even greater social problems) and an unconstitutional intrusion on the privacy of women. Griswold wanted to test the constitutionality of these laws, so she orchestrated a scenario of events that led to her arrest. She opened a Planned Parenthood clinic in New Haven. She did so openly and publicly, practically daring the authorities to arrest her. The clinic was shut down, and Griswold was arrested and convicted.

Much of the oral argument before the Supreme Court focused on the question of due process. Connecticut claimed that the statutes served a legitimate purpose (public morality and public health) under its police powers and that the laws were reasonably connected to those ends. Griswold's lawyers argued that the laws served no legitimate purpose (the regulation of sexual relations between married couples being beyond the reach of the state's police powers) and were therefore irrational and a denial of substantive due process.

The Court sided with the birth control advocates—but for reasons quite different from those based on due process. At least five members of the Court were willing to endorse a right to privacy as a fundamental right protected by the Bill of Rights. This finding involved a creative application of the Court's powers of constitutional interpretation. Nowhere does the Constitution or the Bill of Rights mention a right to privacy. Under a literalist interpretation, then, the Supreme Court could not proclaim the existence of such a right merely because the Justices might deem it good or wise or just.

Literalism proved only a minor obstacle for Justice Douglas. He maintained that privacy is a fundamental right protected by the Constitution. A right to privacy existed in the common law and in the tradition of natural rights that were the principal sources of the Bill of Rights guarantees. Douglas tried to show that this right to privacy was really the seminal spring from which the streams of several specific constitutional rights flowed. Zones of privacy against government intrusion can be found, for example, in the First Amendment. Freedom of religion and speech imply a zone of personal belief beyond the reach of state intervention. Attempts by government officials to inquire into a person's religious beliefs (and, to a lesser extent political beliefs) have usually been viewed as especially odious. The Third Amendment's prohibition against the quartering of troops in peacetime is also based on the presumption of the importance of privacy. Douglas pointed also to the Fourth and Fifth Amendments as sources of a right to privacy. They each prevented or strictly limited intrusions by government upon personal privacy. In sum, Douglas asserted that these specific guarantees in the Bill of Rights had "penumbras formed by emanations from those guarantees that help give them life and substance." The Founding Fathers, then, did not specify a right to privacy only because they believed that the existence of such a right was obvious to any reasonable man. Douglas saw Connecticut's antibirth control laws as violating one of the most fundamental zones of privacy: the sexual relationship between married persons.

Justice Arthur Goldberg and two other colleagues agreed with Douglas on this point: no state should have the power to legislate whether a married couple will have children, or how many children they have, or how to conduct their intimate physical relationship. Goldberg's justification was much simpler than Douglas's assertion of "penumbras" and "emanations." Instead, Goldberg pointed to the Ninth Amendment, which proclaims that the "enumeration in the Constitution, of certain rights, shall not be construed to deny or disparage others retained by the people." Like Justice Murphy before him, Goldberg insisted that the Bill of Rights served only as a catalog of minimal rights. Privacy, to Goldberg, was sufficiently fundamental to merit protection by the Ninth Amendment.

Griswold and its creation of the right to privacy was a controversial decision. Many denounced it as judicial activism in the extreme. Many more wondered what the Court meant by zones of privacy and how far this new right extended. Certainly privacy is not an absolute right any more than the freedoms of speech, press, and religion are. The Fourth Amendment, for example, stipulates that the police may invade the privacy of a home so long as they have a lawful search warrant. By declaring that privacy was a "fundamental right," however, the *Griswold* decision insisted that any future interference with privacy had to be justified by a "compelling" state interest. The reasonableness or even popularity of a law was not sufficient reason.

Do women, as a corollary to the right of privacy, have a right to reproductive choice without government interference? Or does the state have a "compelling interest" that can justify limiting or regulating privacy as regards abortion? These were just two of the myriad social, moral, and political questions raised in *Roe* when it finally went before the Supreme Court.

Certainly the logic of *Griswold* with regard to the inherent privacy of sexual relationships between couples (later extended to single persons as well in *Eisenstadt*) made it clear that choices about child bearing ought not be, in ordinary circumstances, any business of the government.[3] This was a major thrust of "Jane Roe's" argument. A power to prevent abortion might extend to a power to prevent conception or even a power to supervise conjugal relations. Such intrusiveness would transgress the essence of individual liberties as set forth in the Bill or Rights and undermine the constitutional tradition of limited government.

Texas, on the other hand, asserted that while privacy was *a* consideration, it was not the *only* fundamental right at issue. The state maintained that its antiabortion statutes were concerned with protecting the due process rights of the unborn child. Surely, they argued, protecting those rights was an interest sufficiently compelling to justify state legislation.

On this crucial issue—is a fetus a "person" entitled to full constitutional rights?—the Court faced a dilemma that Joel Feinberg has called a "double slippery slope" argument.[4] To illustrate, let us assume that a newborn infant is a "person" with rights that extend at least as far as the right to life. The wrongful death of such a "person" should surely be treated as murder. Does the same quality of "personhood" extend to that same fetus ten minutes before birth? Apart from being attached to an umbilical cord, is there any physiological difference? Is it human life at 9:10 but not at 9:00? One could easily answer that, yes, that is also human life. What about ten minutes before that? And ten minutes before that? Incrementally, there is no real difference between any of these ten-minute phases, yet as we move away from the moment of birth, the slope gets precipitous, until we finally discover that we have agreed that a single-cell organism is a person with full constitutional rights, a proposition considerably less tenable than the original one.

The other side of the slope is equally slippery. We might agree that this one-celled organism is not a person, but how about a two-celled organism? Four-celled? Sixteen-celled? To each we might again say no, but eventually this zygote will begin to look very much like a human being. Can we continue to answer "no" right up to that arbitrary moment we call birth? In short, although each side of the abortion issue begins from a seemingly indisputable truth, those positions become progressively less defensible as they slide down the slope.

The Supreme Court sought to pass through this minefield unscathed. Speaking through Justice Blackmun, they applied a balancing test. Yes, women are entitled to some degree of privacy in their persons. *Griswold* had said at least that. But Texas had convincingly argued that the right to due process and life of the unborn was an area of "compelling interest" to the community. Therefore Blackmun referred back to Douglas's original concept of zones of privacy. In the first trimester of a pregnancy, the privacy interests of the woman were paramount and could not be interfered with by the state. After those first three months, the woman's zone of privacy contracted as the rights of the unborn, as protected by the state, expanded. In the last three months of a pregnancy, this "compelling interest" allowed the state to regulate or even prohibit abortion.

This attempt to have it both ways—to maintain a right of privacy for women and recognize some rights of the unborn—guaranteed that *Roe v. Wade* would not resolve the issue. Antiabortion advocates have made the decision a focus for vigorous political activity, some of it directed specifically at the Supreme Court. Patrick Conley and Robert McKenna offer several of the moral and legal arguments critical of the Court's decision. Feminist groups and other supporters of abortion defend *Roe* as a minimum statement of the "freedom of choice" position. Philip Heymann and Douglas Barzelay offer a measured defense of this highly controversial issue.

$$\begin{bmatrix} \textit{Does a Right to Privacy} \\ \textit{Include the Right to Have} \\ \textit{an Abortion?} \end{bmatrix}$$

Yes: *Roe v. Wade* and Its Critics

Philip B. Heymann
Douglas E. Barzelay

T HE thesis of this article is that the Court's opinion in *Roe* is amply justified both by precedent and by those principles that have long guided the Court in making the ever-delicate determination of when it must tell a state that it may not pursue certain measures, because to do so would impinge on those rights of individuals that the Constitution explicitly or implicitly protects. The language of the Court's opinion in *Roe* too often obscures the full strength of the four-step argument that underlies its decision.

1. Under the Fourteenth Amendment to the Constitution, there are certain interests of individuals, long called "fundamental" in judicial decisions, that a state cannot abridge without a very good reason.
2. The Court has never limited this set of "fundamental" interests to those explicitly mentioned elsewhere in the Constitution.
3. One set of nonenumerated but fundamental rights, which the Court has recognized for 50 years but has only more recently begun calling aspects of "privacy", includes rights of individual choice as to marriage, procreation and child rearing.
4. Since the issue of a right to terminate a pregnancy falls squarely within this long-established area of special judicial concern, the Court was obligated to determine in *Roe* whether the states did in fact have a sufficiently compelling reason for abridging the individual's freedom of choice as to abortion. . . .

The first two propositions of the four-step argument underlying the decision in *Roe* are no longer seriously disputed. The minimal judicial protections

Philip B. Heymann and Douglas E. Barzelay, from "The Forest and the Trees: *Roe* v. *Wade* and Its Critics," 53 *Boston University Law Review* (1973), pp. 765–77.

that are granted an individual whenever a state purports to regulate or abridge any form of his liberty, however unimportant—protections against invidious distinctions, unfair procedures and wholly irrational or arbitrary state impositions—are not the only types of protections the Fourteenth Amendment accords. Some few private interests and liberties have, throughout this century, been declared entitled to a much greater measure of respect at the hands of state legislatures and have been afforded a far more protective measure of judicial scrutiny and concern. Nor has this list of interests specially protected under the vague words of the Fourteenth Amendment been limited to those mentioned or plainly implied in some other clause of the Constitution. . . .

The special protection afforded particular rights has gone far beyond the explicit provisions of the first eight amendments. The right of association is not mentioned in the First Amendment, but the Court has deemed its protection implicit in the several guarantees of that amendment. The Court has also treated the right to travel as fundamental, requiring a showing of a compelling interest to support a state's burdening of the right. Yet no such right is specified in the Constitution; it is apparently enough that it has come to be recognized in a series of cases as "fundamental to the concept of our Federal Union." . . .

In short, the criticism that has been directed at the Court's opinion in *Roe* is not and could hardly be addressed to the first two steps of its argument. It is generally conceded that there are certain interests of individuals that a state cannot abridge without very good reason and that these interests have not been limited to those that were stated explicitly by the Framers of the Fourteenth Amendment nor even to this category as supplemented by a judicial power to incorporate some of the first eight amendments. . . .

The Court in *Roe* held that among the "fundamental" Fourteenth Amendment rights is a category that encompasses protection of individual freedom of choice in matters of marriage, procreation and child rearing. The line of precedent on which it relied begins almost half a century ago. . . .

It may be that these cases could, with some effort, have been individually distinguished on narrow grounds, taken together; however, they clearly delineate a sphere of interest—which the Court now groups and denominates "privacy"—implicit in the "liberty" protected by the Fourteenth Amendment. At the core of this sphere is the right of the individual to make for himself—except where a very good reason exists for placing the decision in society's hands—the fundamental decisions that shape family life: whom to marry; whether and when to have children; and with what values to rear those children.

It is hardly surprising that the Court has come to protect these interests over the last half century. Our political system is superimposed on and presupposes a social system of family units, not just of isolated individuals. No assumption more deeply underlies our society than the assumption that it is the individual who decides whether to raise a family, with whom to raise a family, and, in broad measure, what values and beliefs to inculcate in the children who will later exercise the rights and responsibilities of citizens and heads of families. Any sharp departure from this assumption would cut as deeply at the underlying conditions of acceptance of our society and governing institutions as a broad restriction on the right to vote or hold office.

This point is as important as it is easy to overlook. It is, of course, obvious that the family has historically been a fundamental unit of our society for such purposes as socialization and nature, and that it ranks in importance with the individual as a unit of economic and political decision making. What is far less obvious is that the family unit does not simply co-exist with our constitutional system; it is an integral part of it. In democratic theory as well as in practice, it is in the family that children are expected to learn the values and beliefs that democratic institutions later draw on to determine group directions. The immensely important power of deciding about matters of early socialization has been allocated to the family, not to the government. Thus, if a state government decided that all children would be reared and educated from birth under such complete control of a state official that the parental role would be minimal, the effect of our present notions of democratic government would be immense. The form of our government would not change; elections would go on in the same way and group decisions would be arrived at by the same processes as are now used. The substance of our system, however, would be vastly different. The outcomes of the political system would be radically altered, for the government would then be vested with the capacity to influence powerfully, through socialization, the future outcomes of democratic political processes. The fact that individuals would remain legally free to believe and speak as they wished would not diminish the immense impact of centralizing the processes through which values and beliefs are instilled in the people who will later participate in group decision making. A similar, if less thoroughgoing, alteration of the present allocation of powers in our society could be provided by controlling who is allowed to have children or otherwise regulating the selection of marital partners.

In this light, the long line of precedent in this area under the Fourteenth Amendment is entirely principled. For the Court to have declined strict review of state legislation that limits the private right to choose whom to marry and whether to raise a family, or to decide within wide bounds how to rear one's children, would have been to leave the most basic substructure of our society and government subject to change at political whim. To have treated these matters as rather remote emanations of protections found in the First Amendment or elsewhere in the Bill of Rights would have been disingenuous at best, ineffective at worst.

The similarity of the protected rights in the areas of marriage, procreation and child rearing to the expressly protected rights in the area of religion is striking. Like religious beliefs, beliefs in these areas are often deeply held, involving loyalties fully as powerful as those that bind the citizen to the state. Decisions on these matters tend to affect the quality of an entire lifetime, and may not easily be reversed. The choice of whom to marry or whether or not to have a child, once taken, will have as strong an impact on the life patterns of the individuals involved for years to come as any adoption of a religious belief or viewpoint. Decisions of families in the area of "privacy," like decisions of individuals in the area of religion, cannot easily be controlled by the state; and the devices needed for effective enforcement of state policy may themselves be so intrusive as to be deeply offensive. At the same time, the impact of an individual's decisions on questions of marriage, procreation and child rearing diminishes greatly beyond the setting of the family itself, just as most religious practices affect primarily those who adopt and engage in them. In other words, the impact of such decisions falls largely within one of the basic units of our society and thus does not involve the powerful interest of society in regulating the relationships among its familial and individual units.

In these ways the area that the Court has come to call "privacy" shares with the area of religion sharp distinctions from the areas that the states may regulate with greater freedom. Regulation of economic interests does not invade the basic units of society, nor does it touch emotions as deeply held as those in the areas of religion and family, nor, short of the unconstitutional taking of private property without compensation, does it generally involve decisions with far-reaching effects on the entire life of the individual. Further, economic regulation, unlike regulation of "privacy" interests, deals directly with that interaction among units which is the primary concern of political arrangements. Similarly, the Court would not be required to find that either all consensual sexual activity or the use of soft drugs was protected. To whatever degree such behavior may be socially harmless, it certainly does not produce the same kind of nearly irrevocable effects, nor spring from the same deep well of cultural values as do decisions about marriage, procreation, or child rearing. . . .

Plainly the right of a couple to decide whether or not to prevent the birth of a child by abortion falls within the class of interests involving marriage, procreation and child rearing which the Court has considered "fundamental." . . . The couple's right to decide whether to have a family is the very same right as that established and protected in the cases dealing with contraception; considerations identical to those that justify protecting the broader class require careful scrutiny of regulations concerning abortion. The point is made most clearly by considering what a conclusion that abortion did not fall within a category of special protected interests would have meant. A state, on a slender showing of rationality, could have required abortions—perhaps as incident to limiting a woman to two children—unless of course the fetus's rights were fundamental even though the mother's were not. It could have forced a woman to carry the child of her rapist to term; it could have conditioned the right to an abortion on the payment of a fee or the discretionary approval of a state official.

Recognizing that abortion falls within the class of fundamental interests of "privacy" does not mean that statutes prohibiting abortion had to be considered unconstitutional—only that they had to be justified by compelling state interests. The Court might logically have concluded that the state's interest in protecting the unborn was compelling enough to overrride the parents' rights, without seriously threatening the broad range of individual rights already established under the line of decisions from *Meyer* through *Eisenstadt.* What it could not do, unless it was prepared to discard the principles of those cases, was to avoid evaluating the state's interest to see if it justified taking from the mother all discretion in the matter of abortion. Striking the necessary balance plainly required an agonizingly difficult decision, involving as it it did drawing the line where protection of life may begin, a subject on which public opinion was stridently divided. Yet neither the difficulty nor the impassioned setting of the decision was a principled ground on which the Court could refuse to make an evaluation it was otherwise called upon to make.

The final step of the Court's argument was forced upon it by the prior steps. What the Court had to decide was whether there is an early stage at which the potential of the embryo or fetus is not of sufficient importance to warrant abridging the constitutional right of a woman to decide whether she shall bear children. The Court decided that there was such a stage, and that it ended at about the point at which the fetus was capable of sustaining life outside the womb. One cannot deny, and the Court did not deny, that some would attach great weight to the prospect of life from its earliest days when we have little more than a handful of cells possessing a rich genetic code. But much that we associate with the value of human life is not present at the earliest stages. There is no feeling nor thought of which we know. There is no reciprocal relationship to others that is reflected in need or love. There is no memory or fear. What most of us mean by life, what most of us care about when we think of protecting life, is not true of the 12 or 16 cells present on the third or fourth day after pregnancy nor is it present for some time thereafter. . . .

It is, of course, important that a sharp line be drawn to show where human life begins and ends if we are to maintain a respect for life without regard to differences in intelligence, age, capacity and experience. One may fault the Court for not having drawn such a line with sufficient clarity, but surely it was right that the line can safely be drawn well after the emergence of a fertilized egg. Sometime thereafter there comes a point at which the social interest in the protection of life becomes at least as important as any burden the mother may then have to bear. Clearly, that point has been reached by birth; the Court finds that it may be reached at the point at which life becomes capable of sustaining itself. Perhaps this line is further along than some would like it to be, but that is unlikely to have great practical significance. The overwhelming proportion of abortions will take place in the first few months. What is crucial is the correctness of the Court's determination that there is an early stage at which the potential of the embryo or fetus does not justify overriding the right of the woman to decide whether she will bear a child.

The Court had to go as far as finding that human life with all its claims to importance had not begun in the early days of the embryo and the fetus. But in a very important sense, that is not the consequence of the decision. The consequence is that, subject to the restrictions that states may impose under *Roe,* it is the moral judgment of the mother and her doctor that determines when the life of the fetus shall be considered so substantial as to preclude abortion. One need not be certain how he feels about an abortion at the end of the six weeks or 20 weeks to approve the decision. It is enough to feel that the answer may depend on the woman's age, her marital situation, her financial circumstances and a large number of other factors. It is in light of all these factors, which no statute can incorporate, that the Court has in effect allocated the choice for the first five or six months after conception to the mother and her doctor. It has not decided that the fetus has no moral claim within this period, but simply that the fetus has no legal claim that the state can enforce. This allocation of choice among the mother, the state and the Court was wholly consistent with constitutional precedent and reasoning. . . .

Does a Right to Privacy
Include the Right to Have
an Abortion?

No: The Supreme Court on Abortion: A Dissenting Opinion

Patrick T. Conley
Robert J. McKenna

I N the decade of the 1850s one of the most vexing constitutional questions concerned the status of slavery in the federal territories. For
reasons which historians have not yet fully fathomed, this issue became a
vent for the economic, emotional, psychological, and moral disputes generated by the institution of slavery itself. During this acrimonious debate
three basic positions emerged: (1) the pro-slave argument which held that
Congress had a positive duty to protect a slaveowner's property rights in the
federal territories; (2) a diametrically opposed view, advanced by anti-slavery
Northerners, stating that Congress must ban slavery from the territories; and
(3) the middle ground of "popular sovereignty" which left the decision on
slavery to the residents of the areas in question. Then, in 1857, a Southern-
dominated Supreme Court attempted to resolve this morally-charged dispute
in what it considered to be a rational and impartial manner. The result was
the Dred Scott decision in which the Court novelly employed the procedural
Due Process Clause of the Fifth Amendment to vindicate the pro-slave position. But it did so in disregard of historical precedents which made that view
untenable. To compound its error, the Court contended that Negroes could
not attain citizenship because such status contravened the intent of the
Founding Fathers.

The Dred Scott decision did not resolve the great moral dispute over
slavery and the status of the Negro in American society. It was so patently
unsound that it was overridden—both by subsequent events and by the less
violent process of constitutional amendment.

On January 22, 1973, the United States Supreme Court, in magisterial
fashion, undertook to resolve another moral controversy in the case of *Roe v.*

Patrick T. Conley and Robert J. McKenna, from "The Supreme Court on Abortion: A Dissenting Opinion," 19 *Catholic Lawyer* (1973), pp. 19–27.

Wade, and a companion case, *Doe v. Bolton.* These decisions concerned abortion, and here a right more fundamental than citizenship was at stake—at issue was the right to life. The Dred Scott analogy to *Roe v. Wade* is not an exercise in hyperbole; not only was a more basic right involved, but a much larger class was affected. In 1857, approximately 4,200,000 blacks and their descendants were judicially attainted, while in the year 1973 alone about 5 million living human fetuses will be shorn of their natural right to life for at least the first six months of their existence.

Unlike the Biblical decree of Herod, however, *Roe v. Wade* does not mandate a slaughter of the innocents. The Court, in fact, explicitly denied the contention of appellant Jane Roe (a fictional name), that a woman's right to an abortion is absolute and that she is entitled to terminate her pregnancy at whatever time, in whatever way, and for whatever reason she alone chooses. "With this we do not agree," said Justice Blackmun for the majority. His statement was echoed by the Chief Justice: "Plainly, the Court today rejects any claim that the Constitution requires abortion on demand," affirmed Mr. Burger. Even the libertarian Justice Douglas admitted that "voluntary abortion at any time and place regardless of medical standards would impinge on a rightful concern of society. The woman's health is part of that concern; as is the life of the fetus after quickening."

But, although the decision was not a total victory for the abortion advocates, it was a substantial victory nonetheless. In essence, the Court concluded that a state criminal abortion statute like that of Texas, which "excepts from criminality only a life saving procedure on behalf of the mother, without regard to a pregnancy stage and without recognition of the other interest involved, is violative of the Due Process Clause of the Fourteenth Amendment."

The so-called right which the Texas abortion statute allegedly infringed upon was the expectant mother's right of privacy. In deference to maternal privacy the Court then proceeded to formulate the following abortion schedule: "(a) For the stage prior to approximately the end of the first trimester [the first three months], the abortion decision and its effectuation must be left to the medical judgment of the pregnant woman's attending physician; (b) For the stage subsequent to approximately the end of the first trimester [the second three months], the State, in promoting its interest in the health of the mother, may, if it chooses, regulate the abortion procedure in ways that are reasonably related to maternal health; (c) For the stage subsequent to viability [the final three months], the State, in promoting its interest in the potentiality of human life, may, if it chooses, regulate, and even proscribe, abortion except where it is necessary, in appropriate medical judgment, for the preservation of the life or health of the mother."

Such was the fiat of the Court—a formidable pronouncement indeed. Justice Blackmun's rationale and argumentation, however, were not sufficient to support the Court's foray into the legislative domain because the decision contained several dubious moral, logical, biomedical, and legal contentions.

First, the Court explicitly admitted that it "need not resolve the difficult question of when life begins. . . . the judiciary, at this point in the development of man's knowledge, is not in a position to speculate as to the answer." Later it took notice of the fact that the Catholic Church, "many non-Catholics", and "many physicians" believe that life begins at conception. In view of these considerations and the Court's candid admission of its own ignorance, it seems incredible that the Court could proceed with confidence to schematize abortion according to the trimester system. It chided Texas for arbitrarily selecting conception as a basis for that state's abortion law, and then, in an equally arbitrary manner, chose viability as the basis of its own formula. In effect, the Court said: "We do not know if human life exists prior to viability, but even if it does we choose not to protect it, and we bar the states from protecting it also."

It had often been the practice of the Court when it could not resolve or define a key issue before it (like the nature of a "republican form of government") to declare the matter a political question and therefore non-justiciable. If ever the doctrine of political question should have been invoked, it was when the Court asserted that the question of life's commencement was beyond its ability to resolve. To proceed in the face of that admission was reckless folly. It was, as stated by Justice White in his dissent, "an exercise in raw judicial power"; an "improvident and extravagant exercise of the power of judicial review." White could find "no constitutional warrant" for the Court's action, nor could he accept "the Court's exercise of its clear power of choice by interposing a constitutional barrier to state efforts to protect human life and by investing mothers and doctors with the constitutionally protected right to exterminate it." The Court did rush in, however, armed with its nescience regarding the origins of human life, and the results were disastrous.

Having thus disposed of the question of life, the justices examined four main theories regarding the point in time when the rights of a person attach to a human fetus, namely (1) conception, (2) quickening or first movement, (3) viability, or (4) birth. Justice Blackmun concluded that "the word 'person,' as used in the Fourteenth Amendment, does not include the unborn." Here the Court buttressed its contention with formidable but not insurmountable evidence. With equal effort it could have reached the opposite conclusion, especially in view of the fact that no evidence was adduced to show that the drafters intended to exclude the unborn when they utilized the word "person" in the various sections of the Constitution where it appears. In the absence of a clear constitutional intent, arising no doubt from the fact that the particular problem raised in *Roe v. Wade* never occurred to previous constitutional draftsmen, the Court should have exercised restraint.

The Court has applied the "compelling state interest" standard to those legislatures which have set up classifications or categories, the members of which have been deprived of equal protection of the law. In several recent opinions a majority of the Court asserted that the strictness of the standard for decision in cases involving classifications made by legislative bodies varies according to the nature of the right placed in jeopardy; the more fundamental the right involved, the greater was the judicial requirement to "carefully and meticulously scrutinize" the classification in the light of the following principles:

(a) As the right in jeopardy becomes more fundamental, the more perfect must be the relationship between the classification excluding a human group from the enjoyment of the right and the purpose for which the classification is made.

(b) As the right involved becomes more fundamental, the more "compelling" the state or governmental interest must be in making a classification excluding certain human groups from the enjoyment of the right.

In *Roe v. Wade* the Court has not practiced what it preached. In effect, it has established a *judicial* classification consisting of those unborn humans who have not reached the stage of viability and has deprived these individuals of their right to life by making them fair game for the abortionist. Several learned anti-abortionists who presented an *amicus curiae* brief to the Court for its consideration make this valid observation. They argued that "because of the fundamental nature of life, the most compelling of all interests would have to be shown on the part of the Court in order to carve out such a classification, which would exclude the lives of unborn humans from the protection of the law."

The Court did, indeed, advance a rationale to justify its conclusions by claiming that "the right of personal privacy" is "broad enough to encompass a woman's decision whether or not to terminate her pregnancy," though admitting that the right was "not unqualified and must be considered against important state interest in regulation." When the Court tried to explain why this alleged right of privacy was fundamental enough to override a state's interest in the protection of fetal life, the shallowness of its value system was glaringly revealed.

Justice Blackmun justified abortion on the grounds of privacy because "maternity, or additional offspring, may force upon the woman a distressful life and future," cause psychological harm, bring "distress for all concerned," or place a social "stigma" on the unwed mother. These were the "weighty reasons" for excluding the unborn from the enjoyment of the right to life. Justice Douglas, in a concurring opinion arising out of *Roe v. Wade* and its companion case involving a Georgia abortion law (*Doe v. Bolton*), went to more ridiculous extremes. Childbirth, said Douglas, "may deprive a woman of her preferred life style and force upon her a radically different and undesired future." She would be required "to endure the discomforts of pregnancy; to incur the pain, higher mortality rate, and aftereffects of childbirth; to abandon educational plans; to sustain loss of income; to forgo the satisfactions of careers; to tax further mental and physical health . . . and, in some cases to bear the lifelong stigma of unwed motherhood." One could scarcely imagine a more amoral and hedonistic rationale. For the highest court in a land which professes spiritual values and claims foundation "under God" to use such criteria to justify the extermination of human life is a tragic occurrence in every sense of the word. Here is humanism incarnate—man has become God.

The justifications for abortion expressed by Justices Blackmun and Douglas are the epitome of human selfishness and self-love. The countervailing evils of easy abortion were thrust aside by the Court. Among these baneful effects, according to Dr. Paul Marx, are "the denigration of the traditional sexual morality distilled from centuries of wisdom, the abandonment of self-control as an indispensable human virtue, the substitution of subjective whim for the priceless heritage of human knowledge, the enthronement of utilitarianism over principled morality, the devaluation of life itself, the ruination of the moral basis of natural human rights, and the obvious opening to *euthanasia.*" A society that countenances the brutality of abortion is one in which psychological ills, irreverence for life, and sexual promiscuity are likely to proliferate. In sum, therefore, we have paid an exorbitant price to sustain a woman's right to personal privacy.

That alleged right, however, is more a judicial fiction than a verifiable fact. Even Justice Douglas frankly confesses that "there is no mention of privacy in our Bill of Rights," nor is the type of privacy claimed in *Roe v. Wade* specifically mentioned in any other section of the federal Constitution. The Court invented this right in *Griswold v. Connecticut* when it held that a state law forbidding the use of contraceptives was unconstitutional in as far as the law applied to married persons. The Court advanced the so-called "penumbra" doctrine which held that various guarantees in the Bill of Rights impliedly create zones of privacy. In *Roe v. Wade* a woman's personal decision to abort her child was placed inside that judicially protected private zone.

In their attempt to vindicate this alleged right the appellant used a scattergun approach by claiming that the Texas statute abridged rights of personal privacy protected by the First, Fourth, Fifth, Ninth, and Fourteenth Amendments. One of these random shots found its mark, when the high court held that the right claimed by the appellant was "founded in the Fourteenth Amendment's concept of personal liberty."

In recent years the Court has developed a complex formula to protect from invasion by the states those rights which it uncovers in the mysterious recesses of the Constitution. The test traditionally applied to state social and economic legislation is whether or not the law (for example, the Texas abortion statute) has "a rational relation to a valid state objective." Had this test been employed in *Roe v. Wade* the state statute may have been upheld. However, the Court devised a more stringent standard in *Shapiro v. Thompson* which held that as the right involved becomes more fundamental, the more "compelling" the state interest must be in passing a law which abridges that right. In *Shapiro* and subsequent rulings the "compelling state interest" standard was used only in situations involving the equal protection provision of the Fourteenth Amendment. Justice Harlan attacked this new criteria when he asserted in a *Shapiro* dissent that "when a statute affects only matters not mentioned in the Federal Constitution and is not arbitrary or irrational" the Court is not entitled "to pick out particular human activities, characterize them as 'fundamental,' and give them added protection under an unusually stringent equal protection test." Such action, concluded Harlan, "would go far toward making this Court a 'superlegislature.'" Yet the Court went even beyond this in *Roe v. Wade*—it not only held a woman's private right to abort her unborn child to be "fundamental"; it also expanded the stringent "compelling state interest" test in a novel way to embrace the Due Process Clause (shades of Dred Scott!).

The majority's decision regarding the fundamental nature of the particular right of privacy asserted in this case was vigorously and persuasively attacked by Justice Rehnquist in a dissenting opinion: "The fact that a majority of the States, reflecting . . . the majority sentiment in those states, have had restrictions on abortions for at least a century seems . . . as strong an indication as there is that the asserted right to an abortion is not . . . fundamental. Even today, when society's views on abortion are changing, the very existence of the debate is evidence that the 'right' to an abortion is not so universally accepted as the appellants would have us believe," concluded Rehnquist. . . .

The right of privacy asserted by the Court is not only absent from the express provisions of the original Constitution, the Bill of Rights, and later Amendments, it is not generally recognized by law, by custom, or by majority opinion. How could such an alleged right, therefore, be "so rooted in the traditional conscience of our people to be ranked as fundamental." The Court does not satisfactorily explain its startling judgment. It "simply fashions," says dissenting Justice White, "a new constitutional right for pregnant mothers and, with scarcely any reason or authority for its action, invests that right with sufficient substance to override most state abortion statutes."

The court with equal effort could have "discovered" the unborn's right to life, invested it with "fundamental" status, and clothed it with judicial protection. This right is not explicit in any part of the Constitution, but, unlike the right to abort, it is recognized by law, by custom, and by majority opinion. It can also be inferred from the phraseology of no less a document than our Declaration of Independence: "We hold these truths to be self-evident, that all men are created equal, that they are endowed by their Creator with certain unalienable Rights, that among these are *Life,* Liberty, and the Pursuit of Happiness." Traditionally the term "creation" is applied to conception rather than to the other definable stages of fetal life.

This line of argumentation is at least as formidable as the privacy doctrine which the Court concocted, but, unfortunately, the Court used its legal legerdemain to uphold the right of privacy at the expense of the unborn's right to life—a strange choice indeed, especially in view of the solicitude shown by the Court for criminals under a death sentence in *Furman v. Georgia. . . .*

Our dissenting opinion to the Court's abortion ruling would be merely an intellectual catharsis and an exercise in frustration, if the Court's action could not be overridden. Our purpose thus far has been to show that the decision was patently unsound from either a logical, biomedical, moral, or legal perspective. Hopefully this knowledge of the decision's infirmity will provide an incentive to secure its reversal. . . .

13

San Antonio Independent School District v. Rodriquez:
Do the Poor Merit Special Protections under the Equal Protection Clause?

Linda T. Tudan
Glenn A. Phelps

THE Rodriguez family resided in the Edgewood neighborhood of San Antonio, Texas. The residents of Edgewood were predominantly of Mexican-American heritage and generally poor. Their average family income in 1967 was $4,686, the lowest in the San Antonio metropolitan area. Residents of Alamo Heights also lived in San Antonio. But there the similarities with the Edgewood neighborhood ended. Where Edgewood was Hispanic, Alamo Heights was Anglo. More important for the Rodriguez children, where Edgewood was poor, Alamo Heights was not. The median family income in Alamo Heights in 1967 was $8,001, more than 70 percent higher than in the Edgewood district.

The significance of this wealth differential between the two districts becomes clear when one examines the method of public school funding utilized in Texas. Confronted with the responsibility for financing public education, the legislature enacted a law that supplemented state aid to school districts by utilizing the revenues from local property taxes. This tax was designed to accommodate each district's taxpaying ability.

Under this system Alamo Heights, as the wealthier district of the two, was able to generate much more revenue from property taxes—revenue earmarked for education—than Edgewood was. The average assessed property value per pupil in Edgewood for 1967 was $5,960, the lowest in the San Antonio area. The tax rate was $1.05 per $100 of assessed value, the highest in the area. The district contributed $26 per pupil for the 1967–1968 school year. With the additional funds provided by state and federal sources, total education expenditures for a child from Edgewood equaled $356.

Alamo Heights, on the other hand, had an assessed property value per pupil of $49,000 in 1967. The local tax rate was $0.85 per $100 of assessed value. The district contributed $333 per pupil for the 1967–1968 school year. With state and federal supplements, Alamo Heights spent $594 for each student in its district.

The consequence was that the children residing in wealthier districts were afforded more educational resources. Ironically, residents of Edgewood were required to pay higher taxes to supplement their insufficiently low property values, yet their children continued to receive substantially lower educational funding than the children from Alamo Heights. Thus, deliberate state policy ensured that those children with the most favorable life chances would be further advantaged, while those children with the fewest such opportunities would be further disadvantaged.

Demetrio Rodriguez, along with several of his concerned neighbors, believed his children were not receiving educational benefits proportionate to those being offered to children in wealthier districts. He filed a class action suit on behalf of school children throughout the state who were members of minority groups or who were poor and resided in school districts with a low property tax base (*San Antonio Independent School District v. Rodriguez,* 411 U.S. 1, 1973). Rodriguez claimed that the Texas system of financing public education violated the Equal Protection Clause of the Fourteenth Amendment. He claimed this system discriminated on the basis of wealth (specifically against the poor) by providing to citizens in affluent districts a higher-quality education for their children, while the same group paid lower taxes. Many believe that education is integral to breaking out of the poverty cycle. It is a vital element in creating awareness of cultural values and preparing a child in the skills necessary for successful participation in economic and political life. In contemporary society a child denied access to a good education will have enormous obstacles to overcome—obstacles that, for the poor, are higher to start with than for the rest of us.

The Supreme Court has partially acknowledged this by declaring that public education is a "fundamental interest" of each citizen. A "fundamental interest" is one that, while not necessarily specified in the Constitution, is regarded as an indispensable liberty belonging to all citizens. Other "fundamental interests" include the right to vote and to travel.

Several cases involving "fundamental interests" have appeared before the Supreme Court over the years. The Warren Court was sympathetic toward fundamental interests of racial minorities and the poor. The Court stated in *Harper v. Virginia Board of Election Commissioners* (383 U.S. 663; 1966) that "wealth, like race, creed or color, is not germane to one's ability to participate intelligently in the electoral process. Lines drawn on the basis of wealth or property, like those of race, are traditionally disfavored." The activist Warren Court also ruled in *Griffin v. Illinois* (351 U.S. 12, 1956) that states must provide all indigent prisoners with free trial transcripts. As early as 1954 in *Brown v. Board of Education* (347 U.S. 483), Justice Earl Warren stated, "Education is perhaps the most important function of state and local government. The compulsory attendance laws and the great education expenditures demonstrate the vital nature of education in our society. It is a necessary component to a democratic system." Another federal case decided in 1969 termed education a "critical personal right" (*Hobson v. Hansen,* 269 F. Supp. 401).

These precedents led Rodriguez to believe he would be successful in court. The Supreme Court often utilized a "strict scrutiny" standard when reviewing equal protection claims that involved "fundamental interests." The strict scrutiny doctrine is invoked when the Court believes that a legislative classification is based on "invidious discrimination." Under this "strict scrutiny" of equal protection, a legislative action that classifies people unequally is valid only if it can be demonstrated that the action is vital to the advancement of a compelling state interest. Certain groups in society have been recognized by the Court as requiring special judicial protection due to their vulnerability in the political process. This standard, raised again in *Rodriguez,* maintains that the Fourteenth Amendment prohibits "invidious discrimination" based on such ascriptive characteristics as race or alienage. Such discrimination often prevents or obstructs efforts by the group in obtaining access to the legislative process; thus the minorities in question remain without effective representation. We may ask, then, whether there are certain rights or privileges so essential to the democratic process that their denial (or limitation because of state-mandated policy) effectively violates the Equal Protection Clause.

The federal district court believed Rodriguez's concerns were valid, and it ruled the Texas law unconstitutional. The three-judge panel noted that the state's system of taxation assumed that the value of property in the various districts would be sufficiently equal to sustain comparable expenditures. The adverse effects of this erroneous assumption were higher taxes and lower-quality education for the property-poor districts. The judges also ruled that the method of educational funding employed by the state drew sharp distinctions among citizens based on the wealth of the district in which they resided. They concluded that "lines drawn on wealth are suspect." The importance of education was stressed by the lower court judges. The state was not able to demonstrate a "compelling state interest" for utilizing such a discriminatory system of taxation. The Court believed this system of taxation inhibited the "fundamental interest" in education held by Rodriguez and the citizens of Edgewood.

The state of Texas appealed to the Supreme Court, and in 1973 the Court reversed the decision. Ostensibly the Court adopted a different view of the constitutional questions in the case. Discrimination on the basis of wealth could be invidious only if the state made education available only to those who could afford it. In *Rodriguez* it was not a matter of impoverished children receiving no public education. Rather, they received an education of lesser quality than that offered to children in more affluent communities.

Justice Powell, writing for the majority, stated,

> When government creates a class based on suspect categories, (race, alienage) or abridges a fundamental right, the regulation is subject to "strict scrutiny", placing on government the burden of demonstrating a compelling state interest.

The Supreme Court differed greatly with the lower court's assertion that education was a fundamental right. Justice Powell continued,

> Education is not among the rights afforded explicit protection under our Constitution. It does not fall within any of the categories calling for strict judicial scrutiny. . . . Texas' system abundantly satisfies the constitutional standard for equal protection, since the system rationally furthers a legitimate state purpose or interest. The Texas law does not deny equal protection to school children residing in districts with a low property tax base.

The Burger Court stated in *Rodriguez* that the Court had never held that "wealth discrimination alone provides an adequate basis for involving the strict scrutiny standard." The Texas law had not transgressed a fundamental right that was explicitly or implicitly protected by the Constitution. Poverty is not a "suspect classification." Therefore, laws that discriminate on the basis of wealth need not meet the "strict scrutiny" standard. Texas merely had to demonstrate that its law was reasonable, a standard that the Court agreed the state had met.

In his dissent, Justice Marshall urged the use of a flexible equal protection standard that would focus on the nature of the classification in question. He cited a need for balancing the relative importance of the government benefits an individual does not receive due to any class discrimination against the state's interests asserted in the justification of the classification. Marshall's argument was more in agreement with the lower court's reasoning. Marshall asserted the necessity of recognizing fundamental rights, such as education, as ends rather than means. While the majority believed otherwise, Marshall argued that the standard for review should encompass a broader view of "fundamental interests."

The Court could have declared in *Rodriguez* that education was a fundamental right and poverty was a suspect classification. Either statement would have imposed a burden on the state to demonstrate a compelling state interest to justify its policy. Instead the Court upheld a plan for financing public schools that accommodated substantial disparities in appropriations per pupil among school districts.[1]

The significance of this reasoning for future cases is two-fold. First, the Court has intimated that fundamental rights rarely go beyond those specifically enumerated in the Constitution. Opponents of this view agree with

John Hart Ely's theory of jurisprudence. He refers to "noninterpretivists," or "activists," as those who believe that courts should "go beyond that set of references and enforce norms that cannot be discovered within the four corners of the document."[2] The premise of this argument is that constitutional values should contain substances as well as form.

A second important view is whether the issue of school funding is a political question that should be decided by legislatures, not courts. The issue involves the allocation of municipal services, a concern traditionally reserved for popularly elected legislators. The Court's interventions in equal protection claims under the guise of creating economic equality are, according to this view, often seen as abuses of the power of judicial review.

These significant questions are examined in far greater detail in the two essays that follow. Both Frank Michelman and Ralph Winter are noted professors of law, but they disagree fundamentally on the broad question of whether the Constitution offers any special protections for the poor. Michelman says yes; Winter says no. Their different perceptions are illustrative of this developing area of civil liberties law.

$$\left[\begin{array}{l}\textit{Do the Poor Merit Special} \\ \textit{Protections under the Equal} \\ \textit{Protection Clause?}\end{array}\right]$$

Yes: Welfare Rights in a Constitutional Democracy

Frank I. Michelman

S OME years ago I speculated that persons in our country might have not only moral but constitutional rights to provision for certain basic ingredients of individual welfare, such as food, shelter, health care, and education. That suggestion, which we might call the welfare-rights thesis, has found some strong support, but also has met its share of skeptical, critical, and even derisive rejoinder. Several objections have been lodged: that the concept of welfare rights is fanciful, uncorroborated by legal texts or decisions; that the notion is ill-conceived because there is no justiciable standard for determining when the supposed rights are satisfied; that the courts, in the absence of a justiciable standard, cannot presume to define or enforce these rights without usurping legislative and executive roles; that judicial vindication of these rights would be illegitimate and undemocratic because nothing in our traditional law or written Constitution signifies any general acceptance of the obligations these rights entail; that the claim of rights is misdirected, not in the best interest of the supposed rights-holders; and that the claim is immoral because it attacks the basic liberties of those who would be called upon to satisfy it. These are all forceful objections, and I do not take them lightly. I think, however, that my suggestion about welfare rights can survive them, and ought to be accepted. . . .

Let us turn, then, to the next objection on my list—the asserted want of an adequate basis in law for the welfare-rights thesis. Welfare-rights claims, the objection runs, have no warrant in legally admissible sources construed by legally acceptable methods, as distinguished from, say, the sources and methods of moral philosophy or from mere judicial preference. Because my proposition is one about *constitutional* welfare rights, we can limit the set of admissible sources to the Constitution itself and concentrate on the question

Frank I. Michelman, from "Welfare Rights in a Constitutional Democracy," 1979 *Washington University Law Quarterly* (1979), pp. 659–80. Published by the University of Chicago Press.

of methods for construing it. That, at any rate, is how I intend to proceed, if only because without treating the constitutional document itself as in some sense a first premise, I see no hope of succeeding in the task of opening minds to the welfare-rights thesis. To locate the rights in an "unwritten constitution," or otherwise to deny or repress the distinction in principle between law and morality, would accomplish little toward that end. On this occasion then, I intend to proceed as a legal positivist, though, as you must certainly anticipate, a free-thinking one.

For like reasons I shall abstain from modes of constitutional interpretation that seem too manipulable to prove anything to a welfare-rights skeptic. Thus, I shall have nothing whatsoever to do with any "realist" notion that the Constitution says whatever the judges make it say. Less wholeheartedly, but dutifully, I also foreswear any allegiance to the idea that certain clauses of the Constitution may be correctly read to call for legislative and judicial observance of the tenets of evolving "conventional morality" or "professed public ideals." By so proceeding, one at least leaves open the possibility of satisfying those who . . . believe not only that "a legitimate Court must be controlled by principles exterior to the will of the Justices" (a proposition with which few would take issue), but also that "system[s] of moral and ethical values" cannot, as such, have any "objective or intrinsic validity" on which legitimate adjudication can rest. In short, what follows will be (even if barely) an "interpretivist" argument, in the vocabulary made current by Professors Grey and Ely; that is, an argument that ties its premises into the documentary Constitution.

Interpretivist the argument is, but hardly literalist or, as one might say, contractualist. The argument will not satisfy anyone who thinks political efficacy and group socioeconomic status will enter into the argument now to be offered for identifying welfare rights as among those transtextual rights that ought to be judicially recognized as representation-reinforcing privileges or immunities, or as the negatives of representation-defeating inequalities, under Ely's quasi-interpretivist view of the Fourteenth Amendment.

Consider for a moment the following assortment of transtextual constitutional rights that actually have been recognized and enforced by the Supreme Court: to bear or not bear children as one chooses; to raise and educate one's children as one chooses; to choose freely one's marital status and partner; to live as an "extended" rather than a "nuclear" family; to remain at liberty if not guilty of crime or a threat to anyone's physical safety, even though a genuine annoyance to others; to travel outside the United States; to migrate and resettle within the United States; and to decline participation in patriotic observances.

Should any or all of these be properly regarded as representation-reinforcing rights? Each can certainly be viewed as a "political" right, protecting choices that when exercised can fairly be called political acts—setting up or nurturing what Ely calls "competing power centers," expressing or actualizing values that may or may not be conventional ones, raising consciousnesses, "voting with one's feet," and so on. Although political in the broad sense, however, these acts in themselves do not amount to participation—as do acts of voting, candidacy, officeholding, and legislative lobbying and debate—in representative democracy, the political system of last resort envisioned by the Constitution. Nor do the liberties of family choice, child-rearing, or travel directly enable, enhance, or condition effective participation in that political system. To regard them as constitutionally guaranteed under the rubric of representation-reinforcement would leave that criterion virtually boundless, lacking the constraining force of judicial judgment apparently required by the idea of representative democracy itself. If they are proper constitutional rights—a conclusion I am far from wishing to deny—their sources are unwritten ones beyond the purview of this discussion.

Now contrast those liberties with a person's interest in basic education. Without basic education—without the literacy, fluency, and elementary understanding of politics and markets that are hard to obtain without it—what hope is there of effective participation in the last resort political system? On just this basis, it seems the Supreme Court itself has expressly allowed that "some identifiable quantum of education" may be a constitutional right. But if so, then what about life itself, health and vigor, presentable attire, or shelter not only from the elements but from the physical and psychological onslaughts of social debilitation? Are not these interests the universal rock bottom prerequisites of effective participation in democratic representation— even paramount in importance to education and, certainly, to the niceties of apportionment, districting, and ballot access on which so much judicial and scholarly labor has been lavished? How can there be those sophisticated rights to a formally unbiased majoritarian system but no rights to the indispensable means of effective participation in that system? How can the Supreme Court admit the possibility of a right to minimum education, but go out of its way to deny flatly any right to subsistence, shelter, or health care?

Some may object that I am guilty of confusing the existence or possession of a right with the worth of the right or the capacity to derive value from it. The right to travel, or publish, or worship connotes a freedom to do what one has the means to do, not a social undertaking to provide the means. So it must be with rights of democratic participation, no? Well, no. Rights of democratic participation differ from other rights precisely in that they are rights of last resort, ones that, in the Supreme Court's words, are "preservative of all rights." In Professor Ely's words, they provide a guarantee against "undue constriction" of "the opportunity to participate . . . in the political process by which values are appropriately identified and accommodated," including—and this is crucial—"values" that pertain to the distribution in society of the means of enjoying rights. One might as well say to those who are underrepresented in a malapportioned legislature that their remedy lies through legislative politics, as say to those who lack access to "the basic necessities of life" that their right of democratic participation is not constricted.

If we now let our focus shift from the political-action core to the status-harm core of representation-reinforcement, we find that the argument for welfare rights, as a part of constitutionally guaranteed democratic representation, gains in richness and power. To be hungry, afflicted, ill-educated, enervated, and demoralized by one's material circumstances of life is not only to be personally disadvantaged in competitive politics, but also, quite possibly, to be identified as a member of a group—call it "the poor"—that has both some characteristic political aims and values and some vulnerability to having its natural force of numbers systematically subordinated in the processes of political influence and majoritarian coalition-building. Even if there is no group of "the poor" for which that description holds, it is a blatant fact of national—including constitutional—history that there are groups for which it has held and does hold. It is also a fact—one that can hardly be accepted as accidental—that being a member of, say, the black minority significantly correlates with one's chances of being severely impoverished and, therefore, of carrying marks of poverty that both motivate and facilitate political and social bias. Satisfaction of basic welfare interests thus seems to be a crucial ingredient of any serious attempt to eliminate the vestiges of slavery from the system of democratic representation. The Supreme Court was right on the mark in *Goldberg v. Kelly:* "[W]elfare . . . can help bring within reach of the poor the same opportunities that are available to others to participate meaningfully in the life of the community. . . . Public assistance, then, is not mere charity, but a means to 'procure the Blessings of Liberty to ourselves and our Posterity.'"

Let me now pause to summarize. First, courts can accord recognition to minimum welfare rights in ways that have a practical bearing on adjudication but do not raise judicially inappropriate questions of definition or problems of enforcement. Second, legal argument does exist for judicial recognition of minimum welfare rights as a direct implication of the written Constitution; indeed, it seems to be a stronger and clearer constitutionally based argument than can be found for a number of presently recognized constitutional rights. If in making this latter point I have belabored the obvious, it is only because I want you to share with me the sense of queerness and paradox suffusing this whole discussion: the queerness, on the one hand, of there being so much trouble about admitting that everyone has a right to the means of subsistence at a minimum social standard of decency; and the paradox, on the other, of even thinking to cast the question in the language of rights or even considering the matter as meet for legal disputation. It is a funny feeling repeatedly echoed by the Supreme Court of the 1970s: "The administration of public

welfare assistance . . . involves the most basic economic needs of impoverished human beings," but the questions it raises are questions of "wise economic or social policy," not of right. "We do not denigrate the importance of
decent, safe, and sanitary housing. But the Constitution does not provide
judicial remedies for every social and economic ill." "We are in complete
agreement . . . that 'the grave significance of education both to the individual
and our society' cannot be doubted. But the importance of a service . . . does
not determine whether it must be regarded as [constitutionally] fundamental."

Granting that importance is not determinative, is it not highly signficant?
Obviously, the importance of a service in itself does not *determine* constitutional entitlement to it, precisely because it is *constitutional* entitlement
that is in issue: No constitution, no constitutional right. But once it is allowed
that there are some—any—constitutional rights beyond those literally spelled
out in the constitutional text or rigorously deducible from it, then importance
just has to become a crucial constitutional variable. This is true partly becaue
interests and claims often conflict or, in other words, rights entail costs, and
the significant must take precedence over the petty. It is true also because
some rights presuppose others, and some rights, even if not all, presuppose
one's having passed beyond the struggle for existence and for the marks of
minimum social respect. That is just a simple matter of mundane observation.

Now, if the importance of welfare claims, or the importance of their
importance to the question of whether they are rights, is so clear at the level
of mundane observation, it must be that the trouble about welfare rights
arises not at that level, but at the level of moral and political speculation, or
theory, or (please excuse my mention of it) philosophy. The trouble we share
about welfare rights seems to be evidence of what some assert and others
doubt or deny is an inevitable connection between legal (especially constitutional) reason and speculative or philosophical reflection about matters of
ethics and politics. It seems, in short, that the trouble we have with welfare
rights as legal claims is a direct counterpart of the doubts these rights
engender in a certain sophisticated scheme of political philosophizing that is
widely, if hazily, shared among the educated and reflective public, most or all
of us to some degree included. . . .

No: Poverty, Economic Equality, and the Equal Protection Clause

Ralph K. Winter

S INCE advocates of the reduction of economic inequality through substantive equal protection make no serious claim to historical support,
it will suffice here to confirm in brief fashion that their modesty in
advocacy is fully justified. The Fourteenth Amendment was enacted at a
point in American history when notions of laissez-faire and Social Darwinism
were about to peak and when a number of states (not all Southern) had passed
Black Codes severely restricting the legal rights of blacks and imposing substantial legal burdens upon them. The Amendment was not designed to
reduce inequality in the society generally or to serve as a device by which
government might be compelled to take steps to bring about economic equality. Neither the men involved nor the spirit of the times favored social or
economic equality, much less the notion that government had responsibilities
to rework society along egalitarian lines. Quite the contrary, equality was
invoked in the Amendment out of the fear of government and as a device to
neutralize governmental (and a narrow range of centralized private) power by
compelling it to maintain legal equality when classifications based on race
(or racelike matters) were employed. Had the utterly different philosophy
entailed in notions of income redistribution by government been thought of
as having anything whatever to do with the purpose of the Amendment, it is
safe to say that it simply would have failed of passage.

Much the same can be said of the Amendment's language, although the
conclusions are a shade less definite. "No State shall . . . deny to any person
within its jurisdiction the equal protection of the laws." From that language
proponents of substantive equal protection derive constitutional principles
reducing economic inequality in the society. On its face, the provision seems
remarkably ill-suited to that task, for, to the extent economic inequality is a

Ralph K. Winter, from "Poverty, Economic Equality and the Equal Protection Clause," 1972
Supreme Court Review, pp. 86–102. Published by the University of Chicago Press.

problem, it is a national problem. But the Equal Protection Clause is in terms directed strictly to the conduct of states toward persons within their jurisdiction. If the Equal Protection Clause requires absolute equality—of income or housing or education or anything—the equality thus brought about seems to be equality within each state, not between them. Persons in the richer states will fare better than persons in the poorer states, as indeed they presently do even under *Serrano* and *Shapiro*. What all this accomplishes, apart from encouraging further migration for the purpose of receiving increased public services, is by no means clear. Indeed, there is no guarantee even that the quantum of inequality (if measurable) will not be increased, rather than diminished, by such measures.

If equality is not the goal, but simply minimum protection as to "just wants" or "fundamental interests," it still seems an utterly foolish division of responsibilities to make the identification of these wants or interests a matter for the federal judiciary and leave their fulfillment to the states. The content of these concepts must be related to the wealth of the societal unit involved, but what the citizen of Connecticut views as "basic" housing may well seem a luxury to one in Arkansas. Even notions of subsistence vary widely between the states. Is the Court to adopt the norms of a rich state or a poor state? If the former, how do the poor states pay the cost of providing what are essentially "extras" to their citizens? If the latter, how much can be accomplished in the way of reducing inequality in the richer states? Perhaps the Court ought to fashion an economic norm for each state. But even assuming it was equal to what seems an impossible task, the problem of wide inequalities between the states would remain.

To my knowledge, not a single nonlegal writer on the issue of economic inequality has suggested this sort of division of governmental responsibility. Rather, all seem agreed that if a serious redistribution of income is to take place—whether through direct cash payments or in kind provision of goods and services—the national government is the only appropriate governmental organ to carry it out.

Other aspects of the Amendment are less preclusive than the fact that it is directed to the states rather than the federal government. Nevertheless, they are still suggestive of a purpose far short of the all-embracing scope required by the proponents of the constitutional redistribution of income. The words "No State" and "of the laws" can, I suppose, be read to include all forms of governmental tolerance and thus all forms of private, but regulable, conduct. They seem, however, rather odd choices to that end because they specifically direct attention to formal governmental action. Such emphasis strongly suggests an intended limitation on the scope of the Amendment.

The word "equal" appears on its face more apt to the advocated purpose, for, as Professor Cox has noted, "Once loosed, the idea of Equality is not easily cabined." Nevertheless, Professor Kurland has correctly observed that "its expansionist tendency may be due to its uses as rhetoric rather than as an idea. And the rhetoric is subject to use, if not capture, by anyone on any side of the question." Equality as an idea is in fact not particularly useful, since it is intolerably constraining, for, like virginity, it admits of no degrees. Equality in the provision of "just wants" or the protection of "fundamental interests" means that no person may have more in the way of provision or protection than anyone else, no matter what he is willing to sacrifice in exchange for it. It means equal education, equal housing, equal food, and so on. Few thus go the whole equality route, for it brings the tension between egalitarian notions of justice and the value of individual freedom to the breaking point by promising to suppress vast areas of valuable idiosyncratic behavior. In fact, the rhetoric of equality in stump speeches or stump opinions is really an expression of distaste for inequality rather than an insistence on uniformity and it is that distaste which "once loosed . . . is not easily cabined." Even Karst and Horowitz, having milked equal protection dry, abandon "total equality" as "impossible and undesirable," while Professor Michelman makes explicit that what is at stake in his analysis is "minimum protection," not equality.

The language of the Equal Protection Clause thus seems at best very badly suited, at worst plainly hostile, to the objectives of equality under discussion. The words "No State," "of the laws," and "equal" itself, all must in effect be abandoned as superfluous or meaningless. Indeed, were language the only guide to interpretation, there hardly seems more reason to put the Equal Protection Clause to this intended use than the initial statement of constitutional purpose ("to form a more perfect Union," etc.), or the Ninth Amendment. As a matter of history or language, therefore, focusing on the Equal Protection Clause smacks of random selection, or the content to be given to the law derived from it comes entirely from other sources. . . .

It has been argued that wealth should be assimilated to race as a suspect classification. It is not necessary at this point to wrestle with the problem of precisely what legal result is called for when a classification is labeled "suspect." It may be the equivalent of a conclusive declaration that the statute is invalid; it may call for a searching scrutiny of the motive behind the legislation; it may create a presumption of the statute's invalidity rebuttable only by a showing of a "compelling state interest"; or it may simply shift the burden of demonstrating some legitimate legislative interest to the state. For our purpose, it is enough to say it casts serious constitutional doubt upon the legislation involved.

It would be well at the outset to establish what it is about race that makes it a suspect classification. There is, of course, the history of racial slavery in the United States and, in particular, the clear intent of the Framers of the Fourteenth Amendment to invalidate the Black Codes. Those codes, and a disgracefully large amount of legislation in subsequent years, invoked race as a classification in a way which was intended to operate, and did operate, to discriminate against black people. Race is thus the basis of a stereotype which served as a systematic vehicle of governmental discrimination. Moreover, it is not a stereotype with a pretense at being related to individual merit, even though it is, for the frosting on the cake, unalterable by the individual.

Viewed in these terms, wealth seems by no means assimilable to race. This is so whether we view the issue as classification based on poverty, as in *Griffen* (a free transcript for those who can't afford one) or wealth generally, as in *Harper* (a free vote for all). In either case, the history of the Amendment would seem to cut the other way for there is no evidence that the Framers were concerned with the distribution of income.

Unlike race, moreover, poverty is not absolutely unalterable for all those afflicted by it. The history of this nation is a history of virtually all of its people bettering themselves economically and, for the vast majority, becoming well-to-do or middle-class. Indeed, if income inequality performs the function of increasing productivity at all, income redistribution is then as likely to retard people from bringing themselves out of poverty as it is to cure the evil itself. Beyond that, it cannot be said that poverty has been used like race as the basis for systematic legislative discrimination. There simply has not been any legislation invoking a poverty classification even remotely resembling the widespread, official, racial segregation of schools and other facilities. To the contrary, there is an enormous amount of legislation which, whatever its actual effect, was said—and was intended by most of its supporters—to help the poor. Hour and wage legislation, legislation protecting collective bargaining, social security, the farm program, the creation of the Office of Economic Opportunity, fair employment laws, manpower training programs, unemployment compensation, public assistance, public housing, public education, subsidified health care, etc., have all had as their rationale at one time or another the need to help the poor. In 1970, roughly 47 percent of all governmental expenditures (15 percent of GNP) was allocable to social welfare. Finally, to the extent low income is related to low productivity—and it is to a large extent—poverty is not entirely unrelated to individual merit. One need not adopt productivity as the sole criterion of merit to say that poverty resulting from low productivity is far different from legal exclusion from public facilities because of one's race.

In any event, there is no transcendent income line below which is poverty. The talk we hear of a poverty line refers to an administrative determination by the Social Security Administration, not divine revelation. The fact is that any person who has less material income than someone else will feel relatively deprived. Even if we were capable of raising the income of the bottom 20 percent of the population to that of the lowest income in the twenty-first percentile, we would still have a "poverty problem," because the problem is one of relative rather than absolute deprivation. Thus it is that even as the most disadvantaged in the society have had their lot bettered rather steadily, learned commentators nevertheless speak of those in poverty as being the lowest 20 percent in the population and use the words "getting better" to mean "more equal." This is not to say that one should be indifferent to the plight of those in the lowest 20 percent or that we should ignore their welfare. It is very much to say, however, that the poverty problem is a relative inequality problem rather than some sort of absolute affliction.

Nor is it sensible to think of wealth classifications generally as being suspect. That, of course, abandons the relief of poverty as a goal—the president of General Motors would get a free transcript along with Mr. Griffen—and turns to the even less supportable target of complete equality.

A major theme in the scholarship of constitutional law is the relationship of the Supreme Court, its members appointed for life, to the political branches, their members elected for a fixed term in partisan elections. The principal issue is the identification of the appropriate constraints on the power of judicial review and the resulting spectrum of opinion is large and varied. At one end is the view that the Court must hew closely to the language and specific intent of the Constitution in order to insure that the least democratic branch does not encroach on the powers of elected representatives. Opinions more in the middle call for the "neutral derivation" of constitutional principles or view the Court as "an institution charged with the evolution and application of society's fundamental principles." At the other end are what might be called the super-realists (a term most definitely used for identification rather than descriptive purposes). The only constraint on the exercise of judicial power they recognize is that it should be employed to the end of validation by "tomorrow's history," which is to say, of course, that they recognize no constraint at all, except possibly the need to avoid today's impeachment.

The use of the Equal Protection Clause to reduce economic inequality is not difficult to locate along this spectrum. Having no basis in the history or language of the Amendment and lying well outside what seems the core area of judicial competence, it finds sustenance solely in its alleged wisdom as public policy. Whatever its wisdom, however, it is the kind of policy one concerned with institutional competence would leave to the judgment of the legislative branch.

One area in which legislatures seem institutionally superior to other branches of government is in the representation of interest groups. Indeed, the device of the bicameral legislature seems principally designed to maximize that very function. The reduction of economic inequality, however, seems a classic issue calling for the resolution of the claims of competing groups. Who is to be taxed and how, who is to receive what, and how much sacrifice should society make in the name of equality, are precisely the kind of questions legislatures seem most suited to resolve. To be sure, there may, or may not, be good reason to believe that one interest group is more worthy or deserving than another but it is precisely that judgment, if any, which ought to be the routine grist of the political mill. It is simply impossible for all interested groups to be represented on a body such as the Court and, worse, quite likely that the court will not even be able to identify the groups with the most at stake.

It is for these reasons, I should think, that most students of constitutional law believe the Court's vigorous use of notions of substantive due process to upset economic regulation earlier in the century to be a misuse of the power of judicial review. Substantive equal protection, however, in principle and practice suffers from quite the same defects and has itself created some uneasiness even among its proponents. For that reason, we witness the tragicomic phenomenon of both Justices and commentators nervously seeking to distinguish between what they are doing and the rejected and reviled substantive due process of another era. "Regulation of business or industry" is said to differ from "[t]he administration of public welfare assistance." And we are told that state "economic regulation" is to be distinguished from state imposed "distinctions . . . that run against the poor." Such subtleties, however, are almost patently artificial. All economic regulation involves the allocation of scarce resources and the distribution of income. One may prefer one kind of regulation leading to a particular allocation and distribution over another kind, but the judgment must be based on personal value preferences—the need or worthiness of a group to be helped or the relative lack of merit of one to be injured. These must then be applied in the light of one's judgments about market failure, effect on incentives or on other government policies, etc. In constitutional principle the issues are indivisible. . . .

It may be fairly said then that only those who view judicial review as being without any constraint save that dictated by the pursuit of validation by "tomorrow's history" can view the Court's intervention into questions of the distribution of income without alarm. For if there are constraints on the Court, if we are to maintain any sensible sort of institutional division of labor in the name of either competence or the democratic political process, it would seem that the line must be drawn to exclude income redistribution by judicial fiat. Thus it is that any observer concerned about maintaining constraints on judicial power is likely to view further intervention by the Court in the name of the reduction of economic inequality more as a seizure of power than a legitimate exercise of judicial review.

Notes

Chapter 2

1. Alexis de Tocqueville, *Democracy in America* (New York: New American Library, 1956), p. 154.

Chapter 3

1. Alexander Meiklejohn, *Free Speech and Its Relation to Self-Government* (New York: Harper, 1948).

Chapter 4

1. Thomas I. Emerson, *The System of Freedom of Expression* (New York: Random House, 1970), p. 467.
2. Ibid., p. 486–91.
3. Alexander Meiklejohn, *Political Freedom* (New York: Harper, 1960), p. 36.

Chapter 5

1. Meiklejohn, *Free Speech*.

Chapter 7

1. Richard C. Cortner and Clifford M. Lytle, *Constitutional Law and Politics: Three Arizona Cases* (Tucson: University of Arizona Press, 1971), pp. 10–11.
2. Erwin N. Griswold, *The Fifth Amendment Today* (Cambridge: Harvard University Press, 1955), p. 3.

Chapter 8

1. Leonard W. Levy, *Against the Law: The Nixon Court and Criminal Justice* (New York: Harper, 1979), p. 63.
2. Robert A. Rutland, *The Birth of the Bill of Rights 1776–1791* (New York: Collier Books, 1961), p. 34.

Chapter 9

1. Fred W. Friendly and Martha J.H. Elliott, *The Constitution: That Delicate Balance* (New York: Random House, 1984), pp. 161–72.
2. Bob Woodward and Scott Armstrong, *The Brethren* (New York: Simon and Schuster, 1979), p. 207.
3. Joel B. Grossman and Richard S. Wells, *Constitutional Law and Judicial Policy Making,* 2d ed. (New York: John Wiley, 1980), p. 945.
4. Rupert V. Barry, "Furman to Gregg: The Judicial and Legislative History," 22 *Howard Law Journal* (1979), p. 84–95.

Chapter 10

1. See Graham Hughes, "Reparations for Blacks?" 43 *New York University Law Review* (1968), pp. 1063–74, and Boris I. Bittker, *The Case for Black Reparations* (New York: Random House, 1973).
2. Paul Brest, "Foreword: In Defense of the Antidiscrimination Principle:" 90 *Harvard Law Review* (1976), pp. 1–54; and Charles Murray, "Affirmative Racism," *New Republic,* December 31, 1984, pp. 18–23.

Chapter 11

1. Edward Dumbauld, ed., *The Political Writings of Thomas Jefferson* (Indianapolis: Bobbs-Merrill, 1955), p. 98.
2. Barbara Allen Babcock et al., *Sex Discrimination and the Law: Causes and Remedies* (Boston: Little, Brown, 1975), pp. 4–8.
3. Remarks by Peter Coogan in "Men, Women, and the Constitution: The Equal Rights Amendment," 10 *Columbia Journal of Law and Social Problems* (1973), pp. 82–91.
4. See, for example, *Goesaert v. Cleary,* 335 U.S. 464 (1948).
5. *Cleveland Board of Education v. LaFleur,* 414 U.S. 632 (1974).
6. *Burwell v. Eastern Air Lines,* 450 U.S. 965 (1981).
7. *Rostker v. Goldberg,* 453 U.S. 57 (1981).
8. *Craig v. Boren,* 429 U.S. 190 (1976).

Chapter 12

1. Friendly and Elliott, *Constitution,* pp. 202–08.
2. Louis Brandeis and Charles Warren, "The Right to Privacy," 4 *Harvard Law Review* (1890), p. 193.
3. *Eisenstadt v. Baird,* 405 U.S. 438 (1972).
4. Joel Feinberg, *The Problem of Abortion,* 2d ed. (Belmont, Calif.: Wadsworth, 1984), pp. 1–7.

Chapter 13

1. Alpheus T. Mason and William Beaney, *American Constitutional Law* (Englewood Cliffs, N.J.: Prentice-Hall, 1978), p. 463.
2. John Hart Ely, *Democracy and Distrust* (Cambridge: Harvard University Press, 1980), p. 1.

Case Index

General Index

About the Editors

Glenn A. Phelps is Assistant Professor of Political Science at Northern Arizona University. He earned his B.A. at Lebanon Valley College and later received an M.A. and a D.A. from Lehigh University. Additionally, he has attended Harvard University for postdoctoral study. He is currently studying the political ideology of the Founding Fathers and has published several papers and articles in that area.

Robert A. Poirier is Associate Professor of Political Science at Northern Arizona University. He earned his B.A. from St. Michael's College, Vermont. He later received his M.A. from the University of Arizona and his Ph.D. from the University of Utah. In addition to his work on the First Amendment, he has written in the fields of political risk analysis and political development. He has also served as an officer of the Western Political Science Association.